AGP 0567   4

D0780863

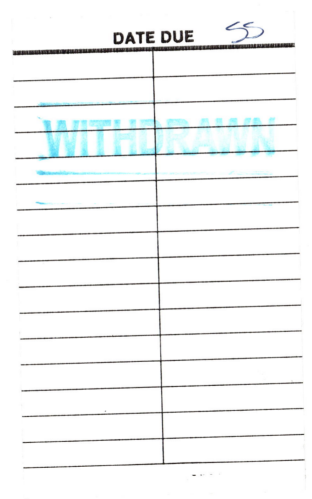

DATE DUE

Design Patterns
for Object-Oriented
Software Development

ACM PRESS BOOKS

This book is published as part of ACM Press Books – a collaboration between the Association for Computing Machinery and Addison-Wesley Publishing Company. ACM is the oldest and largest educational and scientific society in the information technology field. Through its high-quality publications and services, ACM is a major force in advancing the skills and knowledge of IT professionals throughout the world. For further information about ACM, contact:

ACM Member Services
1515 Broadway, 17th Floor
New York, NY 10036-5701
Phone: 1-212-626-0500
Fax: 1-212-944-1318
E-mail: ACMHELP@ACM.org

ACM European Service Center
Avenue Marcel Thiry 204
1200 Brussels, Belgium
Phone: 32-2-774-9602
Fax: 32-2-774-9690
E-mail: ACM_Europe@ACM.org

OTHER TITLES IN THE SERIES

Object-Oriented Reuse, Concurrency and Distribution *Colin Atkinson*

Algebraic Specification *J.A. Bergstra, J. Heering and P. Klint (Eds)*

Object-Oriented Software Engineering: A Use CASE Driven Approach *Ivar Jacobson, Magnus Christerson, Patrik Jonnson and Gunnar Övergaard*

Object-Oriented Concepts, Databases and Applications *Won Kim and Frederick H. Lochovsky (Eds)*

The Oberon System: User Guide and Programmer's Manual *Martin Reiser*

Programming in Oberon: Steps Beyond Pascal and Modula *Martin Reiser and Niklaus Wirth*

Project Oberon: The Design of an Operating System and Compiler *Niklaus Wirth and Jürg Gutknecht*

Advanced Animation and Rendering Techniques *Alan Watt and Mark Watt*

Distributed Systems (2nd edn) *Sape Mullender (Ed)*

Multimedia Systems *John F. Koegel Buford*

Modern Database Systems: The Object Model, Interoperability, and Beyond *Won Kim*

The Stanford GraphBase: A Platform for Combinatorial Computing *Donald Knuth*

Object-Oriented Programming in the BETA Programming Language *Ole Lehrmann Madsen, Birger Møller-Pedersen and Kristen Nygaard*

The Set Model for Database and Information Systems *Mikhail M. Gilula*

The Object Advantage: Business Process Reengineering with Object Technology *Ivar Jacobson*

Database Security *Silvana Castano, Mariagrazia Fugini, Giancarlo Martello and Pierangeli Samarati*

Multimedia Programming: Objects, Environments and Frameworks *Simon J. Gibbs and Dionysios C. Tsichritzis*

Design Patterns
for Object-Oriented
Software Development

WOLFGANG PREE

Johannes Kepler University Linz

▲▼▲ Addison-Wesley Publishing Company

Wokingham, England • Reading, Massachusetts • Menlo Park, California
New York • Don Mills, Ontario • Amsterdam • Bonn • Sydney • Singapore
Tokyo • Madrid • San Juan • Milan • Paris • Mexico City • Seoul • Taipei

Copyright © 1995 by the ACM Press, a Division of the Association for Computing Machinery, Inc. (ACM).

All rights reserved. No part of this publication may be reproduced, stored in a retrieval system, or transmitted in any form or by any means, electronic, mechanical, photocopying, recording or otherwise, without prior written permission of the publisher.

The programs in this book have been included for their instructional value. They have been tested with care but are not guaranteed for any particular purpose. The publisher does not offer any warranties or representations, nor does it accept any liabilities with respect to the programs.

Many of the designations used by manufacturers and sellers to distinguish their products are claimed as trademarks. Addison-Wesley has made every attempt to supply trademark information about manufacturers and their products mentioned in this book. A list of the trademark designations and their owners appears on p. xiv.

Cover designed by Op den Brouw, Design & Illustration, Reading
and printed by The Riverside Printing Co. (Reading) Ltd.
Printed in the United States of America.

First printed 1994. Reprinted 1995.

ISBN 0-201-42294-8

British Library Cataloguing in Publication Data
A catalogue record for this book is available from the British Library.

Library of Congress Cataloging in Publication Data applied for.

Foreword

Wolfgang Pree has written the first book to yield deep insights into the newly emerging field of object-oriented frameworks. He shows how to design framework structures using a hot-spot driven approach which he carefully develops from basic principles. Frameworks are class hierarchies plus models of interactions which can be turned into complete applications through various kinds of specialization. The question Wolfgang Pree adroitly asks is, "What are the appropriate patterns of construction which lead to efficient and elegant frameworks?"

The book goes on to answer this question using an evolutionary approach which unfolds through carefully chosen examples in C++. The result: seven metapatterns which Pree argues are the minimum building blocks necessary to construct elegant software architectures. Using the basic principles of templates and hooks, these metapatterns can express all of the notions of frameworks found in popular architectures such as the ET++ framework and MacApp.

Pree sees existing object-oriented design patterns ranging from Coad Design, coding styles, cookbooks, and class-object methodologies as various attempts to bend a framework to a new purpose. But, these pioneering methodologies fail to lead their users into a deeper understanding of abstract and concrete class hierarchies, and their interactions. Instead, he sees patterns as a way to overcome the steep learning curve of monolithic frameworks. This enterprising author takes the reader on a forcefully convincing tour of the intricacies of object-oriented design. And he backs up his recommendations with detailed C++ code.

What impresses me most is Pree's command of deep technical issues. Yet, he ties concept to practical languages (C++, Ada, Modula-2, Eiffel) using a simple step-by-step progression of ideas. The reader is led down logical pathways which will convince the most astute computer scientist that hot-spot identification is the right way to look at design. While not really a book about software engineering, Pree relates object-oriented programming concepts to good software engineering practice.

Altogether an outstanding contribution by a brilliant young computer scientist. If you want to know the nuts and bolts of modern software development, read this book!

Prof. Ted Lewis, Ph.D.
Naval Postgraduate School
Monterey, California
August 1994

Preface

Object-oriented programming has undeniably become a buzzword. Since the term object is quite generic, the attribute object-oriented can be attached to almost any concept in computer science. As a consequence, there is no consensus on the pros and cons of this programming paradigm: Meyer (1988) states that object-oriented programming is "viewed by some as a typhoon .... and by some as a storm in a teacup."

We have experienced a significant increase in software reusability and an overall improvement in software quality due to the application of object-oriented programming concepts in the development and (re)use of *semifinished software architectures* rather than just single components. Semifinished architectures consist of several single components and the bond between them, that is, their interaction. The term *framework* is used for these architectures.

We have successfully applied framework-centered software development in several projects over the past years and have become enthusiastic about the potential of this way of combining object-oriented concepts. Unfortunately, framework concepts are often not known well enough and thus not used in object-oriented software development projects. One reason for this might be that no methodology directly supports this advanced object-oriented programming approach.

Design patterns recently emerged as a glimmer of hope on the horizon for supporting the development and reuse of frameworks. This book is dedicated to design patterns as a means of capturing and communicating the design of object-oriented systems, especially frameworks.

We view the term pattern as yet another generic buzzword in the realm of object-oriented software development. The definition provided by Merriam Webster (1983) corroborates this point of view:

- a person or thing so ideal as to be worthy of imitation or copying;
- a model, guide, plan, etc. used in making things;
- an arrangement of form; disposition of parts or elements; design or decoration; as, wallpaper patterns, the pattern of a novel;
- definite direction, tendency, or characteristics; as, behavior patterns.

This book first builds a conceptual and terminological basis in Chapters 1 to 3 and goes on to discuss *metapatterns* as a minimal yet sufficient means to meet the goal of capturing and communicating the design of frameworks.

Chapter 1 discusses the principal constructive measures that help achieve satisfying overall software quality.

Chapter 2 describes in detail how to combine the basic object-oriented programming concepts in order to develop frameworks.

Chapter 3 gives an overview of state-of-the-art design pattern approaches in the realm of object-oriented software development.

Chapter 4 introduces an advanced abstraction called metapatterns. This chapter gives a first glimpse of how metapatterns can actively support the design pattern idea in the context of frameworks.

Chapter 5 demonstrates the adequateness of metapatterns for capturing the design of complex frameworks. A hypertext editor with considerable functionality serves as an example of an application built by adapting a graphic user interface (GUI) framework.

Chapter 6 concludes with a vision of how metapatterns can augment existing object-oriented analysis and design methodologies in order to support the development and documentation of frameworks.

Appendix A contains the complete source code listings of the hypertext system discussed in Chapter 5. The relevant coding conventions are outlined.

Appendix B defines important terms in a glossary. Appendix C describes how to access the source files of the hypertext system via ftp.

The intended audience includes anyone who wants to exploit the potential of the object-oriented programming paradigm. The reader should have programming experience in a conventional programming language, such as C or Pascal. Experience with one of the widespread object-oriented languages such as C++ or Smalltalk is helpful but not required. The examples in the book use C++, so that a reading knowledge of C syntax is assumed.

Chapter 2 introduces the fundamental object-oriented concepts together with the language elements of C++ used in the examples. Readers who are familiar with C++ should quickly browse through the mailing framework example before going on to the subsequent chapters on design patterns.

Acknowledgments

Many people helped and advised me in the course of writing this book. I thank Prof. Takayuki Kimura (Washington University in St. Louis, U.S.A.) who motivated me to start writing this book during my stay at WashU. Further thanks go to Prof. Gustav Pomberger and other colleagues at the C. Doppler Laboratory for Software Engineering (Johannes Kepler University Linz, Austria) for numerous discussions on design patterns.

Erich Gamma did pioneering work in his PhD thesis (Gamma 1992) which uses a graphic notation together with an informal textual representation as a basis for describing the design of ET++. His way of describing object-oriented design on an abstraction level higher than the underlying object-oriented programming language stimulated the search for metapatterns.

Günther Blaschek reviewed an early draft version of the manuscript. His detailed hints and suggestions allowed significant improvements.

Bob Bach, a native speaker from Virginia and computer science graduate student at the Johannes Kepler University Linz, not only corrected my English but also provided many useful ideas.

Last but not least, I would like to thank Gustav Pomberger, Timothy Brown, Ernest Wallmüller, Reinhold Plösch, Rainer Weinreich, Christoph Pree, and Peter Sommerlad for their proofreading. Thanks go to the anonymous reviewers for the comments.

It was a pleasure to cooperate with the people from Addison-Wesley (Yvonne Zaslawska, Andy Ware, Alan Grove, Annette Abel, Sheila Chatten) and ACM Press Books (Nhora Cortes-Comerer).

Wolfgang Pree
Linz, Summer 1994
pree@swe.uni-linz.ac.at

Contents

Chapter 3

Chapter 4

Chapter 5

Trademark notice

Apple, Macintosh, and MacApp are trademarks of Apple Computer, Inc.
Eiffel is a trademark of Interactive Software Engineering, Inc.
Objective-C is a registered trademark of Stepstone Corporation.
Porsche is a registered trademark of Porsche Aktiengesellschaft.
PostScript is a registered trademark of Adobe Systems, Inc.
Smalltalk is a trademark of Xerox Corporation.
X Window System is a trademark of Massachusetts Institute of Technology.
UNIX is a trademark of AT&T Bell Laboratories.
Visual C++, Microsoft Foundation Classes, and Windows are
registered trademarks of Microsoft Corporation.
Volkswagen is a registered trademark of Volkswagen Aktiengesellschaft.

Chapter 1

Impact of object-oriented software development on software quality

Over the past decades software has become an important part of an increasing number of technical systems such as airplanes, telephone systems, medical instruments, (nuclear) power plants, rockets, and satellites, as well as economic systems and services such as industrial production and trading systems, stock exchanges, and banking corporations. Inadequate software products underlying these systems may have disastrous consequences. This gives the production of high-quality software top priority.

This chapter discusses the principal *software quality attributes* and the influence of object-orientation on these attributes. Both reduced internal complexity of software systems through well-thought-out structuring and better reusability are viewed as key factors in improving software quality from a technical point of view. This chapter sketches why these factors are so important and how object-oriented concepts prove useful in defining a better internal software structure compared to that produced with conventional software development methods. The remainder of this book focuses on how object-oriented concepts can help to significantly increase software reusability.

1.1 Software quality attributes

The overall quality of software is hard to assess. Though various authors such as McCabe 1976, McCall *et al.* 1977, Ramamoorthy 1982, and Fenton 1991 discuss software quality attributes and software metrics, how to measure software quality remains disputed. Some examples of substantial software quality attributes are:

- correctness: a software product satisfies given needs and is free of errors

1

- ease of use: the ease of learning and using a software product
- reusability: the ability of the whole software system or parts thereof to be reused in other software products
- readability: the effort required to understand a piece of software
- efficiency: optimal use of hardware and software resources
- portability: the ease of transferring software to other hardware and/or software platforms.

Software quality also depends on one's point of view: the criteria relevant for end users in judging software quality differ from those applied by software engineers who have to develop and maintain software. For example, based on these two groups McCall *et al.* (1977) and Meyer (1988) distinguish between external and internal factors of software quality. Among the attributes listed above, correctness, ease of use, efficiency, and portability are especially important for end users.

1.2   Measures for producing high-quality software

We do not discuss interdependencies between the software quality attributes listed above or the various organizational, analytical, and other constructive measures to improve software quality. Instead we focus on two technical aspects which are considered to be crucial in achieving satisfying overall software quality:

(1)   *Well-thought-out structuring* of software systems: Real-world tasks that have to be supported by software products tend to be complex due to the huge number of inherent details. Appropriate structuring of software systems *helps to reduce complexity*. Appropriate structuring means that software is split into pieces that can be looked at almost independently. Furthermore, concepts that allow abstraction from details are necessary. Better structure and reduced complexity make software easier to read and understand and thus to extend and reuse. A better understanding of software components also has a positive effect on the correctness quality attribute.

(2)   *Reuse* of software components in numerous software systems has manifold advantages. The most striking are:

- Already tested and used software components will contain fewer errors than those developed from scratch. Reused components have a positive impact on the correctness of software.
- Development and maintenance costs are reduced, and overruns avoided.
- The development of easy-to-use, consistent, direct-manipulation graphic user interfaces (GUIs) is a difficult and tedious task. Adequate reusable

components for this domain allow improvement in the ease of use of software.

- If components with sophisticated, efficient algorithms can be reused, the overall software product will be more efficient.

- Reusable software components that are already portable across hardware and/or software platforms make it easier to keep the overall software system portable.

Object-oriented software development as presented in this book is a constructive quality assurance measure that addresses both structuring and reusability. The following section discusses the structuring of software systems. The reusability aspect of object-oriented software development sets the tone of the remainder of this book.

1.3 Reduced complexity through structure

In order to cope with the *software crisis*, Doug McIlroy claimed at a NATO conference in 1968 (republished in McIlroy 1976) that "software engineers should take a look at the hardware industry and establish a *software component subindustry*. The produced software components should not be tailored to specific needs but be *reusable* in many software systems." What a software component or software module really is or should be is a subject of controversy.

Figure 1.1 shows schematically a module consisting of a module interface and a module body which represents the implementation of the module. A client of a module only has to understand its interface. As long as

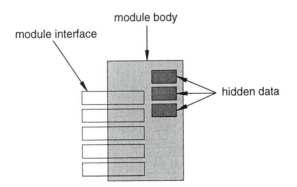

Figure 1.1 Principal components of a software module.

the interface remains unchanged, the implementation part of the module can be changed without requiring any changes in its clients.

From a general point of view, *module-oriented decomposition of software systems* stresses the encapsulation of data and functions. The most important criterion in module-oriented decomposition is *information hiding*, described by Parnas (1972): "A module is characterized by its knowledge of a design decision which it hides from all others. Its interface was chosen to reveal as little as possible about its inner working." The autonomous structure of such software modules is the precondition for their autonomous development and stand-alone testing.

Wirth (1982) identifies three module categories. All three categories rely on the principle of hiding unnecessary details and revealing only the essential aspects:

(1) Modules that offer only procedures/functions and contain no data: A module with mathematical functions such as sin, cos, exp, and sqrt represents an example of this category. Below we use the term *routine* as a generic term for function and procedure.

(2) *Abstract Data Structure* (ADS): An ADS consists of data and routines. Typically, data are hidden and can be accessed only by routines in the module. An example is a module for memory management, whose interface might offer routines to request memory and to free allocated memory. The necessary data to manage the allocated and available memory blocks as well as the required algorithmic details are hidden in the module implementation.

(3) *Abstract Data Type* (ADT): An ADT is like an ADS but represents a type, so that any number of variables of its type can be declared. Take an ADT CharacterStream as an example; it is a sequential file of characters. Clients of the ADT CharacterStream may declare any number of variables of this type and use them with the associated operations such as Connect, WriteChar, and ReadChar. We sketch below how to define the interface of the ADT CharacterStream and how to use this ADT.

Modular software systems especially are based on ADTs. An ADS corresponds to an ADT with exactly one instance. Modules of category (1) have no relevance in the realm of structuring software systems.

Figure 1.2 illustrates the typical structure of a modular software system consisting of instances of ADTs, symbolized by rectangles with rounded corners. (Note that Figure 1.1 depicts a sample ADT. Instances of an ADT mirror its structure, that is, its interface and body.) At run time instances of ADTs invoke each other's routines in order to accomplish certain tasks.

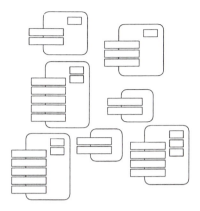

Figure 1.2 Structure of a modular software system.

Well-designed modular systems have almost autonomous modules. Achieving reasonable modularization is a difficult task that requires a lot of experience. There are no specific rules for designing good modularization, only some rules of thumb. The most important rules are presented in Section 4.2.2.

Programming language support for structuring software systems

Wirth (1974) remarks, "We must recognize the strong and undeniable influence that our language exerts on our ways of thinking, and in fact delimits the abstract space in which we can formulate—give form to—our thoughts." Below we outline the influence of programming language concepts on the way software systems are structured.

Functional, top-down design

Before the advent of module-oriented programming languages, the functions of a software system were considered as the primary criterion for its decomposition. Programming languages such as ALGOL, Pascal and C offer routines as their highest-level abstractions.

In connection with these routine-oriented languages, *stepwise refinement*—as described, for example, by Wirth (1971)—is typically applied for decomposing whole software systems. The terms *top-down decomposition* and *functional decomposition* are common synonyms for stepwise refinement.

Top-down decomposition implies the existence of one main routine which uses others for its implementation. Figure 1.3 illustrates the structure

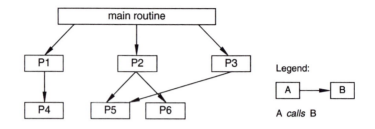

Figure 1.3   Functional, top-down decomposition.

of a stepwise refined software system. Note that the figure depicts no data, only routines. The *data* are usually *separated* from the routines and kept in global variables.

Experience with top-down decomposition has corroborated that the functionality of a software system is most likely to change. Data are much more likely to remain unchanged.

Meyer (1988) describes the problems of top-down decomposition: "Real systems have no top. .... The point is not that you cannot develop a system top-down: you can. But in doing so you trade short-term convenience for long-term inflexibility." Top-down design impedes future changes. Reusing all or parts of software systems designed top-down proves unlikely.

Modularization of software systems
Programming languages that support the modularization of software systems can be divided into two categories:

(1) Languages that offer modules matching the concept of an ADS: Each module formulated in such languages exists exactly once. Providing ADTs is possible but not directly supported. The relevant aspects of how to define ADTs in these languages are outlined below.

(2) Languages that directly support the definition of ADTs: The concepts of inheritance, polymorphism, and dynamic binding are also provided. These concepts are presented in Chapter 2.

Languages of category (1) are termed module-oriented. Typical representatives are Modula-2 (Wirth 1982) and Ada (ANSI 1983).

Languages of category (2) are termed object-oriented. The additional concepts of inheritance, polymorphism, and dynamic binding are primarily intended to improve flexibility and thus reusability.

Both terms—module-oriented and object-oriented—express that these languages support the modeling of real-world building blocks as modules/objects. As a consequence, the semantic gap between entities in the real world and their abstractions in a programming system can be reduced. Note that for many authors this commonality proves sufficient justification to term module-oriented languages as object-oriented. Thus module-oriented languages such as Modula-2 and Ada are sometimes presented as object-oriented. We disagree with this misnomer. A language graduates to the object-oriented camp only if it provides the concepts of inheritance, polymorphism, and dynamic binding.

ADTs in module-oriented languages
In module-oriented languages the definition of ADTs is syntactically not so expressive as in object-oriented languages. Example 1.1 outlines the interface of a Modula-2 module Streams that defines the ADT CharacterStream.

Example 1.1 Interface of a Modula-2 module defining the ADT CharacterStream.

```
DEFINITION MODULE Streams;
    . . .
        (* In an opaque type definition the actual type definition is
            hidden in the module implementation. *)
        TYPE CharacterStream;

        (* Connect opens a sequential file named 'fileName',
            associates it with 'cs' and returns a Boolean indicating
            whether the operation was successful or not. *)
        PROCEDURE Connect(VAR cs: CharacterStream;
                                fileName: ARRAY OF CHAR)
                    : BOOLEAN;

        (* WriteChar writes the single character 'ch' to the sequential
            file 'cs'. *)
        PROCEDURE WriteChar(cs: CharacterStream; ch: CHAR);

        (* ReadChar reads a single character from the sequential
            'cs' into 'ch'. *)
        PROCEDURE ReadChar(cs: CharacterStream;
                                VAR ch: CHAR);

        (* EndOfStream indicates whether the end of the sequential
            stream 'cs' has been reached. *)
        PROCEDURE EndOfStream(cs: CharacterStream):
                    : BOOLEAN;
    . . .
END Streams.
```

A client of module Streams has to declare instances of type CharacterStream and pass them as parameters to all routines provided by module Streams, as shown in Example 1.2.

Example 1.2 Usage of ADT CharacterStream in Modula-2.

```
. . .
FROM Streams IMPORT CharacterStream, Connect, WriteChar,
                    ReadChar, EndOfStream;

VAR cs1, cs2: CharacterStream;   (* Two instances of the ADT
                                    CharacterStream are
                                    generated. *)


IF (Connect(cs1, "File1")) THEN
        WriteChar(cs1, "A");
        WriteChar(cs1, "B");
        . . .
END;

IF (Connect(cs2, "File2")) THEN
        WriteChar(cs2, "M");
        WriteChar(cs2, "N");
        . . .
END;
. . .
```

ADTs in object-oriented languages

Object-oriented languages express the concept of ADTs in a syntactically better way, though the semantics behind ADTs remains the same. Most object-oriented languages provide classes to define ADTs. The class concept is presented in Chapter 2. The ADT CharacterStream can be formulated in C++ as shown in Example 1.3. The routines are written as part of the ADT CharacterStream. This expresses syntactically that routines form an integral part of an ADT.

Example 1.3 Interface of ADT CharacterStream in C++ notation.

```
class CharacterStream {
public:
        bool Connect(char *fileName);
        void WriteChar(char ch);
        void ReadChar(char *ch);
        bool EndOfStream();
};
```

The usage of the ADT CharacterStream in C++ as exemplified in Example 1.4 also expresses that routines form an integral part of an ADT. For example, WriteChar is invoked by the statement **cs1**.WriteChar('A'), requesting the instance cs1 of the ADT CharacterStream to perform this operation since WriteChar is logically a part of the ADT instance cs1.

Example 1.4 Usage of ADT CharacterStream in C++ notation.

```
CharacterStream cs1, cs2;        // Two instances of the ADT
                                 // CharacterStream are
                                 // generated.


if (cs1.Connect("File1")) {
        cs1.WriteChar('A');
        cs1.WriteChar('B');
        . . .
}

if (cs2.Connect("File2")) {
        cs2.WriteChar('M');
        cs2.WriteChar('N');
        . . .
}
. . .
```

Instances of the ADT CharacterStream can be depicted as shown in Figure 1.4. Hidden data might store the file name and details of how to access disk storage.

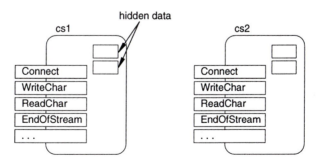

Figure 1.4 Instances cs1 and cs2 of ADT CharacterStream.

1.4   Potential of object-orientation for improving software reusability

The important effect of software reusability on other software quality attributes has already been outlined in Section 1.2. Despite the obvious advantages of software reuse, almost all software systems continue to be developed from scratch. We do not discuss organizational problems and psychological reasons such as the *not-invented-here* (NIH) syndrome which impede software reuse. The NIH syndrome, for example, expresses the fact that programmers tend to rebuild software components rather than reuse existing components. This is especially true if software components do not exactly match the requirements in a particular context.

Technical aspects are viewed by various authors as crucial preconditions for improving software reusability. For example, Meyer (1988) states that without appropriate technology organizational measures are scarcely helpful.

The concepts offered by object-oriented programming languages have the potential to improve software reuse significantly compared to conventional approaches. In general, we discern two principal levels of software reusability:

(1)   reuse of single software components

(2)   reuse of software architectures, that is, several single components and the appropriate glue between them.

Category (1) can be split into routine components and module components as presented in Section 1.3. (Krueger (1992), for example, gives a more fine-grained categorization of software reusability levels, including generator systems, software schemas, and transformation systems. These additional levels have no relevance in the context of this book.)

Conventional routine-oriented programming languages allow construction of reusable routine libraries. They can be viewed as libraries offering small building blocks that might be compared to nuts and bolts in physical systems. Routine libraries with more complex building blocks based on the call-back principle are often inflexible and difficult to use. For example, most libraries offered for programming GUIs based on the X Window system belong to this category.

Though module-oriented languages such as Ada and Modula-2 support the concept of ADTs, the following problem has to be considered: it is almost impossible to construct complex, project-independent modules that meet all future requirements. Typically, a small delta has to be changed so that a module can be reused in software projects other than the one it was originally designed for. Such variants sacrifice compatibility with the original module. Chances are high that such delta changes introduce errors.

As a consequence, module-oriented programming could not lead to the awaited breakthrough in software reusability. Only simple modular components such as linked lists, sets and hash tables are reusable in numerous projects without modifications.

Since object-oriented languages support *programming by difference*, this problem is alleviated: ADTs can often be adapted without touching the source code of the original ADT. The adapted ADTs are compatible with the original.

Even when object-oriented programming languages are used, their real potential is seldom tapped. The concepts of inheritance and dynamic binding are sufficient to construct frameworks, that is, reusable semifinished architectures for various application domains. Such frameworks mean a real breakthrough in software reusability: not only single building blocks but also whole software (sub)systems including their design can be reused. So frameworks enable a degree of software reusability that can significantly improve software quality. Section 2.2 presents the basic concepts and ideas behind frameworks.

Table 1.1 indicates how the concepts offered by programming languages correlate with the degree of achievable reusability. The signs used in the table mean the following: − (impracticable), + (reasonably suited) and ++ (well suited).

Table 1.1 Technical aspects of software reuse.

Reuse of...	Routine-oriented languages	Module-oriented languages	Object-oriented languages
Single components (routines)	++	++	++
Single components (modules)	−	+	++
Frameworks	−	−	(+)+

Design patterns try to describe frameworks on an abstraction level higher than the corresponding code that implements these frameworks. So design patterns should be viewed as complementary to object-oriented languages, and therefore object-oriented languages deserve a ++ rating for supporting the reuse of software architectures.

Chapter 2

Concepts of object-oriented software development

This chapter describes how to combine the basic concepts of object-orientation, that is, data abstraction, inheritance, polymorphism, and dynamic binding in order to develop frameworks. Such frameworks allow the highest degree of software reusability according to the classification given in Chapter 1.

Unfortunately, terms are often misused in connection with object-oriented software development. The term framework is one such example. So this chapter builds both a conceptual and a terminological basis.

Design patterns support the (re)use and development of frameworks. Thus we need a thorough understanding not only of the basic object-oriented concepts but especially of an appropriate combination of them in the realm of frameworks.

This chapter introduces the essentials of the programming language C++ (Ellis and Stroustrup 1990). C++ is used in the examples throughout the book for the following reasons: despite all its deficiencies, C++ has played and will continue to play a crucial role in object-oriented software development in industry and academia. C++ has proved to be "good enough" for programming-in-the-large.

For the reader to understand all the details of the examples presented, we assume a reading knowledge of the C language as described, for instance, by Kerninghan and Ritchie (1988).

For depicting classes, objects, and their relationships we use the graphic notation proposed by Rumbaugh *et al.* (1991) as Object Model Notation. The elements of this notation used and minor extensions to it are explained in the course of this chapter.

2.1   Basic concepts provided by object-oriented programming languages

This section focuses on the essential set of concepts that need to be supported by a language in order for it to be considered object-oriented. The concepts are illustrated by examples. In parallel, the corresponding constructs of the Object Model Notation and of C++ are presented.

2.1.1 Objects

Objects are instances of abstract data types (described in Section 1.3). Thus an object is an entity that has attributes (= data representing an object's state) and provides certain operations that are defined for the particular object. The attributes are called *instance variables*; the operations are called *methods*. An object carries out certain actions when it receives a *message*—a request asking the object receiving the message to do something. The formulation "sending a message" is often used instead of "calling a method". The terms "method" and "method call", which at first glance seem to be equivalent to the terms "procedure/function" and "procedure/function call", express another property of objects: which method is really executed depends not only on the name of the message, but also on the type of the particular object. This property of object-oriented languages, called dynamic binding, is explained in Section 2.1.3.

Objects should adhere to the principle of information hiding: implementation details—the inner structure of an object—should be hidden; data within an object should be accessible for manipulation only by an object's own methods.

Specification of objects
Most of the available object-oriented programming languages use a *class* to describe the scheme of an object (class = abstract data type). Objects are thus instances of classes. Any number of objects (= instances) may be created from a class. These objects have the same behavior, which is determined by the operations defined in the corresponding class. Objects differ in their states as determined by the data stored in the instance variables.

Not all object-oriented languages provide the class construct. SELF (Ungar and Smith 1987, Chambers *et al.* 1989) and Omega (Blaschek 1994) are examples of object-oriented languages without classes. In Omega, for example, new objects are not generated by language constructs, but interactively by means of appropriate object editors. We refrain from a detailed description of these languages since they introduce no essentially new concepts for object-oriented software development. We assume that object-oriented languages always use classes to describe objects.

Object-oriented languages may also be divided into *pure* and *hybrid* languages. Software systems developed in pure object-oriented programming languages consist of objects and nothing else. This means that procedures/functions that do not belong to an object are not supported. Examples of pure object-oriented programming languages are Smalltalk-80 (Goldberg 1984, Goldberg and Robson 1985), Eiffel (Meyer 1988), SELF, and Omega.

Hybrid object-oriented programming languages are usually procedure/function-oriented or module-oriented programming languages with additional language constructs that allow the specification of objects and support inheritance and dynamic binding as described in the course of this chapter. Examples are C++, Objective-C (Cox 1986), Object Pascal (Schmucker 1986), and Oberon-2 (Mössenböck 1993).

Graphic representation
Numerous graphic representations of object-oriented systems have already been proposed. We use the Object Model Notation (Rumbaugh *et al.* 1991) for depicting classes, objects, and relationships between them since this notation proved to be intuitive and sufficient to express the essentials of object-oriented software systems. In this chapter we present the rudimentary elements of the Object Model Notation.

Graphic representation of classes
Classes are drawn as rectangles with the class name in boldface, followed by the instance variables and the methods as exemplified in Figure 2.1. The notation is flexible so that the relevant aspects can be stressed. If the data type of an instance variable can be ignored in a certain context, it need not be specified. Methods are treated analogously.

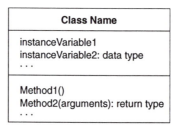

Figure 2.1 Graphic representation of a class.

Object-oriented programming languages support the principle of information hiding. Thus it is possible to specify which instance variables and methods can be accessed from outside and which are hidden in the instantiations (= objects) of a class. This aspect is neglected in the graphic representation shown above. Since classes should adhere to the principle of information hiding, instance variables are assumed to be hidden by default. Methods can be accessed from outside by default.

If an instance variable in an object of class A refers to an object of another class B, the two classes are connected by a solid line. The name of the instance variable is written above this connecting line as shown in Figure 2.2. A diamond is drawn at one end of the connecting line to express that the class at that end defines the instance variable. The use of the diamond deviates from the Object Model Notation where it expresses aggregation. The Object Model Notation provides no means to express the direction of an association between classes since this is considered to be an implementation detail.

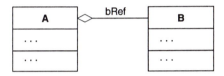

Figure 2.2 An object of class A can refer to exactly one object of class B.

The semantics of the diagram shown in Figure 2.2 are the following: at run time exactly one instance of class B is referenced by an instance of class A. The instance variable bRef of class A stores the corresponding reference. In C++ the instance variable bRef has the type pointer to B.

A solid circle expresses that many, that is, zero or more, B objects can be referenced by an A object (see Figure 2.3). In C++ bList represents, for example, a list or an array containing pointers to B.

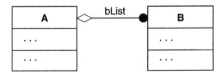

Figure 2.3 A refers to many (zero or more) B.

In pure object-oriented languages, instance variables are always object references. In hybrid object-oriented languages, instance variables may also have simple types (like integer or string). In the examples we define the types either in a C/C++ fashion or by means of a pseudonotation. Table 2.1 gives an overview of these notation details including the notation of methods.

Table 2.1 Notation details for types and methods.

	Pseudonotation	C/C++
String of characters	String	char *
Single character	Character	char
Integer number	Integer	int
Real number	Real	float
		double
Pointer to type T	ˆT	T *
Method M with no return parameter	M()	void M()
Method M with return parameter of type T	M(): T	T M()

It is sometimes necessary to comment instance variables and methods or to attach implementation details to methods. For this purpose we extend the Object Model Notation and use a dashed rectangle connected to the corresponding instance variable or method with a dashed line (see Figure 2.4).

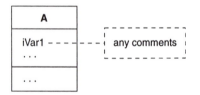

Figure 2.4 Commenting an instance variable.

Which graphic elements are used depends upon their relevance in a given situation. For example, if references between classes are irrelevant in a certain context, they are not drawn.

Text document and folder example

We employ two rudimentary classes—TextDocument and Folder—as the basis of an electronic mail system component which is to become part of an office automation system. A text document stores text characters and has a document name. A folder contains a number of text documents and has a folder name written on a tab as depicted in Figure 2.5.

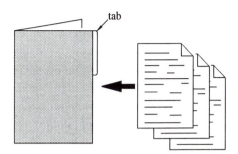

Figure 2.5 Folder storing text documents.

The initial design of the classes TextDocument and Folder is shown in Figure 2.6. This example will be enhanced later in order to illustrate various aspects of object-oriented software development.

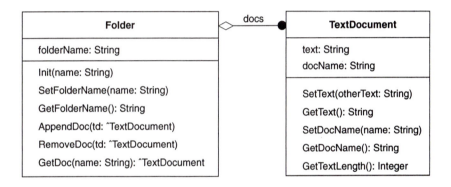

Figure 2.6 Folder and TextDocument classes.

The methods of class Folder serve the following purposes:

- Init(name: String) must be invoked before references to TextDocument objects are appended by calling AppendDoc. The parameter name defines the folder name written on the tab.

- SetFolderName(name: String) allows changes in the folder name.

- GetFolderName(): String returns the current folder name.

- AppendDoc(td: ^TextDocument) adds a text document to the folder. A Folder object stores not TextDocument objects but only references to them. Thus a reference to a TextDocument object has to be passed as a parameter.

- RemoveDoc(td: ^TextDocument) removes the reference to the Text-Document object passed as parameter td if td is stored in the folder. The referenced TextDocument object is not deleted.
- GetDoc(name: String) ^TextDocument searches through all TextDocument object references stored in a particular folder. The reference to the first text document with the name searched for is returned. If no text document name matches the one searched for, 0 is returned.

The methods of class TextDocument serve the following purposes:

- SetText(otherText: String) allows changes in the stored text.
- GetText(): String returns the stored contents of the text document.
- SetDocName(name: String) enables changes in the text document name.
- GetDocName(): String returns the text document name.
- GetTextLength(): Integer returns the length of the stored text.

Graphic representation of objects

Objects are depicted as rounded rectangles with the name of the class they belong to in brackets as depicted in Figure 2.7. Since an object's structure is defined by its corresponding class, the same notation is used to depict an object's instance variables and methods.

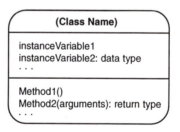

Figure 2.7   Graphic representation of an object.

The Object Model Notation suggests that instance variables can have their values written beside them, separated by the = sign: instVar = **value**. This especially makes sense for instance variables of ordinary types, such as integer. The values of instance variables that have pointer types can alternatively be depicted by letting them point to the entities they refer to. Figure 2.8 demonstrates this extended notation. Assuming that TextDocument is implemented in C++, the instance variables text and docName are pointers to character arrays which store character strings terminated by '\0'.

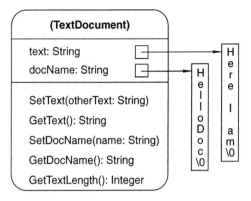

Figure 2.8 A sample instance of class TextDocument.

The necessary C++ code to generate objects and send messages to them is presented later. Nevertheless, we can take a closer look here at the effects of some messages on the object structure.

In order to put a TextDocument object into the state depicted in Figure 2.8, the following steps are required: after generating an instance of class TextDocument, the messages SetText with the string "Here I am" as its parameter value and SetDocName with the string "HelloDoc" have to be sent to that object.

To put that text document into a folder, the following has to be accomplished. An instance of class Folder is generated. That object is initialized by sending the message Init to it with the string "Samples" as the parameter value specifying the folder's name. Now the message AppendDoc has to be sent to the Folder object. The parameter value of this method is the pointer to the TextDocument object we want to put into the folder.

The role of Folder's instance variable docs is worth discussing. Recall that docs is supposed to store zero or more references to TextDocument objects. It was mentioned above that docs represents, for example, a list or an array containing pointers to TextDocument objects. Assuming that an array is used for that purpose, the object structure depicted in Figure 2.9 is obtained after appending the text document named HelloDoc to the folder named Samples.

Note that the implementation decision to use an array can be changed without changing Folder's class interface. This is possible due to information hiding: implementation details can be hidden so that a class' client is not affected if changes occur. The array elements are of type pointer to TextDocument.

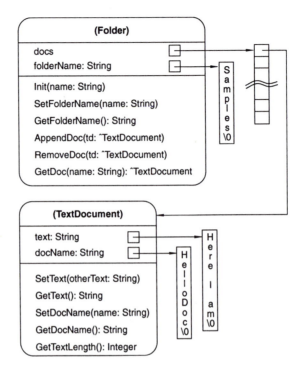

Figure 2.9 Storing the text document HelloDoc in the folder Samples.

Figure 2.9 illustrates details underlying graphically depicted object structures. Figure 2.10 shows the equivalent but more abstract object diagram. Note that the instance variable docs is ignored in the object diagram. Instead, a relation that expresses that the folder Samples refers to exactly one text document is drawn.

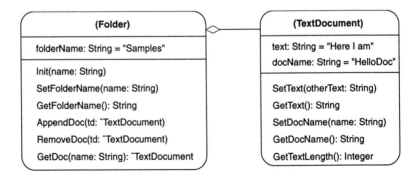

Figure 2.10 Folder Samples containing the text document HelloDoc.

Figure 2.11 illustrates how the class diagram relation zero-or-more ($\diamondsuit$——$\bullet$) is depicted in an object diagram. In the object diagram an A object refers to three B objects.

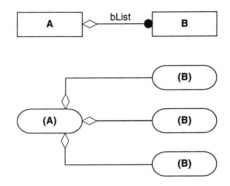

Figure 2.11 Class versus object diagram.

C++ notation
One goal in the development of C++ was to integrate object-oriented concepts into C in a seamless way. The C language element struct reflects a concept known in many programming languages: a struct is a type that allows the collection of any number of *data* elements into one unit. An arbitrary number of instances with the specified structure can be generated. Languages such as Pascal, Modula-2 and Oberon-2 offer the RECORD construct for this purpose. Two properties are missing in the C-struct which prevent it being suitable for class definitions:

- Functions/procedures cannot be components of a struct.
- All components of struct instances can be accessed from outside. Adhering to the principle of information hiding becomes impossible.

Thus the C language element struct was enhanced by these two properties so it could be used for class definitions. C++ introduces the keyword class to express this extension of a struct.

C++ class definition
Components of a class are, by default, hidden so that they cannot be accessed in instances. Components following the keyword public are accessible in objects generated from a class. Further details of the access privilege specification offered by C++ are presented in Section 2.1.2. Example 2.1 shows the general scheme of a C++ class definition.

Example 2.1 General scheme of a C++ class definition.

```
class ClassName {
        hidden instance variables
        hidden methods
public:
        accessible instance variables
        accessible methods
};
```

Like its ancestor C, C++ does not provide language elements for structuring program code in modules. Modula-2, for instance, offers a separation between the accessible and thus visible part of a module and its implementation, which has to be hidden from a module's client according to the principle of information hiding. In C and C++ it is up to the programmer to adhere to some conventions in order to give the program code at least minimal structure. The principal structuring convention in C++ is based on files: class definitions are written in *header files* which end with .h for header. An *implementation file* with the suffix .C includes the corresponding header file. (Include means that a preprocessor simply incorporates the text of the header file named in an #include statement.) The implementation file implements the methods defined in the header file.

The header file defining the TextDocument class could look as shown in Example 2.2. Compare the C++ notation with the graphic representation in Figure 2.6.

Example 2.2 C++ definition of class TextDocument in file TextDocument.h.

```
class TextDocument {
        char *text;
        char *docName;
public:
        void SetText(char *otherText);
        char *GetText();
        void SetDocName(char *name);
        char *GetDocName();
        int GetTextLength();
};
```

Another obvious deficiency of C++ is that the hidden instance variables and methods are visible in a class definition. Separating the class definition and class implementation by using header and implementation files only hides the method implementations from a class' client. In the definition of class TextDocument, for example, a client can see the hidden components text and docName, though these components cannot be accessed in objects generated from that class.

In order to alleviate this problem, another convention is used: the public section is defined first. The C++ keyword private introduces the hidden part, which comes at the end of a class definition. Thus the section which is important for a client is listed first. The definition of class Folder in Example 2.3 adheres to this convention.

Example 2.3 C++ definition of class Folder in file Folder.h.

```
class Folder {
public:
        void Init(char *folderName);
        void SetFolderName(char *name);
        char *GetFolderName();
        void AppendDoc(TextDocument *td);
        void RemoveDoc(TextDocument *td);
        TextDocument *GetDoc(char *name);
private:
        char *folderName;
        List <TextDocument *> *docs;      // uses a predefined class
                                          // List for storing
                                          // references to
                                          // TextDocument objects
    };
```

Before discussing the implementation of these classes and the type of the instance variable docs in class Folder, we take a look at how objects are generated and used from a client's point of view.

C++ object generation
A client of a class needs the class definition in the appropriate header file(s) and a description of the class interface. For our sample classes, TextDocument and Folder, the description at the beginning of this chapter and the self-explanatory names of their methods should be sufficient. In general, the documentation of a class library is a difficult problem. Design patterns represent one powerful possibility for accomplishing that task. The subsequent chapters discuss this issue.

C++ provides two kinds of variables: regular variables and pointer (or reference) variables. A regular variable represents a storage area which contains a certain value. Reference variables contain a pointer (= address) to a storage area where data are stored. This storage area is allocated dynamically in many cases. We assume that the reader is familiar with these concepts and do not go into further detail. From now on we speak of statically declared and dynamically declared variables in order to differentiate these two kinds of variables. The term reference variable is commonly used instead of dynamically declared variable. Note that statically declared variable does not mean declared as variable with the C-specific attribute static.

Many object-oriented languages such as Smalltalk only support reference variables pointing to dynamically generated objects. In C++ variables representing objects can be declared statically or dynamically. Example 2.4 demonstrates this for class TextDocument. The type of the variable sampleDoc is written in boldface in both code fragments. In the left-hand code fragment sampleDoc is a reference variable and has the type TextDocument *. The asterisk expresses the semantics "pointer to".

Example 2.4 Two ways of generating an object in C++.

```
#include "TextDocument.h"                    #include "TextDocument.h"

main() {                                      main() {
    TextDocument *sampleDoc;                      TextDocument sampleDoc;
    sampleDoc= new TextDocument;
    sampleDoc->SetText(...);                      sampleDoc.SetText(...);
    . . .                                         . . .
}                                             }
```

In the case of the statically declared variable sampleDoc in the right-hand code fragment, object instantiation occurs by variable declaration. If we declare sampleDoc as a reference variable, as is done on the left-hand side, an object has to be generated dynamically.

C++ offers the operator new in order to instantiate a class dynamically. This operator can also be used for dynamically allocating storage for simple types, as shown in the implementation of method SetText(...) in class TextDocument for type char (see Example 2.6). The operator delete frees dynamically allocated storage.

The operator new returns a pointer to the allocated storage area. The pointer type corresponds to the argument of the new operator. For example, new TextDocument allocates storage for a TextDocument object and generates that object. The type of the pointer returned by the new operator is pointer to TextDocument.

The use of reference variables in connection with dynamic object generation has to be preferred in the realm of object-oriented software development. The reason for this is explained in Section 2.1.3.

Example 2.5 lists the source code necessary to create the object structure depicted in Figures 2.9 and 2.10, that is, a Folder object Samples containing a TextDocument object named HelloDoc.

Example 2.5 Generation of a TextDocument object and a Folder object.

```
#include "TextDocument.h"
#include "Folder.h"

main() {
        TextDocument *sampleDoc;
        Folder *aFolder;

        sampleDoc= new TextDocument;   // dynamic object
                                       // generation
        sampleDoc->SetText("Here I am");
        sampleDoc->SetDocName("HelloDoc");

        aFolder= new Folder;        // dynamic object generation
        aFolder->Init("Samples");
        aFolder->AppendDoc(sampleDoc);
        . . .
        delete sampleDoc;           // free dynamically allocated
                                    // memory
        delete aFolder;
}
```

The graphic representations of the object structure in Figures 2.9 and 2.10 do not exactly match the code listed above: the reference variables sampleDoc and aFolder pointing to the particular objects are not shown in the object diagrams.

The code fragments in Examples 2.4 and 2.5 also illustrate how messages are sent to objects. The notation used to access a component of a struct instance has been preserved in C++ and is used to access components of a class instance. For example, sampleDoc->SetText(...) is a C-specific shortcut for (*sampleDoc).SetText(...), which means dereferencing sampleDoc and then accessing the component SetText.

Since all instance variables are hidden in the sample classes TextDocument and Folder, we cannot access them from outside in instantiated objects. For instance, writing sampleDoc->docName= "MyDoc"; would be reported by the compiler as a violation of access rights.

From a client's point of view, each object contains all the instance variables and method code specified in the corresponding class. Even though object-oriented language systems internally avoid the duplication of method code, for example, by means of method tables, this view is indeed correct. Objects are really entities that unify data and the behavior associated with them.

As mentioned above, it is good design practice to promote the idea of data encapsulation. This means that the internal state of an object cannot be directly manipulated. It should only be possible to do this by means of methods offered in the accessible interface of an object. TextDocument and Folder are typical examples which pursue the idea of data encapsulation. As a consequence, the hidden data structure used in Folder objects for storing TextDocument objects can be replaced easily without affecting the interface offered.

C++ class implementation

In hybrid object-oriented languages like C++ the only difference between methods and ordinary functions is that methods belong to a class. Thus an object-oriented programming language has to offer a syntactic means of expressing this relationship between a class and its methods. One possibility is to implement C++ methods directly in the class definition, that is, in the header file. We refrain from this possibility, which sacrifices information hiding: a client using such a class definition would be confronted with implementation details.

Methods should be implemented in the implementation file, separated from the class definition. A programmer expresses the semantics that a method belongs to a certain class simply by writing the class name in front of the method name, separating them by two colons. A possible implementation of class TextDocument is shown in Example 2.6.

Example 2.6 Implementation of class TextDocument in file TextDocument.C.

```
#include "TextDocument.h"        // The class interface always has
                                 // to be included in the
                                 // implementation file.
#include "string.h"              // The standard C library offers
                                 // functions such as strcpy for
                                 // copying the characters of one
                                 // string to another and
                                 // strlen for determining the
                                 // length of a string.
void TextDocument::SetText(char *otherText)
{
        if (text != 0)
                delete text;     // Deallocate the storage reserved
                                 // for storing the previous set text.
        text= new char[strlen(otherText)+1];    // Allocate the
                                 // storage for storing otherText.
                                 // Add one element for storing the
                                 // terminating '\0'.
        strcpy(text, otherText); // text <- otherText
}
```

```
char *TextDocument::GetText()
{
        return text;
}
void TextDocument::SetDocName(char *name)
{       // comments analogous to TextDocument::SetText
        if (docName != 0)
                delete docName;
        docName= new char[strlen(name)+1];
        strcpy(docName, name);
}
char *TextDocument::GetDocName()
{
        return docName;
}
int TextDocument::GetTextLength()
{
        if (text != 0)
                return strlen(text);
        return 0;
}
```

Of course, private, hidden components of a class can be directly accessed in the implementation of methods. In the case of class TextDocument the instance variables text and docName can be accessed. The rest of the implementation is straightforward C.

Implementation details: Generating copies of strings for the text and docName instance variables makes the class safer, since string handling is a source of errors in C. For example, a client that passes a pointer to a string as a parameter value to SetText(...) could later deallocate that storage area by accident. This is why managing a separate copy of strings is to be preferred. In the implementation proposed above, a client could do harmful things anyway, since GetText() and GetDocName() return pointers to the relevant internally stored string. The class TextDocument could be made absolutely safe by returning copies of the internally stored strings. The solution presented above can be considered as a compromise between safety and efficiency.

Example 2.7 shows a possible implementation of class Folder. Recall the declaration of Folder's instance variable docs in the header file: List <TextDocument *> *docs. This means that the type of docs is a pointer to a predefined class List. List objects manage elements of any type in a double-linked list. The specific element type is defined by writing <TextDocument *> after the class name List. This notation is based on an experimental design for class templates proposed by Ellis and Stroustrup (1990). Class List—used as a list storing pointers to TextDocument objects—provides the following functionality:

- void Add(TextDocument *td) adds td at the end of the list.
- void Remove(TextDocument *td) removes td if this reference is contained in the list.

The pseudostatement

```
for each td: <TextDocument *> in docs
    td->...
```

iterates over the elements if the variable docs points to the List object.

Example 2.7 Implementation of class Folder in file Folder.C.

```
#include "Folder.h"
#include "string.h"        // The function strcpy (for string copy) is
                           // used for copying the characters of one
                           // string to another.
                           // The function strcmp (for string compare)
                           // is used to decide whether two strings are
                           // equal or not.
#include "List.h"


void Folder::Init(char *folderName)
{
        if (docs != 0) {
                report error: Init has already been called
                return;
        }
        SetFolderName(folderName);   // call method of same class
        docs= new List <TextDocument *>;
}
void Folder::SetFolderName(char *name)
{
        // implementation analogous to TextDocument::SetText
        if (folderName != 0)
                delete folderName;
        folderName= new char[strlen(name)+1];
        strcpy(folderName, name);         // folderName <- name
}
char *Folder::GetFolderName()
{
        return folderName;
}
void Folder::AppendDoc(TextDocument *td)
{
        docs->Add(td);
}
```

```
void Folder::RemoveDoc(TextDocument *td)
{
        docs->Remove(td);
}
TextDocument *Folder::GetDoc(char *name)
{
        for each td: <TextDocument *> in docs
                // document name = name?
                if (strcmp(td->GetDocName(), name) == 0)
                        return td;
        return 0;
}
```

C++ specifics: constructors and destructors

Programmers often forget to call initialization functions. To avoid this pitfall in connection with objects, C++ offers a syntactic construct called a *constructor*. A constructor is simply a special method that has

- the same name as the class
- no return parameter.

A constructor cannot be called directly by sending a message to an object. It is used in connection with object generation and its code is executed immediately after object generation.

In class Folder the method Init(...) represents a typical candidate for a constructor. Class definition and implementation as well as object generation using a constructor are sketched in Example 2.8. Since a constructor is executed immediately after object generation, the parameters needed by the constructor have to be passed at the time an object is generated. Thus parameters have to be passed in connection with new in the case of dynamic object generation, and otherwise in the static declaration of variable aFolder.

Example 2.8 C++ class with constructor.

class definition:
```
        class Folder {
        public:
                Folder(char *folderName);         // instead of 'void Init(...)'
                ...
        };
```

class implementation:
```
        ...
        Folder::Folder(char *folderName)
        {        // There is no need to check whether this method has already
                 // been called since a constructor is invoked exactly once
                 // after object generation!
```

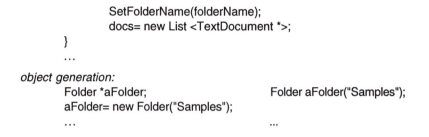

```
                    SetFolderName(folderName);
                    docs= new List <TextDocument *>;
        }
        …
object generation:
        Folder *aFolder;                            Folder aFolder("Samples");
        aFolder= new Folder("Samples");
        …                                            ...
```

A destructor represents the counterpart to a constructor. Its name is the same as the class name but preceded by ~. For example, the destructor of class Folder has the name ~Folder. A destructor is automatically invoked before an object's storage area is deallocated. Thus destructors should be used in classes that allocate storage for their instance variables. For example, class TextDocument allocates storage for text and docName, and class Folder allocates storage for docs and folderName. Destructors free the storage area which is allocated for items referenced by an object's instance variables in addition to the storage for the particular object. Since destructors represent an implementation detail that is irrelevant in the context of this book, we refrain from showing the definition and implementation of destructor methods in the examples.

Destructors help only at the microlevel of memory management, that is, within objects. They are not an alternative for automatic garbage collection as provided, for example, in the Smalltalk and Oberon-2 programming environments.

2.1.2 Inheritance

If a class is to be reused in a software system other than that for which it was originally designed, the class will not fit perfectly in most cases. Inheritance opens the possibility of extending and adapting object descriptions and implementations without changing their source code. According to the levels of reusability introduced in Section 1.4, inheritance increases the likelihood of the reuse of single components. Inheritance in combination with dynamic binding also allows construction of reusable frameworks. This aspect is discussed in Section 2.2.

When class B inherits from class A, the behavior of class B is identical to the behavior of class A. Class B contains the same instance variables and methods as class A. Class B can modify the inherited behavior of A without having to copy and change the source code:

- The implementation of methods of class A can be modified. This is often called method *overriding*. However, the method interface, that is, method name and parameters, cannot be modified.
- New instance variables and methods can be added.

Usually B is called a *subclass* of the *superclass* A; B is derived from A. In the Object Model Notation the inheritance relationship is expressed by a triangle and lines that connect a superclass to its subclasses. Figure 2.12 shows a sample class diagram. In this example SubClassB overrides Method2 of SuperClassA and adds instanceVariable3 and Method3.

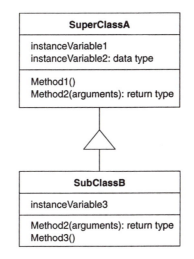

Figure 2.12 SubClassB inheriting from SuperclassA.

Ideally, only a few changes are necessary in order to reuse a particular class. Thus object-oriented programming is often described as programming by difference. A subclass specifies the delta by which it differs from its superclass.

Inheritance allows the definition of *class hierarchies*. These class hierarchies can grow to arbitrary depth.

Furthermore, we must distinguish single and multiple inheritance. With *single inheritance* a class can inherit from exactly one other class. *Multiple inheritance* means that a class can inherit from any number of classes.

We refrain from a discussion of the pros and cons of multiple inheritance and refer to Meyer (1988), Weinand *et al.* (1989), Gamma (1992), and Mössenböck (1993), who represent a sample set of advocates and opponents of multiple inheritance. Chapter 4 discusses some single-inheritance solutions of problems that can be solved with single or multiple inheritance.

Type compatibility and polymorphism
Type checking is also a matter of controversy. In object-oriented languages, static type checking means that the compiler can check whether an object

understands a message, that is, offers the method corresponding to a method call. For example, C++, Object Pascal, Oberon-2, and Eiffel belong to this category. Smalltalk is an example of an object-oriented language with no static type checking: an error does not occur until a message cannot be processed by an object at run time.

We focus on statically typed languages. Variables declared in conventional languages with static type checking, such as Pascal, Modula-2 and Ada, have exactly one data type and they accept only values of that data type. The compiler checks the proper usage of the variables.

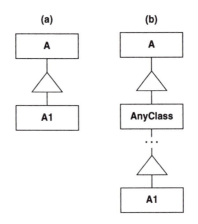

Figure 2.13 A1 as (a) a direct subclass of A and (b) as a descendant of A.

In object-oriented languages that provide static type checking, the following specific situation has to be considered. Subclasses of a class A can only add behavior, that is, instance variables and methods to class A. Thus objects that are instances of a descendant class A1 of A always have at least the instance variables and methods of A: the method names and parameters are the same, though the methods might be overridden. Class A1 being a descendant class of A means that A1 need not be a direct subclass of A, but can be deeper in the class hierarchy. Nevertheless, A1 must inherit from A as depicted in Figure 2.13(b).

As a consequence, an instance of a descendant class of A can be assigned to a variable statically declared of type A as demonstrated in Example 2.9. A variable of type A not only accepts generated instances of class A but also generated instances of all descendants of A. This implies that such a variable accepts not just objects of one type but of *many types*—it is *polymorphic*. Since subclasses are always extensions of their superclasses, objects of descendants of A understand all messages understood by A objects.

Example 2.9 Type compatibility in object-oriented languages with static type checking.

```
A *a;
A1 *a1;
a= new A;
a1= new A1;
a= a1;    // OK assuming that class A1 is a descendant of class A
a1= a;    // type compatibility violation
```

In object-oriented languages with static type checking, we distinguish static and dynamic types of variables:

- The *static type* of a variable is the type according to the declaration of the variable in the (static) program text. For example, the static type of variable a in Example 2.9 is pointer to A, and the static type of variable a1 is pointer to A1.

- The *dynamic type* of a variable is the type of the assigned object at run time. For example, the dynamic type of variable a in Example 2.9 after initialization (a= new A) is pointer to A. After the assignment a= a1 the dynamic type of a is pointer to A1 since a points to an instance of class A1.

Thus a variable has exactly one static type. It may have several successive dynamic types during run time. The number of possible dynamic types depends on the depth and breadth of the particular branch of a class hierarchy.

Type checking at compile time is based on static types. The compiler knows the static type of a variable and determines whether a certain message is understood.

At first glance, this discussion of type compatibility and polymorphic variables seems to be rather theoretical and of secondary importance. However, an appropriate combination of polymorphism and dynamic binding as applied in abstract classes (see Section 2.2.1) offers a fresh look at polymorphism as an important precondition for constructing reusable software architectures.

C++ notation

In order to illustrate the concepts of inheritance and polymorphism, we extend the C++ class definition and implementation of Folder. (Examples 2.3 and 2.7 list Folder's class definition and implementation.)

A class NestedFolder is to be developed which is similar to class Folder but differs in the following respects:

- The name of a folder is limited to 30 characters.

- It should be possible to put not only plain text documents into a folder but also other folders, as illustrated in Figure 2.14.

- The number of items contained in a folder should be made available. A contained folder object should be counted as one item. For example, the folder on the left-hand side in Figure 2.14 contains six items.

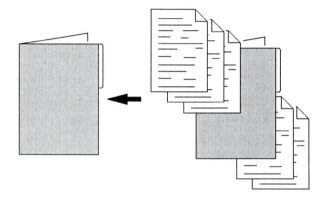

Figure 2.14 Nesting of folders.

A possible implementation of the desired behavior listed above is provided by class NestedFolder, which inherits from class Folder and adds or modifies the following components:

- Method SetFolderName(...) has to be overridden in order to limit the length of a folder name. Additional code is needed to check the folder name length.

- An additional instance variable folders (a List object managing pointers to Folder objects) and the additional methods AppendFolder(Folder *aFolder) and RemoveFolder(Folder *aFolder) implement the recursive structure of NestedFolder objects. GetFolder(char *name) searches the first contained folder whose tab name matches the one searched for.

- An additional method GetNoOfItems() returns the number of contained items, counting contained folders as single items.

Note that this solution is just an intermediate one used to demonstrate a common pitfall in object-oriented design. A significantly better solution is presented in Section 2.2. Nevertheless, building a subclass of class Folder is a good way of illustrating the specification of subclasses.

The C++ class definition of NestedFolder is shown in Example 2.10. The C++ syntax for specifying subclasses is intuitive in the sense that subclass definitions just list the modified and/or additional components.

Example 2.10 Class definition of NestedFolder in file NestedFolder.h.

```
class NestedFolder: public Folder {      // NestedFolder is a
                                         // subclass of Folder.
public:
        NestedFolder(char *folderName);  // constructor
        void SetFolderName(char *name);  // overridden method;
                                         // first task
        // additional methods:
        void AppendFolder(Folder *aFolder);       // second task
        void RemoveFolder(Folder *aFolder);
        Folder *GetFolder(char *name);
        int GetNoOfItems();              // third task
private:
        List <Folder *> *folders;        // additional instance
                                         // variable
};
```

The first line in the definition of class NestedFolder expresses that this class is a subclass of Folder. The word public between the colon and the superclass name Folder means that everything that is public in class Folder also remains public in class NestedFolder.

The rest of the class definition describes the differences with respect to the superclass Folder. Note that the overridden method SetFolderName(...) has the same name and parameter types as the corresponding method in the superclass.

One interesting aspect of class NestedFolder is related to polymorphism: as NestedFolder is a subclass of Folder, NestedFolder objects are also of type Folder. Thus it is sufficient to store the contained folders in a list whose elements are of static type pointer to Folder. Due to polymorphism each array element can store pointers to Folder objects as well as pointers to NestedFolder objects.

A sample implementation of class NestedFolder is shown in Example 2.11.

Example 2.11 Implementation of class NestedFolder in file NestedFolder.C.

```
#include "NestedFolder.h"
#include "string.h"      // The function strlen is used for deter-
                         // mining the string length in the overridden
                         // method SetFolderName(...).
                         // The function strcmp is used for string
                         // comparisons in method GetFolder(...).
#include "List.h"
```

```
NestedFolder::NestedFolder(char *folderName)
                          : Folder(folderName)  ①
                          // The parameter folderName is passed to
                          // the superclass constructor.
{
        folders= new List <Folder *>;
}

void NestedFolder::SetFolderName(char *name)
{
        if (strlen(name) <= 30)
            ②   Folder::SetFolderName(name); // The
                          // superclass method is called.
        else
                report error: folder name > 30 characters
                not accepted;
}

void NestedFolder::AppendFolder(Folder *aFolder)
{
        folders->Add(aFolder);
}

void NestedFolder::RemoveFolder(Folder *aFolder)
{
        folders->Remove(aFolder);
}

Folder *NestedFolder::GetFolder(char *name)
{
        // my folder Name = name?
        if (strcmp(folderName, name) == 0)
                return this;     ③

        for each folder: <Folder *> in folders {
                if (strcmp(folder->GetFolderName(), name) == 0)
                        return folder;
                // The folder hierarchy is searched through.
                if (folder is kind of NestedFolder) {     ④
                        NestedFolder *nFolder=
                                (NestedFolder *)folder; // type cast
                        Folder *tmp= nFolder->GetFolder(name);
                        if (tmp != 0)
                                return tmp;
                }
        }
        return 0;
}
```

```
int NestedFolder::GetNoOfItems()
{
        int items= 1;        // This folder represents one item.
        // The contained folders are counted.
        for each folder: <Folder *> in folders
                // The items are counted in the folder hierarchy.
                if (folder is kind of NestedFolder) {
                        NestedFolder *nFolder=
                                (NestedFolder *)folder;  // type cast
                        items= items + nFolder->GetNoOfItems();
                }
                else      // The instance variable folder refers to
                          // an instance of class Folder.
                        items=  items +
                                1 +  // A folder counts as one item.
                                folder->docs->Size(); // no
                                        // access to 'docs'! ⑤
        // Text documents are counted.
        items= items + docs->Size();   ⑥
        return items;
}
```

Let us discuss important aspects of the code listed in Example 2.11:

①   Constructors are invoked automatically after object generation. If a class is instantiated that is derived from (an)other class(es) the constructor(s) of the superclass(es) must be called first. Appropriate parameters are passed to a superclass constructor by writing a colon and the superclass name followed by the appropriate list of parameters in brackets, that is, : Folder(folderName) in the case of the constructor for NestedFolder. This construct appears between the header and the body of the constructor method. The C++ syntax reflects the fact that the particular constructor body is executed after the constructor of its superclass.

②   When a superclass method is overridden in a subclass, the implementation of the method in the superclass can be used for implementing that method in the subclass. An overridden superclass method is invoked by putting the superclass name in front of the method name separated by two colons. In the implementation of Nested-Folder::SetFolderName(...) the code already implemented in the superclass Folder is used by writing Folder::SetFolderName(...). The additional aspect of checking whether the name is limited to 30 characters augments that code.

In C++ it is possible to skip one or more superclasses in order to reuse method implementations: for example, if a superclass Item of class Folder already provided the SetFolderName(...) method we could—depending on the appropriateness of the implementation—reuse either the Item::SetFolderName(...) or the Folder::SetFolderName(...) method implementation. In general, such a skipping of superclass implementations is not recommended.

③ The keyword this used in the return statement of method GetFolder(...) is a reserved word in C++. It denotes the reference to the current object. If the NestedFolder object that receives the message GetFolder(...) has the name searched for, GetFolder(...) of that object literally returns a pointer to *this* particular object.

④ Unfortunately, the dynamic type of a variable cannot be checked in C++. Though information about the dynamic type should not be necessary in most cases, there are situations where accurate type information is required. For example, folder has the static type pointer to Folder. Since NestedFolder is a subclass of Folder, the instance variable folder can refer to instances of both class Folder and class NestedFolder. Only NestedFolder instances can contain other folders. As a consequence, recursive searching can take place only in NestedFolder instances.

Meta-information is the generic term for information about objects and classes. This includes not only the dynamic type of an instance but also its size, and so on. As C++ does not provide language constructs to obtain meta-information, class libraries implement mechanisms of their own. Sections 5.2.1 and A.2 demonstrate how to handle meta-information in a C++ framework.

Since there exists no standard notation for how to obtain meta-information, we use the statement var *is kind of* A as pseudonotation for checking the dynamic type of a reference variable var. The type check returns TRUE, which means a number ≠ 0 in C++, if the referenced object is an instance of class A or of a descendant of class A.

If folder actually refers to a NestedFolder instance, it is safe to typecast folder after that type check. Instead of the two lines expressing a typecast and then the invocation of GetFolder, we could also write one line: Folder *tmp= ((NestedFolder *)folder)->GetFolder(name).

Note that the temporary variable tmp has to have the static type pointer to Folder for compatibility with the static return type of GetFolder. Of course, the dynamic type of the returned pointer can be either pointer to Folder or pointer to NestedFolder.

⑤ Method GetNoOfItems is logically split into two calculation steps: the contained folders and the contained text documents have to be taken into account. Counting the contained folders and recursively the contained items in these folders causes a serious implementation problem that demonstrates the limits of adapting source code by means of subclasses. If there is a design flaw in the superclass, it often becomes impossible to adapt a class by simply defining a subclass. In such a case the superclass has to be changed, too.

Let us take a closer look at the actual problem. Iterating over the contained Folder objects (references are stored in folders) again implies that the reference variable folder can refer to either an instance of class NestedFolder or one of class Folder. If folder refers to a NestedFolder instance, recursively counting the items contained in this instance is trivial since NestedFolder offers the method GetNoOfItems. Thus we simply have to send the message GetNoOfItems to the NestedFolder object referred to by folder.

If folder refers to an instance of class Folder, we need the number of contained text documents. Now we are in serious trouble. Class Folder does not offer such a method. Exactly this deficiency was fixed by class NestedFolder's additional method GetNoOfItems. Due to information hiding we cannot access from the outside the data structure that stores the references. Recall that folder refers to another Folder object! If this were possible we could write folder->docs->Size(). Besides the methods Add and Remove, class List is also assumed to offer a method Size, which returns the number of stored object references.

Unfortunately, there is no chance of solving this problem without changing class Folder. The best way to do this is to define the method GetNoOfItems already in class Folder. Example 2.12 lists the required changes in the definition and implementation of class Folder and in the implementation of GetNoOfItems in class NestedFolder.

Example 2.12 Necessary adaptations for the implementation of GetNoOfItems.

class definition of Folder:

```
class Folder {
public:
    Folder(char *folderName);
    int   GetNoOfItems();
    ...
};
```

implementation of GetNoOfItems in class Folder:

```
int Folder::GetNoOfItems()
{
    return docs->Size();
}
```

implementation of GetNoOfItems in class NestedFolder:

```
int NestedFolder::GetNoOfItems()
{
    int items= 1;       // This folder represents one item.
    // The contained folders are counted.
    for each folder: <Folder *> in folders
                // The items are counted in the folder hierarchy.
                items= items + folder->GetNoOfItems();
    // Text documents are counted.
    items= items + Folder::GetNoOfItems();
    return items;
}
```

⑥   Though the implementation of GetNoOfItems shown in Example 2.11 is already obsolete, this original code illustrates the access privileges in C++ classes.

C++ supports more sophisticated management of access privileges than discussed up to now. Components which are declared private in a class definition cannot even be accessed in method implementations of subclasses. As a consequence, it would be impossible to access docs in the implementation of NestedFolder::GetNoOfItems() if the component docs were a private component of class Folder. Note that accessing docs in method implementations of NestedFolder is completely different from accessing folder->docs in ⑤. Accessing docs means accessing an inherited instance variable, whereas the statement folder ->docs means accessing the hidden instance variable docs of another Folder object.

Components that should be accessible in method implementations of subclasses but not from outside have to be declared as protected. Thus we have three levels of access privileges in C++: public, protected and private.

The class definition of Folder sketched in Example 2.13 is the precondition for accessing docs in NestedFolder::GetNoOfItems().

Example 2.13 Modified access privileges in class Folder.

```
class Folder {
public:
    ...         // unchanged
protected:
    List <TextDocument *> *docs;
    char *folderName;
};
```

In general, it is often difficult to decide which components can be private without sacrificing the extensibility of a class. When in doubt, a component should be declared protected rather than private. This rule also applies for the instance variable folderName in class Folder.

A sample folder hierarchy
In order to conclude the presentation of implementing class NestedFolder as a subclass of Folder, an example is given of how class NestedFolder can be used. Example 2.14 lists the corresponding code. In lines 7, 10, 15, and 26 of the sample code it is assumed that class TextDocument offers a constructor TextDocument(char *name, char *contents) which initializes the corresponding instance variables by means of the TextDocument methods SetDoc-Name(...) and SetText(...).

Example 2.14 Sample usage of class NestedFolder.

```
1    #include "TextDocument.h"
2    #include "NestedFolder.h"
3    ...
4    NestedFolder *aFolder= new NestedFolder("Samples");
5    NestedFolder *anotherFolder;
6
7    aFolder->AppendDoc(new TextDocument("HelloDoc", "Here I am"));
8    anotherFolder= new NestedFolder("Strictly Private");
9    aFolder->AppendFolder(anotherFolder);
10   anotherFolder->AppendDoc(new TextDocument("1995 Vacation",
11                                             "Kailua, Riva"));
12   anotherFolder->AppendFolder(
13                   new NestedFolder("Former Vacations")
14              );
15   aFolder->AppendDoc(new TextDocument("Arnold's Doc",
16                                       "I'll be back!"));
17   if (aFolder->GetNoOfItems() != 5)
18          report error in the implementation of
19          'NestedFolder::GetNoOfItems()'
20   aFolder->SetFolderName("This is a pretty long name that should not
21                be accepted");
22   Folder *tmp= anotherFolder->GetFolder("Former Vacations");
23   if (tmp && tmp is kind of NestedFolder) {
24          anotherFolder= (NestedFolder *)tmp;
25          anotherFolder->AppendDoc(
26              new TextDocument("1994 Vacation", "Sydney, Cairns")
27          );
28   }
```

According to the method interface in NestedFolder's class definition GetFolder(...) returns a pointer of type pointer to Folder. Line 23 checks the dynamic type of tmp which refers to a folder named Former Vacations. The type check returns TRUE since a NestedFolder instance and not a Folder instance is created in line 13. Due to the type compatibility rules of static types we could not have written anotherFolder= anotherFolder->Get-Folder("Former Vacations") in line 22 instead of lines 22–4.

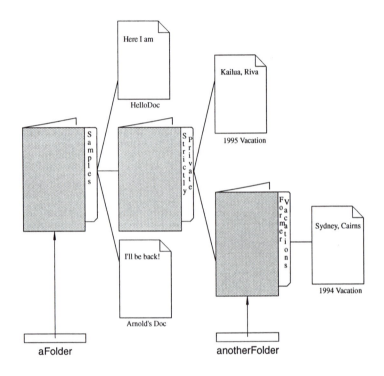

Figure 2.15 Folder and text document structure according to Example 2.14.

After the execution of the sample code, folder and text document structures are built as depicted in Figure 2.15. This figure also illustrates to which folder objects the reference variables aFolder and anotherFolder point at run time after execution of the listed code fragment.

To sum up, the implementation of NestedFolder seems to be a reasonably good solution based on inheriting behavior from the already available class Folder. But if we take a closer look at the implementation of NestedFolder, we notice that we manage two types of references in this class: references to text documents and to folders. An additional document type would require another subclass to manage this additional type. Furthermore, the management of folder names in class Folder is the same as the management of text document names in class TextDocument.

In order to achieve the goal of constructing reusable architectures, we have to introduce a further level of abstraction. The classes TextDocument, Folder, and NestedFolder already abstract important properties of the corresponding real-world objects, but frameworks require another abstraction step that factors out abstract commonalities of these still too concrete classes. Section 2.2 demonstrates the far-reaching effects of this further abstraction step.

Flattened representation of inherited behavior

A disadvantage of an object-oriented language like C++ is that programmers looking at a class derived from another class only see the extensions and modifications. The same approach is usually taken in the Object Model Notation.

To know which protocols, that is, which instance variables and methods, are supported by an object generated from such a class, a programmer must take the class definitions of all the superclasses into consideration. Thus it is absolutely necessary to have tools that provide a *flattened view of classes* in which all inherited instance variables and methods of a particular class are shown. It is also helpful to see which classes define specific components.

NestedFolder	
Folder	folderName: String
	List <TextDocument *> *docs
NestedFolder	List <Folder *> *folders
Folder	GetNoOfItems(): Integer
	SetFolderName(name: String)
	GetFolderName(): String
	AppendDoc(td: ˜TextDocument)
	RemoveDoc(td: ˜TextDocument)
	GetDoc(name: String): ˜TextDocument
NestedFolder	NestedFolder(name: String)
	SetFolderName(name: String)
	GetNoOfItems(): Integer
	AppendFolder(fp: ˜Folder)
	RemoveFolder(fp: ˜Folder)
	GetFolder(name: String): ˜Folder

Figure 2.16 Flattened graphic representation of class NestedFolder.

By means of the example NestedFolder, Figure 2.16 demonstrates how the graphic representation of classes can be extended to provide a flattened view.

The class names on the left-hand side indicate that the components grouped by class are defined in the particular class. For example, the instance variable folders is defined in class NestedFolder, whereas docs and folderName are defined in class Folder. Obviously this flattened representation can be applied in an analogous way in the visualization of object structures.

2.1.3 Dynamic binding

Dynamic binding represents another basic object-oriented concept in the context of inheritance. First we describe dynamic binding in a general way. Then we illustrate the concept in the folder and text document example. We focus on an appropriate combination of dynamic binding and inheritance in the subsequent sections.

Dynamic binding implies a run-time (not compile-time) determination of the method that is to be called. Which method is actually executed depends at run time on

- the message name and
- the dynamic type of the receiver.

In object-oriented languages with static type checking, a reference variable a of static type A can refer to any object that is an instance of a descendant of class A, due to polymorphism. Let us assume that a message M(), whose corresponding method is defined in class A and thus in all of its descendants, is sent to the object referred to by the variable a. The corresponding C++ statement is a->M();.

Methods in most state-of-the-art object-oriented programming languages are dynamically bound by default. If M() is dynamically bound, a->M() does not necessarily mean that M() is executed as implemented in class A. If the object referred to by a is an instance of a descendant of A that overrides M(), the method that overrides M() is executed.

Unfortunately, C++ requires that the programmer explicitly declare methods to be dynamically bound as shown below. Otherwise methods are statically bound, which means that the compiler determines which method is called according to the static type of a variable. Since the reference variable a has the static type pointer to A, method M() as implemented in class A is called no matter what the dynamic type of a is.

In general, dynamic binding is a precondition for development of reusable software architectures that do not depend on specific object types. The basic concepts of constructing such software architectures are presented in Section 2.2.2.

Example and C++ specifics

In order to illustrate the concept of dynamic binding, we take a look at some code samples using the classes Folder and NestedFolder as described in the previous section. Due to polymorphism, a reference variable aFolder of static type pointer to Folder can refer to a Folder instance as well as a NestedFolder instance. In Example 2.15 a NestedFolder instance is assigned to the reference variable aFolder. So aFolder has the dynamic type pointer to NestedFolder. What happens if the message SetFolderName(...) is sent to the object referenced by aFolder? Recall that SetFolderName(...) is overridden in class NestedFolder in order to restrict the folder name length to 30 characters.

Example 2.15   Which method is executed?

```
Folder *aFolder;
aFolder= new NestedFolder("Samples");       // possible due to
                                            // polymorphism
aFolder->SetFolderName("This is a pretty long folder name. Will it be
                       accepted?");
```

According to the concept of dynamic binding, which method is executed depends on the message name and the dynamic type of the object at run time. Thus SetFolderName(...) as implemented in class NestedFolder should be invoked—the folder name is not changed since the string passed as the parameter value is longer than 30 characters. This is the behavior one expects from an object-oriented language. As a consequence, all methods should be dynamically bound. (Note that a correct calculation of the number of contained items in class NestedFolder as listed in Example 2.12 also requires GetNoOfItems to be dynamically bound.)

Example 2.16   Marking a method as dynamically bound in C++.

```
class Folder {
public:
        Folder(char *folderName);
        virtual void SetFolderName(char *name);
        ...
};
```

Unfortunately, C++ methods are implicitly statically bound. The programmer has to mark a method with the keyword virtual in order for it to be dynamically bound. This is why SetFolderName(...) is only dynamically bound if the keyword virtual precedes the method declaration in the class where that particular method is declared first in the class hierarchy. Taking SetFolderName(...) as an example, this method would have to be declared as dynamically bound in class Folder (see Example 2.16). In descendants that override SetFolderName(...), the keyword virtual need not precede the method declaration.

We require all methods to be dynamically bound. Since the Object Model Notation does not mirror this specific C++ deficiency, the keyword virtual does not precede the method names in this notation. All methods are assumed to be dynamically bound.

Another specific issue in C++ is that dynamic binding only works if reference variables are used. SetFolderName(...), for example, would be statically bound in the code shown in Example 2.17 despite a virtual declaration of this method in class Folder.

Example 2.17   Implication of variable declarations on dynamic binding.

```
Folder aFolder("Samples");
NestedFolder aNestedFolder("NestedSample");
aFolder= aNestedFolder;
aFolder.SetFolderName("This is a pretty long folder name. Will it be
                                    accepted?");
```

Thus object-oriented software systems developed in C++ use only reference variables that store pointers to objects. A surprising exception to this rule is Microsoft's Foundation Class Library (Microsoft 1994), where it often does not matter whether reference variables are used. This class library actually circumvents dynamic binding provided by C++ and reimplements dynamic binding in the realm of event handling by means of macros.

Acceptable exceptions to the rule are instances of classes that represent basic data types such as Point, Rectangle, and Complex. In these special cases it is not difficult to define class interfaces that are very unlikely to be modified in subclasses. Typically, no subclasses of these classes are defined and dynamic binding of methods is irrelevant. So variables of these types can be declared statically, for example, in the statement Point p1(10, 20);.

Constructors and dynamic binding

Methods called in constructors are always statically bound in C++. The quick-witted reader will detect a problem in the implementation of NestedFolder's constructor, which passes the parameter folderName to its superclass constructor as listed in Example 2.11. The constructor of Folder calls SetFolderName. This method is declared as dynamically bound, which is useless in this situation. Thus method SetFolderName of class Folder is invoked. Folder::SetFolderName does not check the length of the passed folder name. As a consequence, an instance of class NestedFolder can be generated with a folder name that is longer than 30 characters: NestedFolder *nf= new

NestedFolder("a name that is longer than 30 characters is accepted in the constructor!"). In order to circumvent this C++ problem, we have to check the name length in the constructor of NestedFolder, too.

2.2 Enhancing software reusability by an appropriate combination of object-oriented concepts

Object-oriented programming languages are used in many software projects in a manner similar to module-oriented languages with classes as a means for implementing abstract data types. Inheritance helps to adapt and thus reuse building blocks that do not exactly match the requirements. So adaptations are possible without having to change the source code.

In order to develop the full potential of object-oriented software construction in the realm of constructing reusable architectures, an *appropriate combination* of the basic object-oriented concepts is necessary:

- object/class definition
- inheritance in connection with polymorphism and dynamic binding.

The key idea behind this approach is to find good abstractions of concrete classes. *Abstract classes* as discussed below represent such abstractions. They form the basis of frameworks, which are reusable application skeletons. Frameworks represent the highest level of reusability known today, made possible by object-oriented concepts. A basic understanding of framework mechanisms as explained in this section is necessary in order to grasp the idea of design patterns discussed in the rest of this book. Such design patterns can be viewed in connection with frameworks as a valuable means of documenting existing frameworks and developing new reusable object-oriented software architectures.

2.2.1 Abstract classes

The general idea behind abstract classes is clear and straightforward:

- Properties (that is, instance variables and methods) of similar classes are defined in a common superclass.
- Classes that define common behavior usually do not represent instantiable classes but abstractions of them. They are called *abstract classes*.
- Some methods of the resulting abstract class can be implemented, while only dummy or preliminary implementations can be provided for others. Though some methods cannot be implemented, their names and

parameters are specified since descendants cannot change the method interface. So an abstract class creates a *standard class interface* for all descendants. Instances of all descendants of an abstract class will understand at least all messages that are defined in the abstract class.

Sometimes the term *contract* is used for this standardization property: instances of descendants of a class A support the same contract as supported by instances of A.

- It does not make sense to generate instances of abstract classes since some methods have empty/dummy implementations.

- The implication of abstract classes is that other software components based on them can be implemented. These components rely on the contract supported by the abstract classes. In the implementation of these components, reference variables that have the static type of the abstract classes they rely on are used. Nevertheless, such components work with instances of descendants of the abstract classes by means of polymorphism. Due to dynamic binding, such instances can bring in their own specific behavior.

The key problem is to find useful abstractions so that software components can be implemented without knowing the specific details of concrete objects. Let us redesign the text document and folder example in order to reveal how an abstract class evolves.

DesktopItem: a sample abstraction
The classes TextDocument and Folder as designed and implemented in the previous sections show some similarities:

(1)   Both manage a name: TextDocument is a document name, Folder a name that is attached to its tab.

(2)   In both classes the size of an object, that is, the text length in the case of TextDocument and the number of stored items in the case of (Nested)Folder, can be retrieved.

Another problem in the previous design of the classes Folder and NestedFolder has to be taken into account: the management of additional document types would again imply an extension analogous to the extension of Folder in class NestedFolder in order to manage folder hierarchies. For example, such an extension would be necessary in order to handle instances of a class DrawingDocument. An additional instance variable and corresponding methods like AppendDrawDoc(...) would have to be added in a subclass of NestedFolder to handle that additional document type.

The similarities listed above form the basis of the initial design of an abstract class that defines the commonalities of TextDocument and Folder. We could call the abstract class simply Item. Let us take a look at concrete subclasses of the abstract class: they represent real-world objects like folders and sheets of paper with text written on them. If somebody works with these real-world objects, they are typically placed on desktops. As a consequence, we use the name DesktopItem for the abstract class. This name is more expressive than Item.

The abstract class DesktopItem offers the following contract:

- Due to (1) DesktopItem has the instance variable itemName of type String and two methods to manipulate an item's name, SetItemName(...) and GetItemName().

- Because of (2) we could add the two methods GetSizeInBytes() and GetSizeInItems() to the abstract class DesktopItem. Since GetSizeInItems() only makes sense for Folder objects, we refrain from defining this method in the abstract class.

  GetSizeInBytes() represents a typical example of a method that can only have a dummy implementation in class DesktopItem. The size in bytes of a text document, for example, is its text length; a folder's size in bytes is the sum of the sizes of all the contained items.

  Obviously, no specific instance variables are added in DesktopItem to implement this method. It has to be overridden in subclasses.

Example 2.18 shows the class definition of DesktopItem. Note that the keyword virtual marks all methods except the constructor as dynamically bound.

Example 2.18 Class definition of DesktopItem in file DesktopItem.h.

```
class DesktopItem {
public:
        DesktopItem(char *name= "Untitled");
        virtual void SetItemName(char *name);
        virtual char *GetItemName();
        virtual int GetSizeInBytes();
protected:
        char *itemName;
};
```

In contrast to a dummy implementation of method GetSizeInBytes() (see Example 2.19), the constructor and the methods SetItemName(...) and GetItemName() can actually be implemented in class DesktopItem. A method of an abstract class for which only a dummy implementation can be provided is called an *abstract method*.

Example 2.19 Implementation of class DesktopItem in file DesktopItem.C.

```
#include "DesktopItem.h"
#include "string.h"

DesktopItem::DesktopItem(char *name)
{
        SetItemName(name);
}
void DesktopItem::SetItemName(char *name)
{
        if (itemName != 0)
                delete itemName;
        itemName= new char[strlen(name)+1];
        strcpy(itemName, name);             // itemName <- name
}
char *DesktopItem::GetItemName()
{
        return itemName;
}
int  DesktopItem::GetSizeInBytes()
{
        return 0;                           // dummy implementation
}
```

In the Object Model Notation the attribute {abstract} is written on the right-hand side of abstract methods. We prefer to write abstract methods in *italics*. Analogously, names of abstract classes are written in *italics*. Figure 2.17 shows the class diagram of DesktopItem adhering to these conventions.

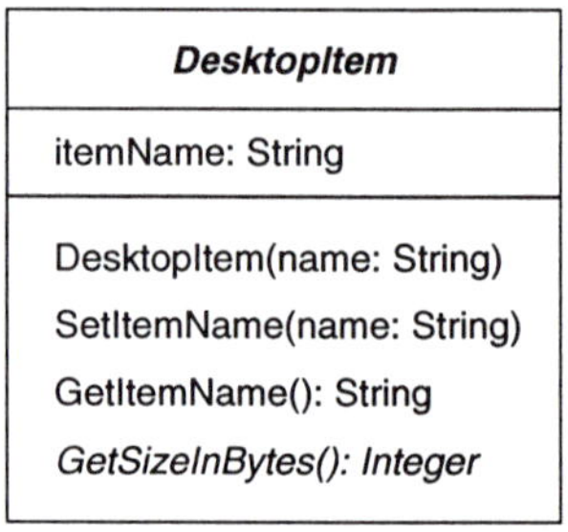

DesktopItem
itemName: String
DesktopItem(name: String)
SetItemName(name: String)
GetItemName(): String
GetSizeInBytes(): Integer

Figure 2.17 Abstract class DesktopItem with abstract method GetSizeInBytes().

Let us consider again the problem that the originally designed classes TextDocument, Folder, and NestedFolder cannot handle additional document types such as instances of a new class DrawingDocument. Each additional document type would imply that another descendant of NestedFolder which manages that particular document type has to be defined.

This severe problem is solved almost automatically by the abstract class DesktopItem. Due to polymorphism, instances of any descendant of Desktop-Item can be referred to by reference variables of static type DesktopItem. We unify the former classes Folder and NestedFolder into one class Folder that manages object references of static type pointer to DesktopItem. The method AppendDesktopItem(DesktopItem *additionalItem) shown in Example 2.20 accepts instances of all subclasses of DesktopItem as a parameter: Text-Document objects, Folder objects (enabling recursive nesting) and instances of *all future* descendants of DesktopItem, such as DrawingDocument, can be handled. This gives a first glimpse of how class design can be drastically improved by means of an abstract class. Example 2.20 lists the source code defining this kind of Folder class as a subclass of DesktopItem.

Example 2.20 Definition of class Folder in file Folder.h.

```
class Folder: public DesktopItem {
public:
        Folder(char *name);
        // Folder-specific implementation of the protocol
        // defined in DesktopItem
        void SetItemName(char *name);   // The superclass method
                                        // is overridden in order to
                                        // limit the name length to
                                        // 30 characters.
        int GetSizeInBytes();

        // additional methods
        int GetSizeInItems();

        // management of contained desktop items
        void AppendDesktopItem(DesktopItem *additionalItem);
        void RemoveDesktopItem(DesktopItem *
                            itemToBeRemoved);
        DesktopItem *GetDesktopItem(char *name);
protected:
        List <DesktopItem *> *desktopItems;
};
```

Since the implementations of the Folder's constructor and the methods SetItemName(...), AppendDesktopItem(...) and RemoveDesktopItem(...) are analogous to the implementations shown in Example 2.11, we focus on the implementation of the remaining methods listed in Example 2.21.

Example 2.21 Relevant implementation aspects of class Folder.

```
#include "Folder.h"
...
int Folder::GetSizeInBytes()
{
        int size= 0;        // A folder itself is supposed to have size 0.
        for each di: <DesktopItem *> in desktopItems
                size= size + di->GetSizeInBytes();
        return size;
}
int Folder::GetSizeInItems()
{
        int size= 1;        // A folder itself represents one item.
        // The items are counted in the contained folders.
        for each di: <DesktopItem *> in desktopItems
                if (di is kind of Folder)
                        size= size +
                                ((Folder *)di)->GetSizeInItems();
                else
                        size++;  // A single DesktopItem is counted
                                 // as 1 item.
        return size;
}
DesktopItem *Folder::GetDesktopItem(char *name)
{
        DesktopItem *item= 0;
        // Am I the desktop item searched for?
        if (strcmp(itemName, name) == 0)
                return this;
        for each di: <DesktopItem *> in desktopItems {
                if (strcmp(di->GetItemName(), name) == 0)
                        return di;
                // The hierarchy is searched through.
                if (di is kind of Folder) {
                        item=
                                ((Folder *)di)->GetDesktopItem(name);
                        if (item != 0)
                                return item;
                }
        }
        return 0;
}
```

Note the elegant recursive structure of method GetSizeInBytes(). Since this method is already defined in the abstract class DesktopItem, no type check is necessary in the overriding method in class Folder. Due to dynamic binding, which method is invoked depends on the dynamic type of di. If di has the dynamic type pointer to TextDocument the corresponding method is executed. If di refers to an instance of any future descendant of DesktopItem that overrides GetSizeInBytes(), the appropriate method is executed. If di refers to an instance of Folder, the recursive calculation is done according to the implementation of GetSizeInBytes() in class Folder.

The other two methods require type checks since these methods are not defined in the abstract class DesktopItem. At the beginning of this section we argued why it does not make sense to define these methods in DesktopItem. The semantics associated with GetSizeInItems() and GetDesktopItem(...) are not appropriate for the other subclasses of DesktopItem.

As some of the behavior of former class TextDocument is defined in DesktopItem, the class definition of TextDocument as a subclass of DesktopItem is also reduced as shown in Example 2.22.

Example 2.22 Definition of class TextDocument in file TextDocument.h.

```
class TextDocument: public DesktopItem {
public:
        TextDocument(char *name, char *contents);
        virtual void SetText(char *otherText);
        virtual char *GetText();
        // TextDocument-specific implementation of the protocol
        // defined in DesktopItem
        int GetSizeInBytes();
protected:
        char *text;
};
```

The implementation of the TextDocument class is analogous to the original implementation. By means of the C function strlen, method GetSizeIn-Bytes() calculates the length of the character string referenced by the instance variable text.

Example 2.23 demonstrates how the classes Folder and TextDocument are used in order to build up an object hierarchy as shown in Figure 2.15. The code in Example 2.23 is more uniform than that in Example 2.14: method AppendDesktopItem(...) appends desktop items to a folder no matter which instance of a subclass of DesktopItem is actually appended.

Example 2.23 Sample usage of classes Folder and TextDocument.

```
#include "TextDocument.h"
#include "Folder.h"
...
Folder *aFolder= new Folder("Samples");
Folder *anotherFolder;
```

```
afolder->AppendDesktopItem(new TextDocument("HelloDoc",
                                "Here I am"));
anotherFolder= new Folder("Strictly Private");
aFolder->AppendDesktopItem(anotherFolder);
anotherFolder->AppendDesktopItem(
        new TextDocument("1995 Vacation", "Kailua, Riva")
);
anotherFolder->AppendDesktopItem(
        new Folder("Former Vacations")
);
aFolder->AppendDesktopItem(
        new TextDocument("Arnold's Doc", "I'll be back!")
);
if (aFolder->GetNoOfItems() != 5)
        report error in the implementation of 'Folder::GetNoOfItems()'
aFolder->SetItemName("This is a pretty long name that should not be
                        accepted");
DesktopItem *tmp=
        anotherFolder->GetDesktopItem("Former Vacations");
if (tmp && tmp is kind of Folder) {
        anotherFolder= (Folder *)tmp;
        anotherFolder->AppendDesktopItem(
            new TextDocument("1994 Vacation", "Sydney, Cairns")
        );
}
...
```

2.2.2 Frameworks

Wirfs-Brock and Johnson (1990) describe the relationship between abstract classes and frameworks in a general way: "Although abstract classes provide a way to express the design of a class, classes are too fine-grained. A framework is a collection of abstract and concrete classes and the interface between them, and is the design for a subsystem."

Abstract classes form the basis of a framework. If abstract classes factor out enough common behavior, other components, that is, concrete classes or other abstract classes, can be implemented based on the contracts offered by the abstract classes. A set of such abstract and concrete classes is called a framework.

The term *application framework* is used if this set of abstract and concrete classes comprises a generic software system for an application domain. Applications based on such an application framework are built by customizing its abstract and concrete classes. In general, a given framework anticipates much of a software system's design. This design is reused by all software systems built with the framework.

GUI application frameworks like MacApp (Wilson *et al.* 1990) and ET++ (Weinand *et al.* 1988, Weinand *et al.* 1989, Gamma 1992, Weinand 1992) provide a reusable, blank *application* that implements much of a given user interface look-and-feel standard. Application frameworks are not limited to the construction of direct-manipulation, graphic user interfaces. Examples are application frameworks for VLSI routing algorithms (Gossain and Anderson 1989), for controlling real-time psychophysiology experiments (Foote 1988), for the development of operating systems (Madany *et al.* 1989, Russo and Campbell 1989), and for visual language systems (Fukanaga *et al.* 1993). Nevertheless, up to now almost all of the publicized frameworks focus on GUIs because GUIs are domain-independent and useful to most programmers.

GUI application frameworks can be viewed as the first test bed for the development of reusable architectures by means of object-oriented programming concepts. They have become one of the main reasons why object-oriented programming enjoys such a good reputation for promoting extensibility and reuse. Applications built on top of a framework reuse its code *and* its design.

Design patterns as discussed in the subsequent chapters help to develop not only applications based on frameworks but also new frameworks by applying design approaches that have already matured in other frameworks. The pain of designing a framework from scratch is described by Wirfs-Brock and Johnson (1990): "Good frameworks are usually the result of many design iterations and a lot of hard work."

A sample mailing framework

In order to illustrate the general presentation of frameworks given above, we sketch the development of a miniframework which is primarily based on the abstract classes DesktopItem and Employee. A mailing framework should manage desktop item mailing between single employees and groups of employees of a corporation. Our initial design of this framework builds upon the following requirements:

(1)   Each employee has a mailbox.

(2)   A mailbox contains a number of desktop items and has a name.

(3)   It should be possible to sort the desktop items contained in a mailbox by name or by (byte) size.

(4)   Every employee must have access to the address list containing all employees and the list of predefined groups such as the management team, secretaries, and part-time employees. Furthermore, an employee should be able to define his or her own groups.

(5)   Access privileges for reading mailboxes, managing the corporation's address list and predefined groups, and changing these access privileges have to be provided.

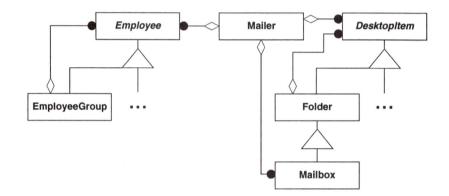

Figure 2.18   Mailing framework classes.

A rough design for the framework is outlined as follows:

- Another class Mailbox is added to the classes DesktopItem, Folder and TextDocument. According to (2) a mailbox is very similar to a folder. Thus class Mailbox becomes a subclass of Folder and adds methods to sort the items contained in a folder by name or size.

- An abstract class Employee is required. Instance variables describe, for example, access privileges. Since these and other aspects of Employee's class interface are irrelevant in this context, we refrain from further detail. Subclasses represent specific types of employees. One subclass called EmployeeGroup manages a group of employees, similar to a folder which manages a group of desktop items.

- A Mailer class is based on the abstract classes DesktopItem and Employee and implements the actual mailing between employees as well as the management of the address list and group lists based on access privileges.

Figure 2.18 shows the class hierarchy and the relationships between the classes that constitute the mailing framework. Recall that abstract classes are written in *italics*.

Let us select some aspects of class Mailer in order to give a glimpse of the interface and implementation of this component. Class Mailer's core data structure could be a list containing all employees. Associated with each employee are a mailbox and a list of groups which are specific to the particular employee. Mailer offers methods to log into the mail system in order to send and read mail and to edit groups and the address list. Edit operations are restricted by access privileges stored with each employee.

A method TransferItem(DesktopItem *item, Employee *sender, Employee *receiver) transfers a DesktopItem instance sent by sender to the receiver and notifies the receiver that mail has arrived. Note that a receiver can also be a group of employees.

Class Mailer does not implement a user interface. For example, an appropriate GUI could support direct manipulation like dragging an iconic mail letter to the iconic mailbox of an employee or employee group. For testing the Mailer component, a simple text-based user interface is sufficient.

An important property of class Mailer is that it need not be modified in order to process instances of additional subclasses of DesktopItem or Employee. In this sense it is no problem to reuse this component when the class hierarchy is extended. For example, no changes are necessary at all in order to mail DrawingDocument, VoiceDocument or EmbeddedDocument instances, to name just a few examples of possible new subclasses of DesktopItem.

Since the classes DesktopItem and Employee provide a convenient grouping mechanism, an easy way of sending a collection of desktop items to a group of employees is provided. When an abstract class and a concrete class are designed with this grouping mechanism built in, we can say that these classes are designed following a *pattern*. Though different objects are grouped in the cases of Folder and EmployeeGroup, the underlying principle of how to group objects is the same. This grouping mechanism also works with all instances of future subclasses of the abstract classes Employee and DesktopItem.

Recall our general definition of a framework: a framework is a set of abstract and concrete classes providing a software system as a generic application for a specific domain. The abstract classes of the mailing framework are DesktopItem and Employee. The concrete classes are Folder, Mailbox and Mailer. Mailer implements a generic mailing system—generic in the sense that it does not handle specific types. Instead, it deals with the abstractions Employee and DesktopItem. The generic mailing system is customized by defining appropriate subclasses of Employee and DesktopItem, for example, the classes TextDocument, DrawingDocument, and Voice-Document as DesktopItem subclasses and the classes Manager, Secretary, and Technician as Employee subclasses. If class Mailer has a good design, it can be adjusted to specific needs by specifying the desired differences in a subclass of Mailer. This illustrates the property of frameworks that applications based on a framework are built by customizing its abstract and concrete classes.

Figure 2.19 stresses the fact that frameworks rely on abstract classes and are made possible by the object-oriented concepts of polymorphism and dynamic binding. Abstract classes define a certain contract symbolized as a plug type. Any objects having this interface can be plugged in. Instances of classes that are based on plugs, such as Mailer, manage only these plugs and their implementation relies on the abstract contracts. Which concrete objects are plugged in at run time does not matter: due to dynamic binding, objects have the appropriate behavior.

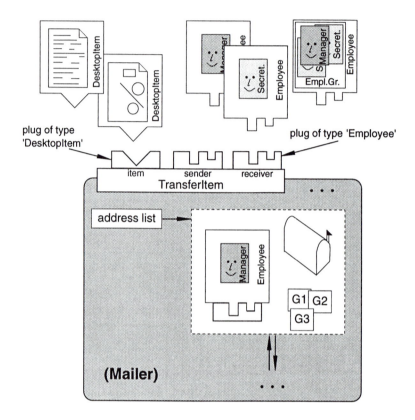

Figure 2.19 Generality of a Mailer object.

For example, one entry in the address list managed by a Mailer object consists of a plug of type Employee, a mailbox, and some mailing groups defined by the particular employee. Which concrete object of type Employee is plugged in does not affect the implementation of class Mailer. Figure 2.19 shows an instance of class Manager (presumed to be a descendant of Employee) plugged into the first entry of the address list.

The threshold for what constitutes a (minimal) framework is a matter of dispute. As such, whether class Folder and DesktopItem together constitute a framework can be disputed. Class Folder is a generic application managing DesktopItem instances. The question is whether item management together with size calculations have the critical mass to be an application/system.

In order to build a terminological basis, we distinguish between two categories of framework. Frameworks that constitute a generic application for a domain area are called application frameworks. Frameworks are those that represent a micro-architecture consisting of only a few components. The mailing framework described above would not be an application framework since mailing is only a basic task. The mailing framework could be part of an office automation application framework. Of course, it is often hard to decide whether a framework migrates to the category of application frameworks or not—it is almost impossible to draw a sharp line. From now on we use the term framework as a generic term for application framework and framework. Only in cases where a distinction is necessary do we use the term application framework explicitly.

The example of the mailing framework outlined above gives an idea of how object-oriented systems relying on abstract classes are developed. These concepts are crucial to understanding the design patterns presented in the remainder of the book.

Chapter 3

Survey of design pattern approaches

There exists no standardization of the term *design pattern* in the realm of object-oriented software development. This chapter makes an effort to give a definition of this vague term by presenting and discussing relevant state-of-the-art approaches.

In general, patterns help to reduce the complexity in many real-life situations. For example, in some situations the sequence of actions is crucial in order to accomplish a certain task. Instead of having to choose from an almost infinite number of possible combinations of actions, patterns allow the solution of problems by providing time-tested combinations that work. For example, car drivers apply a certain behavior pattern to set a manual-transmission vehicle in motion. This balance of clutch and gas is applied no matter whether the vehicle is a Volkswagen Beetle or a Porsche 959.

Patterns appear in a vast variety of domains in daily life. In fashion, various patterns exist that describe good-looking combinations of various aspects like colors. More or less mandatory rules (for example, behavior patterns and traffic rules) might be derived from usable patterns.

Each culture has a set of behavior patterns outlining how to behave in certain situations. For example, behavior patterns describe how to eat a meal. In the European culture, knife and fork are used together for eating, while in the U.S. these tools are used together only for certain tasks. People belonging to the cultural complex of the Far East use different tools for eating. Another example of a behavior pattern is how people interact. For example, people in the U.S. commonly greet each other differently than people in Japan. Traffic rules can be viewed as patterns prescribing how moving vehicles have to interact. How can the pattern concept be applied to software development, and especially to object-oriented software development?

3.1   The role of design patterns

Programmers tend to create parts of a program by imitating, though not directly copying, parts of programs written by other, more advanced programmers. This imitation involves noticing the pattern of some other code and adapting it to the program at hand. Such imitation is as old as programming.

The design pattern concept can be viewed as an abstraction of this imitation activity. In other words, design patterns constitute a set of rules describing how to accomplish certain tasks in the realm of software development. As a consequence, books on algorithms also fall into the category of general design patterns. For example, sorting algorithms describe how to sort elements in an efficient way depending on various contexts.

If the idea sketched above is applied to object-oriented software systems, we speak of design patterns for object-oriented software development. This book deals only with these design patterns. From now on we use the terms pattern and design pattern synonymously with object-oriented design pattern and always mean the latter.

The various design pattern approaches presented in the rest of this chapter reflect increasing levels of abstraction. Higher abstraction also brings higher rewards in terms of framework development and reuse. Truly useful design pattern approaches to framework development start with Section 3.4.

3.1.1   A brief historical overview

The roots of object-oriented design patterns go back to the late 1970s and early 1980s. The first available frameworks such as Smalltalk's Model-View-Controller (MVC) framework (Krasner and Pope 1988) and MacApp (Schmucker 1986, Wilson *et al.* 1990) revealed that a framework's complexity is a burden for its user. (By the term user we mean the programmer who uses a framework to produce a specific application.) A framework user must become familiar with its design, that is, the design of the individual classes and the interaction between these classes, and maybe with basic object-oriented programming concepts and a specific programming language as well. This is why framework cookbooks have come to light. Their recipes can be seen as design patterns that describe typical ways to use a particular framework (see Section 3.4).

In the early 1990s more advanced design pattern approaches gained momentum. Available object-oriented analysis and design methods appeared to be insufficient to construct reusable software architectures. For example, Richard Helm *et al.* (1990) described interactions between objects of different classes in a formal way. Pioneering work was accomplished by Erich Gamma (1992) in his doctoral thesis which presents patterns incorporated in the GUI application framework ET++ (Weinand *et al.* 1988, Weinand *et al.* 1989, Eggenschwiler and Gamma 1992, Weinand 1992).

At the 1991 Object-Oriented Programming Systems, Languages and Applications (OOPSLA) Conference—a major forum for researchers and practitioners in the field of object-oriented technology—Bruce Anderson headed the workshop "Towards an Architecture Handbook". Participants were encouraged to describe design patterns in a manner similar to the descriptions of architecture patterns presented in Christopher Alexander's books *A Pattern Language* (Alexander *et al.* 1977) and *The Timeless Way of Building* (Alexander 1979). These books show non-architects what good designs of homes and communities look like. One pattern, for example, recommends placing windows on two sides of a room instead of having windows only on one side. Alexander's patterns cover different levels of detail, from the arrangement of roads and various buildings to the details of how to design rooms.

Inspired by this architecture handbook workshop, Ralph Johnson (1992) documented the HotDraw framework in a cookbook style. Peter Coad organized the OOPSLA'92 and OOPSLA'93 workshops on object-oriented patterns. The '93 workshop was co-organized by Bruce Anderson and Peter Coad. A separate conference on design patterns was held near Urbana-Champaign, Illinois, in August 1994. In a nutshell, design patterns became a hot topic in the object-oriented community.

3.1.2 Categorization of design pattern approaches

As the design pattern approach in the realm of object-oriented software development has just emerged recently, there is no consensus on how to categorize design patterns. In order to categorize the design pattern approaches presented in this chapter, we distinguish between the purpose of a particular design pattern approach and the applied notation.

Purpose
As outlined in Section 1.4, the concepts offered by object-oriented programming languages are sufficient to produce reusable single components and reusable frameworks. The appropriate design of single components is a precondition for constructing frameworks. Some design pattern approaches focus on the design of single components or of a small group of components, ignoring the framework concept.

The design of reusable frameworks is more challenging. Thus we consider design pattern approaches as more advanced and more important if the framework aspect is stressed.

Design patterns and frameworks

Experts in the field of object-oriented software development have intuitively recommended that novices learn basic object-oriented concepts first and then proceed to take a close look at various frameworks. Of course, frameworks have to be used (for example, by modifying and extending sample applications built with a particular framework) before implementation details can be examined. Though the term design pattern is not used explicitly, novices actually gain their experience in object-oriented software development by abstracting design patterns from various specific frameworks. From this they learn how to design class interfaces and how to let abstract and concrete classes interact.

The major disadvantage of this approach is the enormous effort required. Since the first step of this method of learning is to use a framework, software engineers first have to learn the details of a framework. Often this involves learning a new programming language. Poor documentation of available frameworks makes the second step—studying implementation details—even more painful and time consuming. Abstracting design patterns which have been obscured by many implementation details requires an in-depth look at a framework. Sometimes it even becomes impossible to understand particular design decisions without any hints.

The main purpose of the framework-centered design pattern approaches is to describe the design of a framework and its individual classes without revealing implementation details. Such abstract design descriptions constitute an indispensable vehicle for communicating mature designs to novices and experts in an efficient way. As a result, these design patterns can help to

- adapt a framework to specific needs
- construct new frameworks incorporating mature and proven designs.

Design patterns help to achieve the first goal since they constitute a roadmap for understanding the specific implementation details of a framework. If a software engineer grasps the design of an existing framework, it will be possible to apply this experience in the development of new frameworks.

Notation

The following notations or combinations of them are applied in state-of-the-art design pattern approaches:

- informal textual notation
- formal textual notation, that is, a formalism or a programming language
- graphic notation.

Table 3.1 Categorization of state-of-the-art design pattern approaches.

			Purpose	*Notation*
Object-Oriented	Components:	+		Informal textual notation
Patterns (Peter Coad)	Frameworks I:	–		Graphic notation
	Frameworks II:	±		
Coding Patterns	Components:	±		Programming language
	Frameworks I:	–		Informal textual notation
	Frameworks II:	–		
Framework Cookbooks	Components:	–		Informal textual notation
	Frameworks I:	+		Programming language
	Frameworks II:	–		
Formal Contracts	Components:	±		Formal textual notation
(Richard Helm *et al.*)	Frameworks I:	±		
	Frameworks II:	±		
Design Pattern Catalog	Components:	±		Informal textual notation
(Erich Gamma *et al.*)	Frameworks I:	–		Graphic notation
	Frameworks II:	+		Programming language

By informal textual notation we mean a plain English description. For example, an informal description summarizes specific situations where a design pattern can be applied.

A formal textual notation might be either a particular formalism or a programming language such as C++. Code fragments written in a specific programming language only complement other notations. Bear in mind that design patterns have to abstract from programming language code, which should thus be reduced to a minimum in design pattern descriptions.

A graphic notation in the realm of object-oriented software development usually depicts class/object diagrams and complements the other notations.

Application to state-of-the-art design pattern approaches
Table 3.1 categorizes the design pattern approaches presented in this chapter according to their purpose and notation. The Purpose column indicates which goals a particular design pattern approach pursues:

- "Components" rates how a particular design pattern approach focuses on the design of single components or of a small group of components, ignoring the concept of abstract classes and frameworks.
- "Frameworks I" rates how a particular design pattern approach focuses on achieving the goal of describing how to use a framework.

- "Frameworks II" rates how a particular design pattern approach focuses on achieving the goal of capturing the design of frameworks so that the design can be reused in the development of new frameworks.

We employ the ratings – (goal not pursued), ± (goal pursued to some degree) and + (goal pursued).

The Notation column lists notations applied in the various design pattern approaches. If one notation dominates another, it is listed before the less important one. For example, in the Design Pattern Catalog an informal textual notation and a graphic notation dominate by far the use of a programming language.

3.2   Object-oriented patterns

In 1992 Peter Coad published his first article on design patterns, entitled Object-Oriented Patterns (Coad 1992). The overview of Coad's design pattern approach provided in this section is based on this article and on personal discussions about his upcoming book which is a practical guide to object modeling.

According to Coad, design patterns are identified by observing the lowest-level building blocks, that is, classes and objects and the relationship established between them. Coad applies a general scheme in order to describe a particular design pattern:

- a brief introduction and discussion of the typical problem that a pattern helps to solve, including an analogy if suitable;
- an informal textual description of the pattern accompanied by a graphic representation;
- guidelines on when (not) to use a pattern, and on which patterns are suited for combination with a particular pattern.

We categorize Coad's patterns into

- basic inheritance and interaction patterns
- patterns for structuring object-oriented software systems
- patterns related to the MVC framework.

In order to give a glimpse of Coad's design pattern approach, we have chosen some representative examples and discuss them.

3.2.1 Basic inheritance and interaction patterns

Patterns belonging to this category encompass primarily the basic modeling capabilities offered by object-oriented programming languages. For example, inheritance patterns state that the behavior of a class can be modified and/or augmented in subclasses. For this purpose, object-oriented programming languages offer the mechanisms of overriding methods, adding instance variables, and adding methods in subclasses as explained in Chapter 2. Furthermore, the concept of an abstract class is presented as a pattern.

At a similar abstraction level, basic interaction patterns describe message sending if more than two objects are involved. If a message is not sent directly from one object to another, one or more translator objects mediate between them thus producing a cascaded effect.

3.2.2 Patterns for structuring object-oriented software

Most of Coad's patterns belong to this category. They describe how a small group of classes supports the structuring of software systems if certain conditions hold.

Description of an item
The purpose of this pattern is to put instance variables of a class Item into a separate class ItemDescriptor. Item instances refer to an instance of ItemDescriptor. If several Item objects refer to *one* ItemDescriptor object, changes to the latter affect all corresponding Item objects.

Thus this design pattern can be used "when some attribute values may apply to more than one object in a class" (Coad 1992). If each Item object has its own ItemDescriptor object, the design pattern becomes superfluous: all instance variables of ItemDescriptor can be defined in class Item.

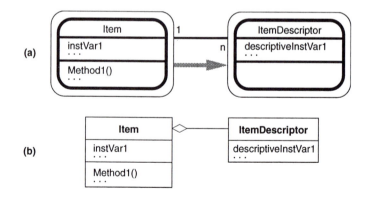

Figure 3.1 Item description pattern.

Figure 3.1(a) illustrates this pattern using Coad's notation. The most important elements of this notation are outlined in (Coad 1992), for example.

Figure 3.1(b) shows the equivalent diagram based on Object Model Notation. Though Coad uses his notation for describing his design patterns, we will only use the Object Model Notation for the other examples in order to avoid confusing the reader.

The gray arrow in Coad's notation expresses that a message is sent from Item instances to their corresponding ItemDescriptor instance. The connections between the graphic representations of Item and ItemDescriptor in both diagrams express that any number of Item objects refer to exactly one ItemDescriptor object. The graphic notation abstracts from the details of how such an association is established. For example, an instance variable in class Item can store a reference to the particular ItemDescriptor object.

This design pattern is close to features offered by some object-oriented programming languages. Smalltalk, for example, provides *class variables* for the case where *all* Item instances refer to a common pool of attribute values: a class variable exists once for all instances of a class. Changes affect all instances.

Changeable roles

Coad (1992) motivates the significance of this pattern by means of an analogy. "A *player* object .... *wears different hats*, playing one or more *roles.*"

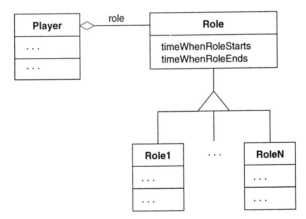

Figure 3.2 Design pattern facilitating changeable roles.

An instance of class Player refers to one Role object at a time. The Role object may be changed. Figure 3.2 shows the corresponding graphic representation in the Object Model Notation.

We consider another aspect important in the realm of this design pattern: class Role constitutes a typical example of an abstract class. Since the description of this pattern is too general, no hints can be given as to which behavior can be defined in class Role. The design pattern description only mentions that the two instance variables timeWhenRoleStarts and timeWhenRoleEnds are common attributes of various roles.

If this pattern is applied, additional common behavior should be defined in class Role as demonstrated in an enhanced version of this pattern in Section 3.6.1. Otherwise the implementation of Player will be cluttered with case statements where the role a Player object plays has to be checked. Which operations of the Role object to which the instance variable role refers can be invoked by a Player object depends on the result of the dynamic type check of instance variable role. This design would encumber extensions such as handling further Role objects in addition to the originally planned ones.

Patterns dealing with object collections

In many situations elementary objects can be grouped and managed by a supervisor object. In the example sketched in Chapter 2, a folder manages an arbitrary number of contained desktop items. For example, in order to calculate the size of a folder measured in bytes, the folder asks each contained desktop item its size and calculates the overall folder size.

This sample of an object collection incorporates a general pattern: a class Container provides an instance variable containedItems. Instances of Container can store references to an arbitrary number of Member objects as shown in Figure 3.3.

Figure 3.3 Gathering Member objects in a Container object.

If this pattern is used, class Member should be designed such that instances act on themselves, that is, the behavior of instances does not depend on other instances. A DesktopItem instance, for example, can calculate its own size.

Coad recommends encapsulating Member objects, that is, making them accessible only via the corresponding Container object when they are not needed as single objects. Other objects have to deal with the Container object as a kind of mediator.

The Container pattern discussed so far is independent of abstract classes and frameworks: neither Container nor Member has to be an abstract class. A more advanced Container pattern migrates to the framework camp: if Member is the abstract superclass of Container as shown in Figure 3.4, class Member typically defines methods common to both.

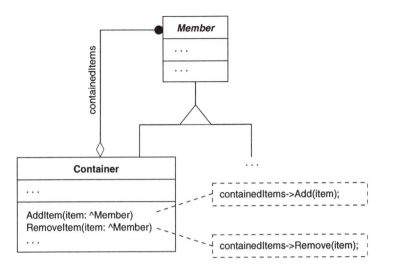

Figure 3.4 Pattern allowing the treatment of a group of objects as one.

The abstract class DesktopItem and its subclass Folder presented in Section 2.2.1 are based on the pattern depicted in Figure 3.4. This pattern allows the treatment of a Container object as a single Member object. As a consequence, hierarchies of Member objects can be built.

Typically, class Member represents an abstract class in this pattern. The management of Member objects in an instance of class Container constitutes a framework.

3.2.3 Patterns related to the MVC framework

Those of Coad's patterns that stress the framework aspect are derivatives of the Model/View/Controller (MVC) framework (Krasner and Pope 1988), so we discuss this framework first.

The MVC framework reflects the fact that GUI applications consist of three components: the model, the view, and the controller. These components are used to impose a structure on interactive applications.

The *model* stores application-specific data. For example, a text processing application stores the text characters in the model; a drawing application stores a description of the graphic shapes there.

A *view* component presents the model on a display, usually the screen. Any number of view components might present the model in different ways. Each view has to access the information stored in the model.

Finally, the *controller* handles input events such as mouse interaction and key strokes. Each view has an associated controller that connects the particular view with the input devices mouse and keyboard. This implies that a model has any number of associated view/controller pairs, but at least one. Figure 3.5 sketches the MVC components and the control flow between these components.

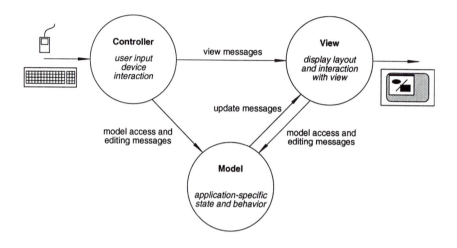

Figure 3.5 Model/View/Controller components.

The view and controller components can access the model component. They can inform themselves about the data stored in the model and are allowed to change these data.

    The model cannot access its controller(s) or view(s). The model itself does not care how it is shown. The model can have an arbitrary number of view/controller pairs associated with it, so that the user can have many views (= visible representations) of one model.

    If a user provides input actions via the mouse or keyboard, a controller sends a message to the model or occasionally directly to the view. The model changes its data if necessary and informs all view/controller pairs associated with it. The object-oriented implementation of this update operation forms a typical framework.

    A view component is represented by the abstract class View. This class offers a method Update. If a change in the model occurs, the model, an instance of class Model, iterates over all associated View objects and sends the Update message to them. Descendants of View have to override the Update method accordingly. Thus the update operation can be implemented in class Model. This framework works with any future View descendants that show the data stored in a model. Class Model remains unchanged.

    Of course, View and Controller also implement other typical properties. They are described together with their methods in Schmucker (1986) and Krasner and Pope (1988).

The MVC framework has some deficiencies in the realm of GUI programming:

- A strict separation of the three components model, view, and controller is sometimes too rigid.
- The update mechanism of views is inefficient due to inaccurate information about necessary updates.

Despite MVC's deficiencies, Smalltalk's MVC classes together with about 25 subclasses can be considered as the first application framework for GUI programming. The MVC framework had an undeniable impact on later frameworks which refined its ideas. For example, state-of-the-art GUI application frameworks unify the controller and view components.

Coad (1992) calls the update framework outlined above Broadcast pattern and renames it to Publisher/Subscriber. Figure 3.6 depicts the Publisher/Subscriber pattern. Class Publisher corresponds to class Model in the MVC framework; class Subscriber corresponds to class View.

Specific implementations of this pattern might add parameters to method Update. If Subscriber objects have no instance variable referring to their corresponding Publisher object, this reference can be passed as a parameter of method Update. Update might also be augmented by specific parameters that give hints about the kinds of changes that are published by the Publisher object. Some Subscriber objects might only be interested in specific changes, so that they do not have to access the Publisher object for changes that are irrelevant to them.

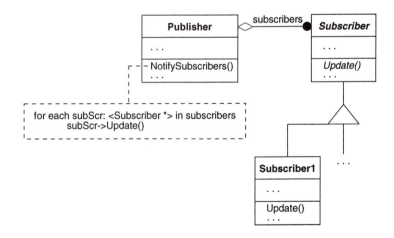

Figure 3.6 Publisher/Subscriber pattern derived from the MVC framework.

Compare the Publisher/Subscriber pattern to the simple Container pattern shown in Figure 3.3. The Publisher/Subscriber pattern is based on the

Container pattern. It enhances the Container pattern by specifying that class Member (now Subscriber) is abstract and offers the method Update. Furthermore, the interaction between the two components participating in the pattern is defined: if a Publisher object changes, it sends Update to each Subscriber object. Though a Publisher object refers to many Subscriber objects, the semantics of "contains" is not adequate in this context. A Publisher object is just associated with its Subscriber objects. Nevertheless, the same mechanism, that is, an instance variable storing any number of references to Subscriber objects, is used to implement the relationship between the two classes.

Another pattern proposed by Coad involves all three components of the original MVC framework, that is, the model, view, and controller.

3.2.4 Summarizing remarks

Most of Coad's patterns suggest how to structure object-oriented software systems. Unfortunately, the importance of abstract classes and frameworks is not stressed—most pattern descriptions and examples do not mention these aspects, though some patterns are close to frameworks. To sum up, Coad's design pattern approach

- helps in the design of single components or of a small group of components, ignoring the framework concept;
- describes aspects of the MVC framework;
- is not aimed at describing adaptations of frameworks.

3.3   Coding patterns

The term coding pattern expresses that the abstraction level of these patterns is quite close to code formulated in object-oriented programming languages. Patterns presented in this section help to solve specific tasks effectively in the realm of a particular object-oriented programming language. We use coding pattern, style guideline and coding convention synonymously. This section focuses on coding patterns for the language C++.

Coplien (1992) states that "most of what guides the structure of programs, and therefore of the systems we build, is the *styles* and *idioms* we adopt to express design concepts."

The principal goals of coding patterns are

- to demonstrate useful ways of combining basic language concepts
- to form the basis for standardizing source-code structure and names

- to avoid pitfalls and to weed out deficiencies of object-oriented programming languages, which is especially relevant in the realm of C++.

3.3.1 Coding patterns for C++

C++ is a language monster that requires coding patterns to tame its monstrosity. Ironically, contradicting coding patterns are recommended for C++.

One reason for conflicting coding conventions is the question of whether dynamic binding represents a crucial language feature. Since abstract classes and frameworks rely on dynamic binding we recommend those coding patterns that do not sacrifice dynamic binding.

To give the reader an example of a coding pattern belonging to the opposite camp, we selected a coding pattern from Coplien (1992) that assumes that variables are statically declared in C++ programs. Thus dynamic binding is sacrificed. Most of the C++ styles and idioms proposed by Coplien (1992) only prove useful for software projects that deny the importance of abstract classes and frameworks.

Appendix A discusses further C++ coding patterns for structuring source code and for dealing with meta-information.

Variable declaration and object generation ...
The two conflicting coding patterns presented in this section result from different points of view on how to declare variables in C++.

... Coplien's recommendation
Readers who are not interested in C++ tricks and pitfalls should skip the following discussion of Coplien's coding pattern: orthodox, canonical class form (Coplien 1992). We briefly present this example for those readers who want to get an impression of the impact of C heritage on the C++ language via the possibility of static and dynamic declaration of variables of a class type.

Note: Bear in mind that Coplien's recommendation implies giving up dynamic binding, which we consider fatal for *advanced object-oriented* software development.

Coplien (1992) assumes that variables are declared statically in C++ as demonstrated in Example 3.1. In order to avoid problems in connection with assignment operations, declarations, and parameter passing, he proposes the orthodox, canonical class form. Coplien states that this coding pattern "is one of the most important C++ idioms, and is a common theme that underlies much else presented in this [his] book."

Example 3.1 Static variable declaration and object instantiation.

```
#include "SampleDoc.h"

SampleDoc aSampleDoc(...);    // declaration and instantiation
. . .
```

According to Coplien (1992) a class adheres to the orthodox, canonical form if the class definition contains

(1)   a default constructor

(2)   an assignment operator and a copy constructor

(3)   a destructor.

We discuss these coding patterns together with C++ language specifics that explain why such coding patterns make sense in the realm of statically declared variables:

(1)   A *default constructor* is invoked by the C++ language system if an array of objects is statically generated from a class. For example, the following statement generates an array of 100 A objects: A objectsOfClassA[100].

Recall how constructors are handled: the constructor method is called when an object is instantiated. All necessary parameters have to be passed to the constructor method at that time.

One C++ inconsistency is that it does not provide the syntax for passing necessary parameters to the constructor method(s) in the case of a static array declaration. The clumsy C++ solution of this problem is that a default constructor of the corresponding class is called for each generated object. A default constructor is a constructor without parameters. In the case of class A it would be A(). (Note that C++ allows *function overloading* which means in the realm of classes that methods with the same name can exist for a class as long as they differ in type and/or number of parameters. So a class may have several constructors.) If the programmer does not define the default constructor, the C++ compiler automatically generates it with an empty implementation, that is, { }.

In order to avoid problems in the case where an array of objects is statically declared, rule (1) of Coplien's coding pattern recommends that the default constructor always be defined. For example, an automatically generated default constructor with an empty implementation does not allocate memory for dynamically declared instance variables of an object such as those referring to a character string.

(2)   If statically declared variables are assigned (see Example 3.2), the following problem has to be considered. Instance variables of class A

might refer to dynamically allocated storage areas like character strings, other arrays, or dynamically allocated objects. Assigning variables means that the values of the instance variables are assigned. In the case of instance variables that refer to dynamically allocated storage areas, the stored references are assigned.

Example 3.2 Assignment of statically declared variables.

```
. . .
A a1, a2;        // static declaration and instantiation
a1= a2;          // assignment
. . .
```

For example, after the assignment a1= a2, the memory previously referred to by instance variables of a1 is not disposed of, as illustrated in Figure 3.7.

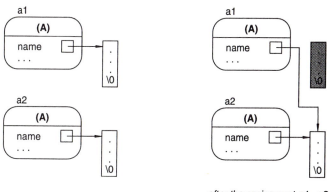

after the assignment a1= a2

Figure 3.7 Memory that is no longer required after an assignment operation has not been disposed of.

Thus the assignment operator = has to be overloaded according to rule (2). The C++ language feature *operator overloading* was inspired by Ada. The overloaded operator = has to dispose of memory that is not referred to any more after an assignment operation.

An analogous problem arises if a variable is passed as a *call-by-value* parameter to a function. In this case a *copy constructor* is used by the C++ language system. Since a discussion of the recommended definition of a copy constructor reveals no additional aspects, we refer to Coplien (1992).

(3)   A class should have a destructor in order to free memory that its
instances have dynamically allocated and that is not referenced by others.
Of course, this rule is applicable independent of whether variables are
declared statically or dynamically.

So a class adhering to the orthodox, canonical form helps to avoid problems
that clients of a particular class might have if variables are declared statically.

If variables are declared dynamically according to our recommendation
(see below), rules (1) and (2) of this coding pattern become superfluous. The
declaration of an array of pointers causes no problem since no object
generation is involved. Assigning a reference variable a2 to another reference
variable a1 implies that both refer to the same object after the assignment, as
shown in Figure 3.8.

The object originally referred to by a1 is not referenced by this variable
any more. The programmer has to dispose of that object before the
assignment operation a1= a2 if no other references to that object exist. The
operator = is not overloaded in connection with dynamically declared variables
since operator overloading works only with statically declared variables.

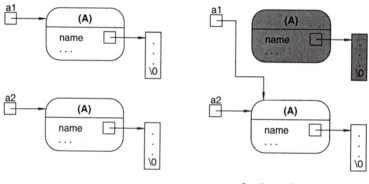

after the assignment a1= a2

Figure 3.8   Assigning reference variables.

... our recommendation

In order to enable dynamic binding, state-of-the-art class libraries and
application frameworks such as ET++ rely solely on the declaration of
reference variables that store pointers to dynamically allocated objects, as
exemplified in Example 3.3.

Example 3.3   Declaration of a reference variable and dynamic object allocation.

```
#include "SampleDoc.h"
SampleDoc *aSampleDoc;
```

```
aSampleDoc= new SampleDoc(...);   // Classes are only
                                  // instantiated dynamically.
. . .
```

For example, ET++ defines two basic data types represented by the classes Point and Rectangle. Since these classes are not supposed to be subclassed, their methods are not dynamically bound. As a consequence, these classes form an exception to the rule stated above. Objects of these classes are typically created by a static declaration (see Example 3.4). In order to reduce the binary size of applications, frequently used instances of these classes are declared as global constants such as const Point gPoint0(0, 0) and const Rectangle gRect0(gPoint0, gPoint0).

Example 3.4 Static declaration of Point and Rectangle variables.

```
. . .
... = new SampleDoc(..., Point(50, 70), ...);
Rectangle  r1(gPoint0,  Point(20,  60));
. . .
```

An object of class Point has two public instance variables, x and y, of type int. Rectangle represents a rectangle parallel to the axes with the public instance variables origin, representing the upper left corner of the rectangle, and extent, representing the diagonal vector from the origin to the lower right point.

Since these two basic data types are extensively used in the GUI application framework ET++, numerous operations are defined in these classes. For example, the operators +, +=, −, and −= are overloaded in class Point so that Point objects can be added and subtracted. The overloaded operator + of class Rectangle allows the addition of a point delta to a rectangle. Point delta has to be interpreted as a translation vector, meaning that the origin of the rectangle is moved by delta. Example 3.5 illustrates how operators can be used in connection with class instances as if Point and Rectangle were already built-in types in C++.

Example 3.5 Operations with Point and Rectangle objects.

```
Point p(10, 40);
Rectangle r(gPoint0, p+gPoint10);
r= r + p − Point(50, 80);
p+= gPoint1;
```

Other operations of class Rectangle allow the calculation of union and intersection of two rectangles, checking whether a point is inside a rectangle, and so on. These operations can be viewed as coding patterns in the realm of the classes Point and Rectangle. They form an ET++-specific mini-language for working with these basic data types.

3.3.2 Naming conventions

Conventional procedure/function libraries already apply certain naming conventions. This aspect is even more important in the realm of application frameworks since programmers think in the high-level design incorporated in them. Thus consistent naming schemes become essential. The most striking naming conventions applied in ET++ are presented below.

Class names and method names start with a capital letter followed by lower-case letters, such as the class name Application. Instance variables and local variables start with a lower-case letter. If a name consists of several words, the second and subsequent words start with a capital letter, such as the method name DoLeftButtonDownCommand or the instance variable name shapeList. Similar to naming conventions used in the GUI application framework MacApp, the following names start with a special prefix in ET++:

- Global variables start with the prefix g: gFileDialog, gApplication, gWindowSystem.

- Constants start with the prefix c, for example, cIdFirstUser and cIdNone. Constants that identify predefined ET++ commands also start with c followed by upper-case letters, such as cSAVEAS, cPRINT and cPASTE.

- Constants belonging to an enumeration type start with the prefix e: eVObjHLeft, eVObjHCenter and eVObjHRight.

These general naming conventions apply to method names:

- Methods that define the value of an instance variable start with Set such as SetOrigin(...). Methods that return the value of an instance variable start with Get such as GetOrigin().

- Abstract methods that have to be overridden in subclasses start with Do: DoKeyCommand(...), DoRead(...).

- Methods implementing dynamic object creation as discussed in Section 3.6.1 contain Make or Create, such as DoMakeManager().

- Methods that actually draw on the screen start with Gr for graphic: GrLine(...), GrPaintRect(...), GrFillRect(...), GrFillOval(...), GrShow-BitMap(...), GrFillPolygon(...).

3.3.3 Summarizing remarks

Coding patterns presented in this section depend on a particular programming language and/or class library. They primarily give basic hints on how to structure a software system from a syntactical point of view. These patterns are not suited to helping in the design of classes. The latter involves decisions about methods and instance variables grouped in a class, the meaning of the methods, and so on.

Obviously, coding patterns do not support a programmer in adapting or developing a framework either. Naming conventions are just a basic approach to standardizing names in a class library. Such conventions serve as a precondition for not getting confused when using a class library.

3.4   Framework adaptation patterns—cookbook recipes

This section illustrates *application framework cookbooks*. We use the short form *cookbook*.

Cookbooks contain numerous *recipes*. They describe in an informal way how to use a framework in order to solve specific problems. The term framework usage expresses that a programmer uses a framework as a basis for application development. A particular framework is adapted to specific needs. Recipes usually do not explain the internal design and implementation details of a framework.

Cookbooks exist for various frameworks. For example, Krasner and Pope (1988) present a cookbook for using the MVC framework. The MacApp cookbook (Apple 1989) describes how to adapt the GUI application framework MacApp in order to build applications for the Macintosh. Ralph Johnson (1992) wrote a cookbook for the HotDraw framework, developed by Kent Beck and Ward Cunningham for implementing various kinds of graphic editors.

We use ET++ as an example to demonstrate the cookbook concept. An overview of how hypertext systems can support the cookbook approach concludes this section.

3.4.1 Structure and use of cookbook recipes

Recipes are rather informal documents. Nevertheless, most cookbook recipes are structured roughly into the sections purpose, procedure (including references to other recipes), and source code example(s).

A programmer has to find the recipe that is appropriate for a specific framework adaptation. A recipe is then used by simply adhering to the steps that describe how to accomplish a certain task.

Sample recipe: creating documents in ET++

As an example we present a recipe which describes how to create documents in the GUI application framework ET++. In order to understand this recipe, it is necessary to outline some aspects of ET++ first. More details regarding ET++ are discussed in Chapter 5. Bear in mind that the following brief introduction to ET++ is not part of the recipe presented below.

ET++ integrates elementary user interface building blocks such as various kinds of buttons, menus, and text fields, as well as high-level application components. These components are mainly represented by the classes Application, Document, and View, which implement the generic frame of ET++ applications. These strongly related classes define much of an application's control flow.

An Application instance controls the *event loop*. Furthermore, it can manage objects of static type Document. For example, a running spreadsheet application may have any number of opened documents at a time.

Document is an abstract class managing data. For example, typical spreadsheet document data includes numbers, text and formulas. A document in a graphic editor manages the figures.

Document roughly corresponds to the model component in the MVC framework. Data managed by a Document object are usually displayed in a View object on the screen. ET++'s View class corresponds to both the view and controller components in the MVC framework.

At the start of an application, an appropriate Document object has to be generated. Furthermore, Document objects have to be created every time a New or Open menu command is submitted by the application user.

The contract of class Document allows the implementation of various user interface look-and-feel aspects in the abstract classes Application and Document, for example:

- The menu item Save is only enabled in a running application if any changes occurred in a document.

- The menu command Revert discards all changes in a document.

- When quitting an application, it checks whether all modified documents have been saved. If not, the application user is asked whether the changed documents are to be saved.

Class Document as an abstract class standardizes the protocol for subclasses and provides dummy or preliminary implementations for some of its methods. Each application built with ET++ has to define a subclass of Document for handling application-specific data. For example, class SpreadSheetDoc is defined for a spreadsheet application.

The cookbook recipe shown below describes how to create an application-specific Document subclass and pass it to an Application object so that the newly created document is managed in the way described above. The word Your is included in variable and type names that *your*—the client's—application has to define. Analogous recipes can be found in cookbooks for GUI application frameworks that have a structure similar to ET++.

Purpose

A Document object manages the data set of an application independently of how it is displayed or printed. It also provides methods to save the data in files and read it back (for details see the recipe "Saving and restoring data in documents").

ET++ asks your application to create a new application-specific document when the user starts the application or chooses the New or Open menu commands.

Steps how to do it

(1) Declare the file type of your document as an instance of Symbol. This is usually done by an extern declaration in the header file where your Document class is defined:

> extern Symbol cYourDocType;

The actual declaration is done in the implementation file of your Document class:

> Symbol cYourDocType("YourTypeName");

If you use a file format that is predefined in ET++, use the predefined file type. For example, a file made up of ASCII characters is of type cDocTypeAscii.

The file type has to be passed to the constructor of class Application. It becomes the principal file type of your application. If your application must deal with various file types, see the recipe "Handling different file types in an application".

(2) Implement YourApplication::DoMakeManager in the subclass YourApplication of Application. ET++ calls this method every time a new document needs to be created. You need the following declaration as part of the definition of YourApplication:

> Manager *YourApplication::DoMakeManager(Symbol
> managerType);

The parameter managerType is the principal file type. Usually this file type is passed on to the created document.

Recall that Document is a subclass of Manager. Thus references to Document objects are type compatible with the required return type of DoMakeManager.

A sample implementation is given in the source code example for this recipe.

(3) If you have menu commands other than the standard File menu commands, that is, New, Open, Save, Save As, and Revert, that apply to the document or its contents, override the methods DoMakeMenuBar, DoMenuCommand and DoSetUpMenu of class Document. See the "Creating menus and handling menu commands" recipe for details on these methods.

Source code example

```
. . .
#include "YourApplication.h"
#include "YourDocument.h"

YourApplication::YourApplication(...) : Application(...,
                                        cYourDocType)
{
    . . .
}
Manager *YourApplication::DoMakeManager(Symbol
                                        managerType)
{
    YourDocument *aDoc;
    aDoc= new YourDocument(managerType, ...);
    return aDoc;
}
. . .
```

Besides this sample recipe and the recipes referred to by the "Creating documents" recipe, numerous other recipes are useful in the realm of the application framework ET++. To name just a few, there are recipes to

- create, initialize and draw a view
- create a window
- define and handle dialogs
- handle mouse and keyboard events.

Corresponding recipes describe how to adapt ET++ in order to accomplish these tasks.

Summarizing remarks

Note that a programmer using the "Creating documents" recipe does not get the background information provided before the presentation of this recipe. Though step (2) of the recipe mentions when DoMakeManager is invoked, a *description of the overall design is missing*; for example, why method DoMakeManager has to be overridden is not explained. In order to answer this question, the design of class Application regarding DoMakeManager needs to be explained: the abstract class Application cannot know in advance which concrete subclass of Document has to be instantiated in the case of a New or Open menu command. This problem is solved by defining the object creation method DoMakeManager, which creates the appropriate Document object; thus the creation is kept flexible and actually accomplished in method DoMakeManager of class YourApplication by overriding the abstract method of Application. DoMakeManager, which returns a pointer of *static* type Manager, is called in the Application component every time a document has to be generated. So a subclass of Application always has to override method DoMakeManager as described in the recipe.

Also note the *references to other recipes* in the "Creating documents" example. Both properties, that is, almost no description of the overall design and numerous references to other recipes, characterize the cookbook recipe style.

3.4.2 Cookbooks as hypertext

Cookbook recipes with their inherent references to other recipes lend themselves to presentation as hypertext. A hypertext system allows the creation of and navigation through a directed graph. The nodes of such a graph are different parts of documents, such as texts and drawings. The edges link these document nodes. Links are unidirectional. They are typically represented in a document as buttons or as text written in *italic style*. If a user pushes a link in a document, the hypertext system presents the corresponding linked part. In this context we speak of the user following a link. Hypertext systems are discussed, for example, in Garett *et al.* (1986), Goodman (1988), and Shneiderman and Kearsley (1989).

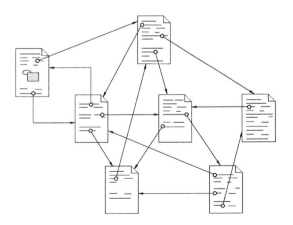

Figure 3.9 Cookbook recipes stored in a hypertext graph.

Cookbooks written with a hypertext system can contain the recipes as nodes (see Figure 3.9). Parts of these recipes, like the code samples, might be separated from the actual recipes. This information is presented if the cookbook user wants to access these code samples by activating the corresponding links. This splitting avoids information overload.

In an analogous way hypertext cookbooks might contain more information about design details without overwhelming a cookbook user with undesired details. Some cookbook users may only want to know how to accomplish a certain task without being confronted with details. Others might want to know why certain methods have to be overridden. A well-structured hypertext recipe can be split into parts dealing with various levels of detail information. For example, a core recipe contains the absolutely necessary information. Cookbook users interested in more details follow the links to additional information.

Example: a hypertext cookbook for ET++

ET++ itself was used to implement a hypertext editor for editing a prototype of a hypertext ET++ cookbook. The ET++ hypertext cookbook discussion and all the screenshots shown in this section resulted from a reimplementation of the ET++ hypertext cookbook prototype. This reimplementation was done by the author and is based on the cookbook descriptions in Weinand *et al.* (1989) and Gamma (1992).

The ET++ cookbook editor is an advanced hypertext system that allows the definition of nodes that are

- text documents or parts of text documents;
- drawings for graphically portraying various aspects of the application framework such as relationships between classes;
- source code files or parts of source code files.

All nodes in a hypertext edited by the ET++ hypertext editor are ET++ documents. Links in the ET++ cookbook are marked by a push button. Special symbols are used for the various link types. A brief textual description of the link follows the link type symbol. Figure 3.10(a) shows a see-also link that refers to a node "Flexible object creation". Figure 3.10(b) shows a code-example link named YourDocument.h, expressing that the file YourDocument.h is displayed when the button is pressed.

(a)   (b)

Figure 3.10 Representation of link buttons.

The ET++ hypertext cookbook provides the following link types:

- *See also:* This reference to another node where a feature is also explained is marked by a balloon. Figure 3.11 shows the cookbook recipe "Creating documents". Activating the see-also link named "Flexible object creation" shows the design pattern underlying the DoMakeManager method. This design pattern is explained in Section 3.6.1 and Section 4.2.3.

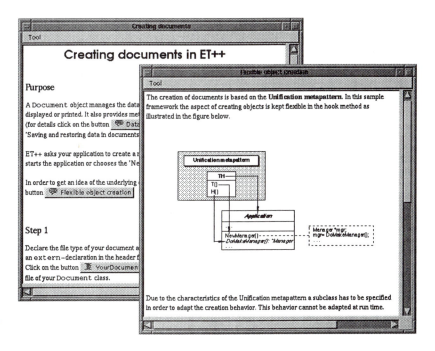

Figure 3.11   Screenshot demonstrating see-also links.

- *Code example:* Code-example links are connected to source code files. Code-example links correspond to the source code example section in ordinary cookbook recipes. Figure 3.12 illustrates this link type. Activating the code-example link named YourDocument.h opens the corresponding text document and selects the relevant portion of the source code.

Hypertext systems involve the danger of getting lost in the hypertext graph structure. Thus navigation support is essential for a hypertext cookbook to be usable. The ET++ hypertext cookbook offers two navigation utilities:

- *Table of contents*. The table of contents can be hierarchically structured as shown in Figure 3.13. For example, the recipe "Handling docu-

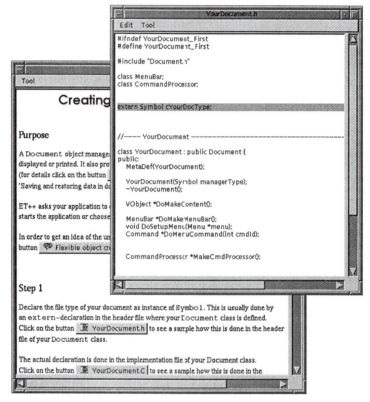

Figure 3.12   Screenshot demonstrating code-example links.

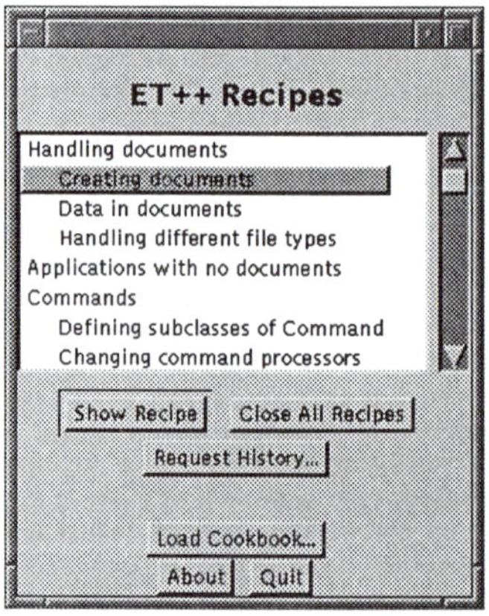

Figure 3.13   Cookbook topics.

ments" describes in general the role of Document objects in the realm of ET++. A more detailed recipe such as "Creating documents" explains how document creation is adapted.

- *Request history*. This list displays the document names of the nodes that have been visited during a session. The user can choose any document in the table of contents or the request history in order to go there.

3.4.3 Summarizing remarks

Though the concept of cookbooks proved to be an adequate means for adapting application frameworks, some problems have to be considered. Cookbooks have to cover a wide range of typical framework adaptations, and they are hardly ever complete.

The more adaptations are described in a cookbook, the harder it is to find the appropriate recipe. In many cases adaptations can be accomplished in several different ways. Cookbooks that encompass various different adaptations for solving a particular problem tend to become too complex: usually several adaptations have to be combined during application development using a framework. A programmer can easily become confused in searching for reasonable adaptation combinations.

In order to alleviate such problems, cookbooks have to be written by people who have an in-depth understanding of a framework. Ideally, of course, a cookbook is authored by the framework developers.

An advanced hypertext system like the ET++ cookbook editor lends itself as a basis for going beyond the scope of mere adaptation cookbooks. Hypertext cookbooks can also document the design of a framework based on design pattern approaches like the Design Pattern Catalog (see Section 3.6) or Metapatterns (see Chapter 4). The result of such an effort could be termed a *recipe and design book*.

3.5   Formal contracts

A principal goal of this chapter is to give an overview of design pattern approaches in the realm of object-oriented software systems. Formal approaches should not be neglected, though many software engineers resent them. One reason might be that, despite expected breakthroughs, formal program specification and program verification remain limited primarily to the realm of small programs.

The formal approach presented by Helm *et al.* (1990) is chosen in this overview of design pattern approaches for the following reasons:

- Contracts are aimed at frameworks. The goal of this approach is a formal description of frameworks and their components, not a verification. Thus this approach can be applied to describe the design of software systems that go beyond the scope of Mickey Mouse systems.

- The few elements of the notation are not too difficult to grasp.

An example of another approach that describes object-oriented systems based on a formal notation is the object-relationship modeling language called "Data Structure Manager" (Shah *et al.* 1989). This language is close to C++. Garlan and Shaw (1993) give an overview of approaches for describing software architectures.

This section starts with a presentation of the Publisher/Subscriber pattern using formal contracts. The Publisher/Subscriber pattern has already been described in Section 3.2.3 by means of the Object Model Notation, so the reader can compare two different notations applied to one example. Another goal of this section is to derive the pros and cons of this formal approach by means of the examples presented. An attempt to formalize the DesktopItem-Folder framework gives a glimpse of the limits of formal contracts. We discuss only those elements of the formal notation that are required for the examples and refer to Helm *et al.* (1990) for other details regarding the notation.

Chapter 2 introduced contract as an alternative term for class interface. Helm *et al.* (1990) broaden this definition: behavioral compositions represent "groups of interdependent objects cooperating to accomplish tasks.... Patterns of communication within a behavioral composition are often repeated throughout the system with different participating objects.... Contracts are a construct for the explicit specification of behavioral compositions."

Bertrand Meyer uses the term contract in connection with preconditions and postconditions supported by the Eiffel language (Meyer 1988). In the following section contract and formal contract are used as synonymous terms expressing the meaning defined by Helm *et al.*

3.5.1 Formal contracts: their notation and associated operations

Recall the Publisher/Subscriber pattern (see Figure 3.14). A Publisher object notifies its dependent Subscriber objects whenever changes occur by invoking the Update() method for each Subscriber object.

The Publisher/Subscriber pattern serves as an example to introduce the most important elements of formal contracts. Example 3.6 shows the contract that corresponds to the Object Model Notation of the Publisher/Subscriber pattern in Figure 3.14.

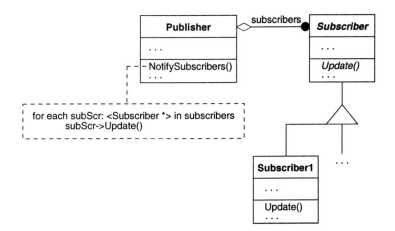

Figure 3.14 Publisher/Subscriber pattern derived from the MVC framework.

Example 3.6 PublisherSubscriber contract.

contract PublisherSubscriber
     Publisher **supports** [
           NotifySubscribers() =>
                  < ‖ s: s ∈ Subscribers: s->Update() >
           AttachSubscriber(s: Subscriber)   =>
                  { s ∈ Subscribers}
           DetachSubscriber(s: Subscriber)   =>
                  { s ∉ Subscribers}
     ]
     Subscribers: Set(Subscriber) **where each** Subscriber
               supports [
     Update() =>
     ]
     contract invariant
        -
     contract establishment
           < ‖ s: s ∈ Subscribers:
                <Publisher->AttachSubscriber(s) > >
  end contract

Basic elements of the notation

Participants in a contract constitute its first part. In our example the
participants are Publisher and a set of Subscriber participants. For each
participant the contractual obligations have to be defined. They consist of *type*

obligations, which correspond to instance variables and methods, as well as *causal obligations* which describe actions and conditions associated with type obligations.

The type obligations of the participant Publisher are NotifySubscribers(), AttachSubscriber(), and DetachSubscriber(). Causal obligations ensure behavioral dependencies between objects. Causal obligations are specified after =>.

We borrow the high-level language used in contracts described by Helm *et al.* (1990). The principal elements of this language allow expression of

- *method calls*: For example, a call of method Update of a subscriber s is expressed by writing s->Update().

- *setting of instance variables*: Δ v means that a value is assigned to an instance variable v.

The operator $\parallel$ expresses that the order of actions is irrelevant. A semicolon between actions means a sequential ordering of the actions. Conditionals are denoted by an if-then-else construct.

The construct < o v: c: e > means repetition of an expression e separated by the operator o for all variables v that satisfy c. In the Publisher/Subscriber contract the construct < $\parallel$ s: s $\in$ Subscribers: s->Update() > is an example of < o v: c: e >, with

- $\parallel$ as operator o
- s: s $\in$ Subscribers as v: c, and
- s->Update() as e.

It means that all s_1, s_2, ...: s_i $\in$ Subscribers have to form an expression with operator $\parallel$ and e, resulting in s_1->Update() $\parallel$ s_2->Update() $\parallel$ ... . This means that the message Update() has to be sent to all objects in the set Subscribers. The order of these method invocations does not matter.

Conditions which have to be met by participants are written in { }. For example, { s $\in$ Subscribers} means that the condition "s is an element of the set named Subscribers" has to be true after the invocation of AttachSubscriber with s as parameter. Such conditions are also used in the realm of value settings. For example, Δ v { v = ... } allows the specification of details regarding the value of v which cannot be expressed in Δ v.

The description of a contract's participants is followed by an invariant section that defines the contract invariant that has to be maintained by the participants. The Publisher/Subscriber contract does not define an invariant. The ModelView contract shown in Example 3.7 demonstrates a contract invariant section.

The last section of a contract specifies what has to be done in order to establish a contract, that is, after generating objects of the classes that correspond to the contract participants. In the Publisher/Subscriber contract, Subscriber objects have to be attached to the Publisher object they depend on.

Contract refinement

Complex behavioral compositions are built of simpler ones. The operations contract refinement and contract inclusion allow the reuse of contracts as a basis for or part of others. We pick the operation contract refinement as an example.

Contract refinement allows adding participants and extending type obligations as well as invariants. Extended invariants have to be compatible with the original one. Thus a contract is specialized by refinement.

We specialize the Publisher/Subscriber contract to express the relationship between the model and view components in the MVC framework: if the model component changes, all view components that display the model have to be updated. The original contract PublisherSubscriber is refined by specifying

- the condition that causes updates of the dependent view objects

- how the update operation of the dependent view components is defined.

For example, a linked list of integers could be the model component which can be presented in various ways by means of different view components (see Figure 3.15). Changes to the model, such as adding and removing integers, have to be reflected in all views that depend on the model component.

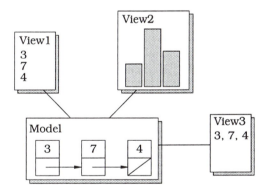

Figure 3.15 Sample model and view components according to MVC.

Example 3.7 refines the PublisherSubscriber contract and describes its specialization ModelView:

Example 3.7 ModelView contract as refinement of the PublisherSubscriber contract.

```
contract ModelView
        refines PublisherSubscriber (Model = Publisher,
                                     Views = Subscribers)
```

```
                    Model supports [
                        value: Value      // Value can be a simple type such
                                          // as a String or a complex data
                                          // structure such as a linked list.
                        SetValue(val: Value) => Δ value { value = val };
                                                 NotifySubscribers()
                        GetValue(): Value =>     return value
                    ]
                    Views: Set(View) where each View supports [
                        Update( ) =>     Draw()
                        Draw()    =>     Model->GetValue()
                                         { View reflects Model.value }
                    ]
                    contract  invariant
                        Model.SetValue(val) => < for all v: v ∈ Views:
                                            v reflects Model.value >
                    contract  establishment
                        < || v: v ∈ Views: <Model->AttachSubscriber(v) ;
                                            v->Draw()> >
            end  contract
```

The refines statement expresses that contract ModelView refines contract PublisherSubscriber. All obligations are inherited from PublisherSubscriber and can be re(de)fined. The participants Publisher and Subscribers of contract PublisherSubscriber are renamed Model and Views. Model adds the type obligations value, SetValue(...) and GetValue(). Update() of participant View is more specific. Its causal obligation is not defined at all in Publisher-Subscriber. The type obligation Draw() is added in participant View which refines Subscriber of contract PublisherSubscriber.

In the following, some details of contract ModelView are explained. The causal obligation of value is to be of the unspecified type Value. Value can represent a simple type such as a character string, but also a complex data structure such as a linked list or tree. The causal obligation of SetValue(val: Value) is specified after =>. Δ value { value = val } denotes that the type obligation value is set so that the condition "value is equal to val" holds afterwards. The action NotifySubscribers() has to follow the setting of value. Thus these two actions are separated by a semicolon.

Also note that participants refer to each other, ignoring implementation details of how such references are resolved. For example, in the causal obligation of Draw(), method GetValue() of participant Model is invoked.

Conformance declaration

Conformance declarations map contracts onto classes. This becomes necessary if class names and participant names are not identical. Furthermore, obligations of contract participants can be spread over several classes such as an abstract class and its subclasses.

The PublisherSubscriber contract could be implemented in one abstract class Object, which is the root of a single-rooted class hierarchy. Example 3.8 shows a conformance declaration that describes the mapping of the PublisherSubscriber contract onto class Object. Other methods of class Object could conform to participants of several different contracts.

Example 3.8 Conformance declaration of class Object.

```
class Object conforms to Publisher, Subscriber
in PublisherSubscriber
        Object supports
                NotifySubcribers();
                AttachSubscriber(s: Subscriber);
                DetachSubscriber(s: Subscriber);
                Update();
        requires subclass to support
                Update();
end conformance
```

The ModelView contract which refines the PublisherSubscriber contract represents another example. An abstract class View corresponds to participant View. The implementation of the Draw() method is left to specific subclasses of View (see Example 3.9).

Example 3.9 Conformance declaration of class View.

```
class View conforms to View
in ModelView
        inherits from Object
        View supports
                Update( );
                Draw();
        requires subclass to support
                Draw();
end conformance
```

Thus conformance declarations make abstract classes explicit. A conformance declaration for a class with the section "requires subclass to support" marks that class as an abstract class.

3.5.2 Sample contract for the DesktopItem-Folder framework

Let us try to apply the concepts of formal contracts described above for the abstract class DesktopItem and its subclass Folder, which constitute a framework for the management of DesktopItem objects (see Section 2.2). The formal description of this framework will also reveal some disadvantages of formal contracts.

We call the formal contract of this framework simply Desktop. One problem already arises at the beginning of the contract definition: what are the participants of the Desktop contract? Of course, DesktopItem and Folder play a key role. But we have to express a specific relationship between these two participants. Class Folder as a *subclass* of the abstract class DesktopItem contains a list of DesktopItem objects. Due to polymorphism, recursive nesting of Folder objects becomes possible.

Contract specifications do not allow the expression of subclass relationships. This has to be done in conformance declarations. Thus we have the following choices:

(1)   We define two participants DesktopItem and Folder, duplicating common type obligations, that is, the methods SetItemName(...), GetItemName(), GetSizeInBytes() and the instance variable itemName. This solution introduces redundancies without expressing the essential relationship between the participants.

(2)   We define only DesktopItem in the formal contract. The fact that Folder is a subclass of DesktopItem is expressed in a conformance declaration.

(3)   A Folder contract refines a contract called DesktopItem.

Example 3.10 shows a formal contract according to (1).

Example 3.10   Contract Desktop with participants DesktopItem and Folder.

```
contract Desktop
        DesktopItem supports [
                itemName: String

                SetItemName(name: String) => Δ itemName
                                        { itemName = name }
                GetItemName(): String => return itemName
                GetSizeInBytes(): Integer => return 0
        ]
```

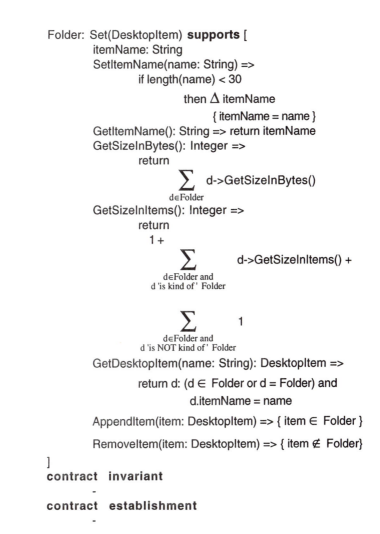

Folder: Set(DesktopItem) **supports** [
  itemName: String
  SetItemName(name: String) =>
    if length(name) < 30
      then Δ itemName
        { itemName = name }
  GetItemName(): String => return itemName
  GetSizeInBytes(): Integer =>
    return
    $$\sum_{d \in \text{Folder}} \text{d->GetSizeInBytes()}$$
  GetSizeInItems(): Integer =>
    return
    1 +
    $$\sum_{\substack{d \in \text{Folder and} \\ d\ '\text{is kind of}'\ \text{Folder}}} \text{d->GetSizeInItems()} +$$

    $$\sum_{\substack{d \in \text{Folder and} \\ d\ '\text{is NOT kind of}'\ \text{Folder}}} 1$$
  GetDesktopItem(name: String): DesktopItem =>
    return d: (d $\in$ Folder or d = Folder) and
      d.itemName = name
  AppendItem(item: DesktopItem) => { item $\in$ Folder }

  RemoveItem(item: DesktopItem) => { item $\notin$ Folder}
]
contract   invariant
  -
contract   establishment
  -

As already mentioned, this contract specification does not express that Folder objects can be recursively nested by means of AppendItem(...). There is no element in the formal contract specification language to make explicit that class Folder is a subclass of DesktopItem. This deficiency also causes problems in the formal contract specification, for instance, in the causal obligation of GetDesktopItem(...). The type associated with d is unspecified. If it were possible to specify that Folder is a subclass of DesktopItem, d would have the polymorphic type DesktopItem which can represent objects of all subclasses of DesktopItem.

Example 3.11 outlines an appropriate conformance declaration which expresses that Folder is a subclass of DesktopItem.

Example 3.11 Conformance declarations of DesktopItem and Folder.

```
class DesktopItem conforms to DesktopItem in Desktop
        DesktopItem supports
                all type obligations of participant DesktopItem
        requires subclass to support
                GetSizeInBytes();
end conformance

class Folder conforms to Folder in Desktop
        inherits from DesktopItem
        Folder supports
                all type obligations of participant Folder
end conformance
```

Choosing approach (2), that is, defining only participant DesktopItem in the contract specification in the same way as in Example 3.10 and leaving out participant Folder, does not lead to a satisfying solution either. Folder would be specified in a conformance declaration as a subclass of DesktopItem as sketched in Example 3.11. Though redundancies can be eliminated in this case, the description of the important subclass relationship is still split between the contract and the conformance declaration. Analogous arguments are valid for approach (3).

In this simple example it even seems that the formal notation reduces the understandability compared to a description based on an object-oriented programming language. The formal specification of the mailing framework outlined in Section 2.2.2 would cause comparable problems. Component Mailer is based on the abstract classes DesktopItem and Employee, which both support recursive nesting by means of the corresponding subclasses Folder and EmployeeGroup.

3.5.3 Pros and cons of formal contracts

Helm *et al.* pioneered the abstract description of what they call behavioral compositions in object-oriented systems. The proposed formal notation has the following advantages:

+   The suggested notation consists of few elements. The concepts introduced mirror those of object-oriented programming languages. For example, participants are close to objects.

+   Formal contracts take into account the fact that complex behavioral compositions are built of simpler ones. The operations contract refinement and contract inclusion support the adaptation of contracts and contribute to the flexibility of this approach.

Nevertheless, formal contracts have several limitations, too:

– Formal contracts can be difficult to apply in certain situations. For example, expressing the DesktopItem-Folder framework in the previous section appeared to be rather cumbersome with formal contracts. Introducing new notational elements could alleviate this problem, but the formal notation would become more complex.

– A formal notation imposes a sense of exactness which may hide flaws in the specification. In the PublisherSubscriber contract, for example, participant Subscribers is a set of participants of type Subscriber. The data structure Set is supposed to be an elementary type. As a consequence, type Set would have to provide appropriate operations for its management, such as adding and removing elements. Thus the type obligations AttachSubscriber(...) and DetachSubscriber(...) of participant BroadcastingItem are superfluous. Such redundancies are often caused by lack of a clear indication of where to define certain aspects of behavior.

– Essential aspects become cluttered with many details. The abstraction level of the formal notation appears to be too close to object-oriented programming languages.

To sum up, formal contracts offer one way of describing framework designs, that is, the interrelationships of objects constituting a framework. Helm *et al.* (1990) view formal contracts as a means for *interaction-oriented design*. This idea has inspired other notations. The following section discusses an informal notation.

3.6   Design pattern catalog

Erich Gamma pioneered a catalog-like presentation of design patterns in his Ph.D. thesis (Gamma 1992). This thesis built the basis of an advanced catalog-like presentation of more than 20 design patterns published in Gamma *et al.* (1993) and Gamma *et al.* (1994). We refer to the design patterns listed in these two publications as a *design pattern catalog* or simply *catalog*.

The design pattern catalog attaches importance to abstract classes and frameworks. Actually, most of the patterns constitute frameworks for a particular purpose. As a consequence, Gamma *et al.* (1993) view these patterns as "reusable micro-architectures that contribute to an overall system architecture" that "... provide a common vocabulary for design."

Each pattern in the catalog is described by means of informal text, one or more diagrams in the Object Model Notation, hints regarding the implementation, and code examples in C++ and/or Smalltalk. In essence, a pattern description starts with a sample usage of a particular pattern in a certain context. Usually a graphic diagram and an informal textual description provide a brief overview of the pattern and show the advantages offered by the pattern. A more abstract informal description of the pattern participants and their collaborations follows, accompanied by a corresponding class/object diagram. Relevant clues outlining typical situations when to use the pattern, including caveats, follow the abstract description. Code examples and examples of object-oriented systems where the pattern was successfully applied conclude the pattern description. References to other pattern descriptions point out related patterns and their differences.

In this section we give a glimpse of the design pattern catalog. Deviating from the fine-grained pattern classification proposed in the catalog, we apply the following classification of the listed patterns:

- patterns relying on *abstract coupling*
- patterns based on recursive structures
- other patterns.

3.6.1 Patterns relying on abstract coupling

Most of the patterns in the catalog are based on *abstractly coupled classes*. Figure 3.16 illustrates the concept of abstract coupling. At least class B of the two coupled classes A and B has to be an abstract class.

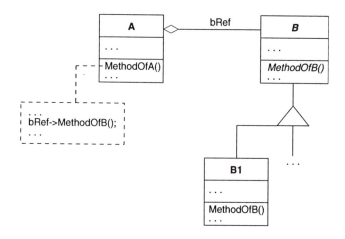

Figure 3.16 Abstract coupling of class A and abstract class B.

In the example shown in Figure 3.16, an object of class A maintains a reference to a B object by means of the instance variable bRef. At run time bRef does not refer to an instance of B since B is an abstract class. Instead, bRef refers to an instance of a descendant of B. Figure 3.17 demonstrates the variations of abstract coupling without depicting methods and subclasses of abstract classes as in Figure 3.16.

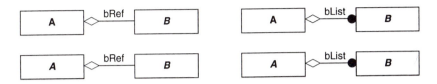

Figure 3.17 Variations of abstract coupling.

State pattern

The State pattern in the catalog is similar to Coad's Changeable Roles pattern described in Section 3.2.2. Recall the remark regarding the Changeable Roles pattern: class Role should be an abstract class. Coad's pattern is considered to be too general to give hints on which behavior should be defined in the abstract class Role. The State pattern eliminates this deficiency.

Figure 3.18 shows the enhanced Changeable Roles pattern. In the design pattern catalog, class Player is called Descriptor; class Role corresponds to class State.

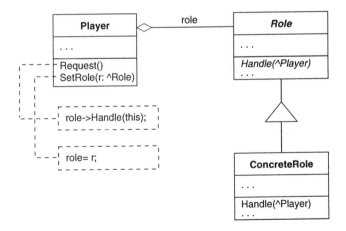

Figure 3.18 State pattern as an enhanced Changeable Roles pattern.

The design pattern catalog outlines a sample usage of this pattern in the realm of networking: a class TCPConnection corresponds to Player, an abstract class TCPState to Role. TCPClosed and TCPEstablished are two subclasses of TCPState. Depending on the actual object referred to by the instance variable role, an object of class TCPConnection handles requests differently, like opening a connection.

Factory Method pattern

This pattern underlies, for example, the creation of documents in ET++ as described in the corresponding cookbook recipe in Section 3.4.1. Figure 3.19 depicts the creation of SpreadSheetDoc objects in a sample ET++ application.

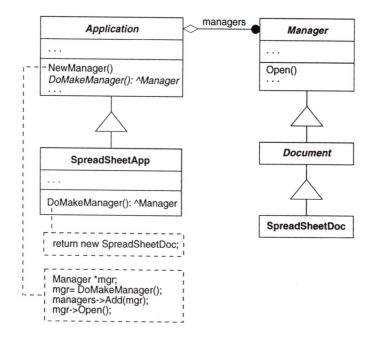

Figure 3.19 Factory Method pattern applied in the realm of a sample ET++ application.

The Factory Method pattern makes object instantiation more flexible compared to direct object instantiation. "However, a potential disadvantage of factory methods is that there are now two points of evolution .... Consequently, two class hierarchies must evolve in coordinated fashion" (Gamma *et al.* 1994).

Observer pattern

The Observer pattern in the catalog corresponds to Coad's Publisher/ Subscriber pattern (see Section 3.2.3) and the Publisher/Subscriber contract (see Section 3.5.1).

Most patterns in the catalog contain useful hints regarding their implementation. For implementing the Observer pattern, Gamma *et al.* (1994) discuss hash-linking, "in which a dictionary maintains a subject-to-observer mapping. Thus a subject with no observers does not incur storage overhead. On the other hand, this approach increases the cost of accessing the observers."

Analogous patterns

Numerous other patterns in the catalog are based on abstract coupling. Typically, the semantics, that is, the method names and the entities represented by the classes, differ in these patterns. For example, in the State pattern the classes Player and Role cooperate via the Handle method provided by class Role. The part that is kept flexible in this pattern is the way a request is handled by a specific Role object. Analogously, the participants of the Observer pattern interact based on the Update method of the observers. The part that is kept flexible in this pattern is the way an update operation is accomplished.

Below we summarize the other related patterns in the catalog, pointing out the particular flexible aspect of these patterns.

- *Bridge pattern*: describes the concept of abstract coupling.

- *Builder pattern*: is useful to maintain flexibility in the creation of parts of a complex entity.

- *Command pattern*: how a task (= command) is accomplished is kept flexible.

- *Iterator and Visitor patterns*: are useful to keep flexible the action that is carried out while iterating over objects in data structures such as linked lists or trees.

- *Interpreter pattern*: used in the realm of interpreting regular languages. How a parse node is interpreted constitutes the flexible part in this pattern.

- *Mediator, Adapter patterns*: is used for flexible protocol adaptations of (a) class(es).

- *Prototype pattern*: is useful to keep object instantiation flexible.

- *Proxy pattern*: is useful to keep the (local) representation of an object flexible.

- *Strategy pattern*: helps to keep a strategy, that is, a behavior or an algorithm, flexible.

To sum up, all these patterns are quite domain-independent sample frameworks demonstrating various semantic aspects that can be kept flexible by applying the concept of abstract coupling.

3.6.2 **Patterns based on recursive structures**

The grouping of DesktopItem objects by means of class Folder as shown in Figure 3.20 is a sample application of the Composite pattern presented in the catalog.

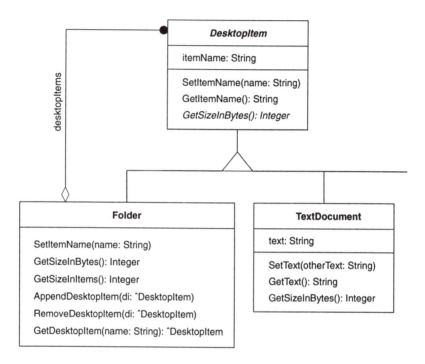

Figure 3.20 Sample usage of the Composite pattern.

As discussed in detail in Chapter 2, this pattern allows recursive building of a hierarchy of folders. A Folder object can be treated as a single DesktopItem object since it *is a* DesktopItem (= inherits from DesktopItem).

Figure 3.21 illustrates the Composite pattern in a more abstract manner. The Composite pattern presented in the catalog deviates from the figure as the methods for adding and removing items are defined in the abstract class SingleItem. Coad also describes this pattern as outlined in Section 3.2.2.

The Chain of Responsibility and Decorator catalog patterns are also based on recursive structures. Patterns dealing with recursive structures are discussed in detail in Chapter 4.

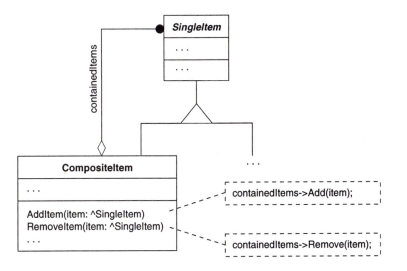

Figure 3.21 Composite pattern.

3.6.3 Other catalog patterns

The remaining catalog patterns can be summarized as follows. An Abstract Factory pattern is close to the Factory Method pattern. Flyweight represents a pattern similar to Coad's Item Description pattern presented in Section 3.2.2. The Solitaire pattern represents a coding pattern that limits the number of createable instances of a class to one.

The Template Method pattern forms the basis of all patterns dealing with abstract classes. Template methods are discussed in detail in Chapter 4.

3.6.4 Summarizing remarks

The design pattern catalog constitutes a pioneering work in the realm of design patterns for frameworks. Most of the patterns focus on frameworks. Gamma *et al.* (1993) point out the difference between frameworks and design patterns: ".... frameworks are implemented in a programming language. .... In this sense frameworks are more concrete than design patterns. .... Mature frameworks usually reuse several design patterns."

Since experienced object-oriented designers collected these patterns, the catalog represents a valuable resource of micro-architectures. Knowing these design examples can help in the development of new (application) frameworks.

Nevertheless, numerous patterns in the catalog are similar. In the following chapter we present a more advanced abstraction that allows us to categorize the catalog patterns and to describe them on a metalevel.

Chapter 4

Metapatterns

Design patterns in the realm of frameworks provide the essence of this book. So far, we have examined some example patterns. Except for the coding patterns and the framework adaptation patterns discussed in Chapter 3, all other design pattern approaches try to describe frameworks on an abstraction level higher than the corresponding code that implements these frameworks.

State-of-the-art design pattern approaches essentially attempt to select frameworks that are not too domain-specific. Such frameworks are presented as examples of good object-oriented design that can be applied in the development of other frameworks.

For example, the Publisher/Subscriber pattern is quite domain-independent and can be used in many frameworks. We use the term *framework example (design pattern)* for those design patterns in Chapter 3 that describe sample frameworks. Some of Coad's patterns, the frameworks formally described in the notation proposed by Richard Helm *et al.*, and most patterns in the design pattern catalog of Erich Gamma *et al.* belong to this category.

We consider these catalogs of framework examples to be a useful means of constructing new frameworks. Nevertheless, a more advanced abstraction is helpful, for example, in order to actively support the design pattern idea in the realm of tools. Chapter 6 discusses this aspect.

We introduce the term *metapatterns* for a set of design patterns that describes how to construct frameworks independent of a specific domain. Actually, constructing frameworks by combining the basic object-oriented concepts proves quite straightforward. Thus these metapatterns turn out to be an elegant and powerful approach that can be applied to categorize and describe any framework example design pattern on a *metalevel*. So metapatterns do not replace state-of-the-art design pattern approaches, but complement them.

The goal of this chapter is to present and illustrate the concept of metapatterns. In order to grasp metapatterns, the reader should be familiar with some frameworks such as those presented in Chapters 2 and 3.

4.1 Metapatterns and (application) frameworks

Recall the characteristics of (application) frameworks: they consist of ready-to-use and semifinished building blocks. The overall architecture, that is, the composition and interaction of its building blocks, is predefined as well. Reusing a framework usually means adapting building blocks to specific needs by overriding methods of some framework classes in subclasses. Application frameworks are discussed below.

In general, an application framework standardizes applications for a specific domain. Usually, various aspects of an application framework cannot be anticipated. These parts of an application framework have to be generic so that they can easily be adapted to specific needs. Figure 4.1 shows schematically this property of an application framework with the generic, flexible parts in gray.

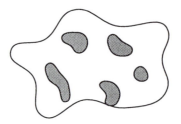

Figure 4.1 An application framework with flexible hot spots (gray).

The difficulty of good object-oriented design is to identify the *hot spots* of an application framework, that is, those aspects of an application domain that have to be kept flexible. We consider a framework to have the quality attribute "well designed" if it provides adequate hot spots for adaptations.

Primarily, *domain-specific knowledge is required* to find these hot spots. Only domain analysis can help to acquire this knowledge. However, framework examples and metapatterns are useless during this domain analysis. Patterns can only outline how to design and implement frameworks that match these hot spots, that is, frameworks that are adaptable where required.

Concepts offered by object-oriented programming languages allow implementation of application frameworks with hot spots. Examples that demonstrate how flexibility is gained in object-oriented design have already been presented in Chapters 2 and 3. Metapatterns highlight the essential constructs for building frameworks, that is, reusable, flexible, object-oriented software.

4.2   Class/object interfaces and interaction metapatterns

In general, a class interface is made up of several methods and possibly instance variables that can be accessed in instances of a particular class. We use again the term contract synonymously with class interface or protocol. We ignore the special meaning of the term contract in the realm of formal contracts discussed in Section 3.5.

Template and hook methods form the metapatterns required to design frameworks consisting of single classes or groups of classes together with their interactions. The terms template method and hook method are commonly used by various authors such as Wirfs-Brock *et al.* (1990), Pree (1991), Gamma *et al.* (1993), and Gamma *et al.* (1994).

The *narrow inheritance interface principle* (Weinand *et al.* 1989) as a fundamental design guideline is strongly related to this distinction between hook and template methods. General considerations and specific examples illustrate how to combine these two metapatterns in order to develop well-designed frameworks.

4.2.1   Template and hook methods

The implementation of the framework concept depends heavily on dynamically bound methods. Recall that all methods are assumed to be dynamically bound. Let us take a closer look at how to develop frameworks by means of basic object-oriented concepts applied at the microlevel, that is, in the implementation of methods.

In the implementation of frameworks the following kinds of methods have to be distinguished:

- *template methods* which are based on
- *hook methods*, which are either
    - *abstract methods*,
    - *regular methods*, or
    - template methods.

These class interface and interaction metapatterns are described in detail below. In general, template methods implement the *frozen spots* and hook methods implement the hot spots of an application framework, according to Figure 4.1. Note that the term template method, or simply template, must not be confused with the C++ template construct, which has a completely different meaning. In the remainder of this book we *ignore* the C++ meaning.

With some imprecision, we can say that complex methods called *template methods* can be implemented based on elementary methods which are called *hook methods*. Template methods are a means of defining abstract behavior or generic flow of control or the relationship between objects (in the case where they are applied across class borders as explained below).

Flexibility within one class

Let us consider the example shown in Figure 4.2(a): a class B offers three methods M1(), M2() and M3(). M1() constitutes the template method based on the hook methods M2() and M3(). For method M2() only the method interface, that is, its name and parameters, can be defined, not an implementation. The term *abstract method* has already been introduced in Chapter 2 for such a method. Abstract methods are written in *italic style* in the graphic representation. Method M3() is assumed to provide a meaningful default implementation.

Since M2() is an abstract method, it does not make sense to generate instances of class B. B is an abstract class.

Class B could, for example, correspond to a class RentalItem, which could be part of an application framework for reservation systems (see Figure 4.2(b)). Class B's template method M1() corresponds to PrintInvoice() of class RentalItem. For method CalcRate() only the method interface can be defined, not an implementation. Method GetName() is assumed to provide a meaningful default implementation.

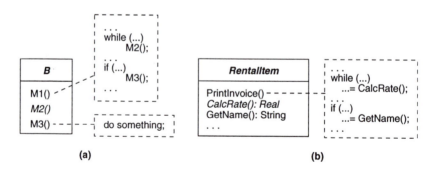

(a)   (b)

Figure 4.2 Template and hook methods unified in one class.

B must be adapted in a subclass where at least the abstract method M2() of B is overridden, as shown in Figure 4.3(a). The default implementations of M1() and M3() hopefully meet the requirements of the specific application under development. RentalItem is adapted in an analogous way (see Figure 4.3(b)).

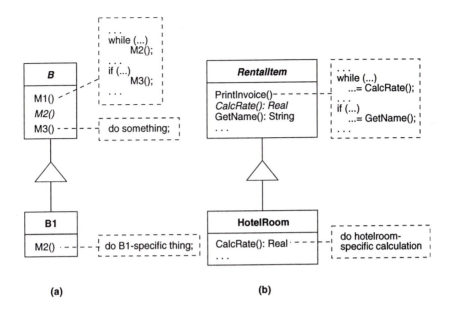

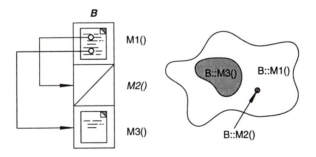

Figure 4.3 Adaptation of hook methods in subclasses.

The concept of template methods is illustrated in Figure 4.4. Method calls are expressed by arrows: M1() calls the abstract method M2() and method M3(). M2() is depicted as a gray spot that has to be filled. M3() is depicted as a gray spot that can be replaced.

Figure 4.4 A template method calling its hook methods.

Subclass B1 shown in Figure 4.3(a) adapts the template method M1() by overriding M2(). The template method M1() of class B is adapted without changing its source code, as illustrated in Figure 4.5.

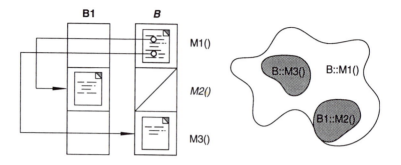

Figure 4.5 Adaptation of template method M1() by overriding B::M2().

Of course, method M3() can also be overridden in a subclass of B in order to adapt this hot spot of template method M1(). Figure 4.6 illustrates this adaptation assuming that class B1 overrides the methods M2() and M3() of class B.

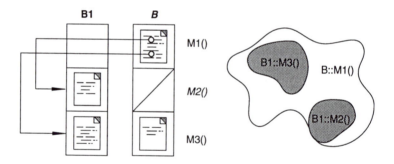

Figure 4.6 Adaptation of template method M1() by overriding B::M2() and B::M3().

Template methods and hook methods are not only suited to introducing flexibility within a single class. If template and hook methods are unified in one class the behavior of this class can only be modified by defining a subclass. For example, the behavior of printing an invoice can be changed by defining a subclass of RentalItem and implementing its hot spots in a specific way.

In some situations more flexibility is required to allow adaptations at run time. In order to achieve this degree of flexibility, frozen spots (template methods) and hot spots (hook methods) have to be put into separate classes as explained below.

Flexibility across class borders
The contract of a class B can only be augmented in subclasses. Subclasses of B can modify method implementations or add new methods. Either methods of class B itself (as demonstrated with B::M1() in the examples above) or of any other class can be based on the contract of B. Other classes based on the contract of B means that variables of static type B are used in these classes so that the corresponding objects can refer to B objects. Messages corresponding to the contract of B are sent to these B objects. If B is an abstract class such as in our example, these variables will never refer to B instances but only to instances of descendants of B.

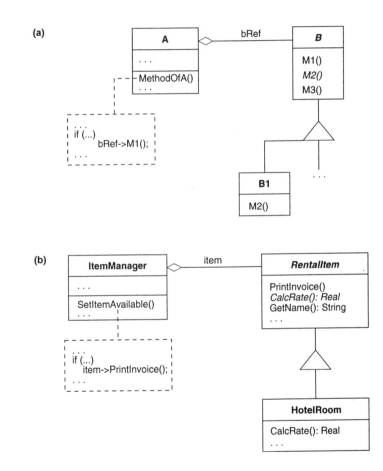

Figure 4.7 Abstract coupling based on template and hook methods.

The example in Figure 4.7(a) illustrates a case where another class A is based on the contract of class B. Class A could, for example, correspond to a class

ItemManager in an application framework for reservation systems (see Figure 4.7(b)).

In the example in Figure 4.7(a), objects of class A maintain a reference to objects of class B by means of the instance variable bRef. Note that the way class A and class B are coupled via bRef is one example of *abstract coupling* outlined in Section 3.6.1.

Ideally, MethodOfA() is adapted to specific needs by only overriding B::M2() in a subclass of B. The instance variable bRef then has to refer to the appropriate instance of a subclass of B.

What constitutes a template method and a hook method is a matter of point of view. A hook method is elementary compared to the template method in which the particular hook method is used. In another context, the template method can become a hook method of another template method. For example, MethodOfA() is a template method using M1() as a hook method. In the realm of class B, method M1() is a template method.

As a consequence, we use the term *template method* for both. Template methods call at least one other method. If it is necessary to distinguish between the elementary hook method and the template method based on that hook method, we explicitly use the term hook method. Hook methods can be abstract methods, regular methods (see below) or template methods.

The remaining methods that do not call other methods and that provide a meaningful implementation are *regular methods*. We use the term regular method only if it is necessary to stress this aspect. In the examples illustrated in Figures 4.2–6, B::M3() represents a regular method if do something does not call other methods.

Note that template methods are not restricted to abstract classes. For example, class A in Figure 4.7(a) offering MethodOfA() is a concrete class. Methods in any class can be template methods for the following reasons: the methods a template method is based on can be defined

- within the same class as the template method
- in one of the superclasses of the class where the template method is defined
- in another class.

The DesktopItem-Folder framework in Section 2.2 represents another example where template and hook methods are involved across class borders. Method GetSizeInBytes() in class Folder is a template method that implements in advance the generic algorithm for calculating the Folder object size without knowing how the size of the particular objects contained in the folder is calculated. This means that the template method Folder::GetSizeInBytes() has as its hot spot the size calculation of the contained objects.

GetSizeInBytes() is defined as an abstract method in Folder's superclass DesktopItem. This method has to be overridden in all descendants of Desktop-Item. Due to the inheritance relationship between Folder and DesktopItem, the template method GetSizeInBytes() in class Folder has the same name as its hook method, the abstract method GetSizeInBytes() in class DesktopItem.

Folder::GetSizeInBytes() can be implemented in advance since Folder objects store the references to all contained DesktopItem objects. How the dynamically bound method GetSizeInBytes() is overridden in descendants of DesktopItem determines the calculation in Folder objects.

4.2.2 Interface and interaction design guidelines

The *narrow inheritance interface principle* is the primary design guideline for frameworks. As discussed below, this principle is strongly related to the distinction between template methods and hook methods. Besides the narrow inheritance interface principle, only a few rules of thumb can assist in interface and interaction design.

Narrow inheritance interface principle

Weinand *et al.* (1989) describe the narrow inheritance interface principle employed in frameworks: "Behavior that is spread over several methods in a class should be based on a minimal set of methods which have to be overridden." Otherwise clients deriving subclasses would have to override many methods to adapt that behavior.

Lalonde (1989) uses the term *design by primitives* instead of narrow inheritance interface principle. We prefer the latter since we consider this term more descriptive.

In the example shown in the Figures 4.2–6, programmers who derive a subclass from B ideally have only to override the hook method B::M2() and maybe also the hook method B::M3() in order to adjust the behavior of the template method B::M1(). The narrow inheritance principle expresses that overriding the smaller hook methods has to be sufficient in order to adapt the more complex template methods. If the template method B::M1() had to be overridden in order to adapt class B to specific needs, the narrow inheritance principle would be violated. In an analogous way it should be possible to adapt MethodOfA() in Figure 4.7(a) by overriding only B::M2() and maybe B::M3() in a subclass of B.

Template method Folder::GetSizeInBytes() in the DesktopItem-Folder framework also adheres to the narrow inheritance interface principle. The size calculation defined by this template method is adapted by overriding the hook method GetSizeInBytes() of class DesktopItem in subclasses of DesktopItem; the template method in class Folder remains unchanged.

Obviously, the design of class interfaces should follow the narrow inheritance interface principle. Unfortunately, designing classes with narrow inheritance interfaces involves conflicting goals: good design of class interfaces in the realm of frameworks should find the optimal balance between flexibility and the effort required to adapt classes.

A class that provides powerful template methods which are only based on a few hook methods implies minimal effort for adaptation. Behavior is adapted by overriding some or all of these few hook methods in subclasses. However, powerful template methods could sacrifice the flexibility of a class. If their hook methods are not sufficient to modify the template method's behavior, a class becomes inflexible, implying that the whole template method has to be overridden. Thus template methods have the potential of reducing adaptation effort without sacrificing flexibility, but add the danger of making classes too rigid, which again drastically increases the adaptation effort.

As a consequence, classes in a mature framework should contain powerful yet flexible template methods—they have to be flexible where necessary in the particular domain. Programmers ideally only have to override a few hook methods in order to adapt a framework to their specific needs. The design of the corresponding class interfaces typically requires many iterations, caused by the use of a framework in specific situations. During such iterations, template methods might appear to be too rigid, so that more hook methods have to be integrated. It is also possible that the usage of classes provides insights into how to define additional template methods. If programmers have to implement similar control flow repeatedly in the course of adapting a framework, additional template methods should be defined in framework classes.

It is impossible to describe general guidelines for getting template methods right from the start. Class interface design depends very much on the specific domain for which a framework is developed. Descriptions of sample frameworks can illustrate how to do it right in specific situations.

Above all it is important to grasp the conflicting goals of combining template and hook methods according to the narrow inheritance principle. The optimum balance depends on domain-specific adaptations of frameworks.

The structure of template methods sometimes depends on the way objects are composed in object-oriented systems. This aspect is pointed out in Section 4.3.

Some rules of thumb

In the realm of module-oriented software development, numerous rules of thumb have been proposed for modularizing software systems. These rules can also be applied to structuring object-oriented software. Various authors discuss such guidelines, for example, Meyer (1988), Hoffman (1990), and Gamma (1992). The most important rules of thumb are:

- *Weak coupling between classes, that is, their corresponding objects.*
  This principle restricts communication between objects. Objects should

exchange as little data as possible. Adhering to the principle of weak coupling between classes reduces the complexity of the overall system.

- *Strong coupling within a class.* This means that there should be no methods and data without any relationship. Strong coupling within a class is usually achieved by defining a class for only one abstraction with methods that are closely related to the instance variables. Classes with weak inner coupling should be split into independent classes.

- *Minimal, adequate class interface.* Redundant features, that is, offering a service via several slightly different methods, should be avoided.

- *Testability.* It should be possible to test the correctness of a class without knowing in which context a class will be used. Weak coupling between classes and a minimal class interface simplify testing.

Besides these considerations, choosing appropriate and uniform names for classes, methods and instance variables greatly contributes to the understandability of a framework. Since frameworks already incorporate much of the design and control flow, they are more than a set of reusable basic software components. Actually, frameworks can be thought of as high-level languages going far beyond the scope of their underlying object-oriented programming language.

As a consequence, framework design and especially class interface design also means language design. Thus names should not only be semantically expressive but also consistent throughout a framework, as described in Section 3.3.2. A good idea is to mark related methods uniformly in different classes. For example, in a GUI application framework the names of all methods that draw on the screen could start with Gr for graphics.

4.2.3 Example: flexible object creation

This section demonstrates how template methods, hook methods and the narrow inheritance principle are applied in a framework example. This sample framework is called Factory Method in the design pattern catalog of Erich Gamma *et al.* (1994). Other authors term this framework example virtual constructor (Ellis and Stroustrup 1990, Coplien 1992). Let us briefly discuss this naming issue. The term virtual constructor is avoided in this book since it causes confusion in connection with the C++ constructor construct. A C++ constructor is a method for object initialization. The design pattern for flexible object creation has nothing to do with object initialization. Factory Method could be confused with a meaning that is sometimes associated with classes: classes are viewed as object factories. As a consequence, we use the term *flexible object creation* for this framework example in the remainder of this book.

This framework example is typically applied when a template method has to generate objects without prescribing exactly the class which is instantiated. Instead of hard-coding the object instantiation, a hook method is called that generates an object. Variations of flexible object generation are possible. Some of them are discussed below. Figure 4.8 depicts one object creation pattern. In this case template method Template1() uses the hook method CreateB() in order to keep the creation of B objects flexible.

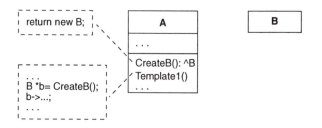

Figure 4.8 Flexible creation of B objects by means of the hook method CreateB() in method Template1().

Note that class B is not an abstract class. As a consequence, the hook method CreateB() used for object creation does not have to be an abstract method. A::CreateB() can provide the instantiation of class B as a default implementation. Clients of A have to override method CreateB() in a subclass of A if the object creation behavior of class A is to be adapted.

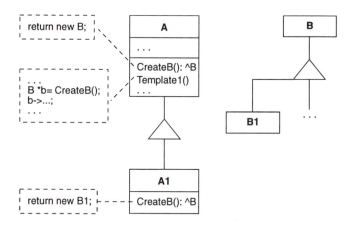

Figure 4.9 Adaptation of A's object creation behavior.

Figure 4.9 illustrates such an adaptation of class A. Class A1 overrides the hook method CreateB(), so that a B1 instance is created in A::Template1() instead of an instance of B.

The template method Template1() need not be overridden in subclasses in order to adapt its behavior regarding object creation. Thus the design of A adheres to the narrow inheritance interface principle. In instances of A1 the template method Template1() creates B1 instances since its hook method CreateB() is overridden.

If Template1() did not use the hook method CreateB() for object creation and hard-coded the creation instead (in this example B *b= new B), problems would arise, if this aspect were considered important in the realm of adaptations of class A. In this case A would have to be redesigned. Otherwise, Template1() itself would have to be overridden every time an instance of a specific subclass of B is handled in the template method, whereby the narrow inheritance interface principle is violated.

Recall the guideline that names should not only be semantically expressive but also consistent throughout a framework. This rule of thumb can be applied in the realm of the Flexible Object Creation pattern. For example, all hook methods in a framework that are intended to keep object creation flexible could start with the semantically expressive word Create. The application framework ET++ also adheres to that rule of thumb. In ET++ these hook methods contain the word Make, as in DoMakeManager().

Some pattern variations
Document creation in ET++'s class Application represents a slight variation of the pattern shown in Figures 4.8 and 4.9. Class Application corresponds to class A; class Document corresponds to class B. Method CreateB() corresponds to DoMakeManager() in class Application. Since Document is an abstract class in ET++, DoMakeManager() cannot be implemented in advance. So DoMakeManager() is an abstract method in the abstract class Application. Both Application and Document have to be subclassed. A subclass of Application has to override DoMakeManager() accordingly so that an appropriate instance of a Document subclass is generated. The template method NewManager() of class Application is based on this flexible object creation and corresponds to the template method Template1().

Also consider some other variations of the Flexible Object Creation pattern: Method CreateB() could be an abstract method, though class B is not an abstract class. Thus clients of A always have to subclass A and define the object creation behavior by overriding CreateB(). Another variation of this specific framework pattern is that Template1() is not in class A but in another class C which maintains a reference variable of static type A. C objects can refer to an instance of A or any subclass of A that overrides CreateB(). Depending on the dynamic type of the referenced A object, Template1() of C objects will behave differently as far as the creation of B objects is concerned.

4.2.4 Summarizing remarks

The Flexible Object Creation pattern illustrated above (and slight variations thereof) is yet another example of how to construct a framework for a specific domain by means of template and hook methods. The minidomain of these frameworks is object creation. This reveals an interesting aspect that is worth considering.

Object creation is one example that occurs in all frameworks whatever their particular purpose. As a consequence, the Flexible Object Creation pattern is not really domain-specific. Above we sketched how to design template methods in order to keep them flexible with regard to object creation and to adhere to the narrow inheritance interface principle.

The application of the template method and hook method metapatterns is unchanged in other situations where frameworks have to be developed: generic behavior, that is, control flow that should be flexible, has to be packed into hook methods. In the case of the Flexible Object Creation pattern, object creation is the behavior that should be flexible. Hook methods can be viewed as place holders or hot spots that are invoked by template methods.

Again, the difficulty lies in finding out which behavior should be kept flexible in domain-specific frameworks and which behavior should be standardized by means of template methods. Finding the right balance usually requires profound domain-specific knowledge and numerous design iterations.

4.3 Class/object composition metapatterns

The standardized frozen spots of a framework are represented by template methods. Hook methods are the flexible, gray spots within these frozen spots. This section introduces the terms *template* and *hook classes* based on the distinction between template and hook methods explained above.

Section 4.3.2 discusses the few attributes that influence class/object composition. Based on these attributes, metapatterns are presented for composing objects of template and hook classes. These composition metapatterns often influence the structure of template methods as will be demonstrated in Section 4.4.

4.3.1 Template and hook classes

Sometimes, template methods and hook methods are unified in one class. For example, this is the case in some variations of the Flexible Object Creation pattern.

In many situations it is better to put frozen spots and hot spots into separate classes. In this case, the class that contains the hook method(s) can be considered as the *hook class* of the class that contains the corresponding template method(s). We call the class that contains the template method(s) a *template class*. In other words, a hook class *parameterizes* the corresponding template class.

Analogous to template and hook methods, the particular situation determines which class is a template and which a hook class. If the template methods of a class are used as hook methods by methods of another class, the template class becomes a hook class (see Section 4.2.1 for details).

4.3.2 Composition attributes

Several attributes influence how to compose template and hook classes and their corresponding objects:

- Can an object of a template class refer to exactly one object of the hook class or to any number of objects of the hook class?
- Is one class a descendant of the other class?
- Are the classes abstract classes?

Reference relationships between objects of template and hook classes
A precondition for allowing message sending between objects is the existence of a reference between these objects. Of course, this is also true for coupling the objects of template and hook classes. In most cases an object of a template class has to maintain a reference to the object of the corresponding hook class, since a template method sends messages to the object of the hook class.

In general, a reference between an object of template class T and an object of hook class H can be established in the following ways:

(1)   by means of an instance variable of static type H in class T

(2)   by passing object references via method parameters

(3)   by means of a global variable referencing the object of class H.

Typically, reference relationships are established by applying possibility (1). For example, in Figure 4.7 class A is a template class, class B a hook class. Objects of A refer to B objects by means of the instance variable bRef.

Possibility (2) allows only short-term relationships between objects. For example, recall the State pattern discussed in Section 3.6.1 and depicted in Figure 4.10. Here class Player is the template class with Request() as a template method. Class Role constitutes the hook class with Handle(...) as the hook method—handling requests is the hot spot in that framework example. A long-term relationship between a Player object and a Role object is established according to possibility (1) via the instance variable role. A short-term relationship between a Role object and a Player object is established by applying possibility (2): in the statement role->Handle(*this*) a reference to the actual Player object is passed to the Role object, which can use it only in the Handle(...) method to access the particular Player object. This short-term relationship might be needed in order to implement Handle(...) in specific Role subclasses.

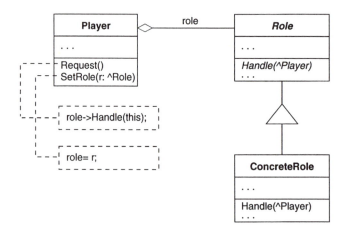

Figure 4.10 Short-term reference relationship in a sample framework.

Possibility (3) is only used in special situations. For example, some frameworks contain classes that are instantiated exactly once. A reference to such an instance is sometimes stored in a global variable. Template methods might use this global variable to establish a reference to the corresponding object.

According to the discussion above, the realm of metapatterns encompasses only possibility (1), that is, the establishment of a reference between objects of template and hook classes via an instance variable.

The number of referenced objects as reference attribute

Based on possibility (1), by means of an appropriate instance variable an object of a template class can refer to

- exactly one object of a hook class
- any number of objects of a hook class (= a group of objects of a hook class).

Figure 4.11 depicts these two situations. In the class diagram on the left, instance variable hRef of an object of template class T can refer to exactly one object of hook class H. An object of template class T with the instance variable hList can refer to any number of objects (zero or more) of class H.

Figure 4.11 Template class with different types of instance variables.

Semantic aspects of reference relationships

Another aspect of references between objects has to be considered. Object references express various semantic relationships between objects. For example, it is distinguished whether an object *uses* another object or whether an object *is part of* another object. For example, in the MVC framework the model component *uses* view components so that the model can be displayed and changed. In the Desktopltem-Folder framework the desktop items contained in a folder are viewed as *parts of* the folder object. In the case of the State framework example the answer is not so obvious: is a Role object part of a Player object or does a Role object use a Player object?

In general, such semantic relationships depend on the specific domain. As a consequence, these semantic aspects of object references are not considered in the realm of metapatterns.

Inheritance relationships between template and hook classes

As far as the inheritance relationship between a template class and its hook class is concerned, two cases have to be distinguished: those with and those without inheritance relationships (see below).

Whether an instance variable that can refer to one object or a group of objects is chosen has no influence on the different inheritance relationships. We randomly chose the particular reference relationship where an instance variable in a T object refers to exactly one H object.

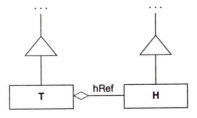

Figure 4.12 No inheritance relationship between template and hook classes.

(1)   There is no inheritance relationship between the template class and the hook class at all. Both classes are in separate branches of the class hierarchy, as depicted in Figure 4.12.

A special case of no inheritance relationship is where the template class and the hook class are unified in one class, as shown in Figure 4.13.

Figure 4.13 Unified template and hook classes.

(2)   The template class is a descendant of its hook class or vice versa (see Figure 4.14).

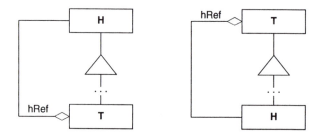

Figure 4.14 Template class inheriting from its hook class and vice versa.

We conclude that only the template class inheriting from its hook class makes sense. Subclasses are more specific than their superclasses. For example, abstract methods in a class define abstract behavior that takes shape in subclasses. Hook methods might be abstract methods. According to the narrow inheritance principle, template methods are never abstract methods. They are based on hook methods. We can say that template methods are more concrete than hook methods; hook methods have to be overridden in subclasses. Thus the more concrete template classes should never be superclasses of their more abstract hook classes.

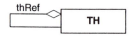

Figure 4.15 Unified template and hook classes with reference relationship.

Again, hook and template classes can be unified. The instance variable then has the static type of the unified class, as shown in Figure 4.15.

Note that this case is different from Figure 4.13, where template and hook classes are simply unified. In the case of the simple unification, any number of TH objects can be generated. These objects are not related to each other except that they belong to the same class. If template and hook classes are unified and a reference relationship exists as shown in Figure 4.15, chains of TH objects can be built. This issue and the implications of the other inheritance relationships presented above are discussed in detail in Sections 4.4 and 4.5.

Kinds of template and hook classes

We have to distinguish between concrete classes and abstract classes. Assuming that both a template class and a hook class can be concrete or abstract, four combinations result as listed in Table 4.1.

Table 4.1 Combinations of different kinds of template and hook classes.

Template class	Hook class
Concrete	Abstract
Abstract	Abstract
Abstract	Concrete
Concrete	Concrete

At first glance, only the combinations where the template classes are concrete seem to make sense. Hook methods may be abstract methods or concrete methods, that is, regular ones or other template methods—both offer a concrete, meaningful default implementation. Thus hook classes can be abstract classes or concrete classes.

Since template methods should never be abstract methods according to the narrow inheritance interface principle, template classes have to be concrete classes. This is only half of the truth: template classes typically contain more methods than the particular template method that is considered in a specific context. These classes might also contain abstract methods, although these abstract methods are not used by the particular template method. Nevertheless, the overall class is then an abstract one. So template classes are either concrete or abstract.

For this reason, we think that distinguishing abstract and concrete classes in connection with template and hook classes is not helpful. Thus this attribute is not considered further in the realm of composition metapatterns.

4.3.3 Resulting composition metapatterns

According to the discussion in the previous section, the following questions concerning class/object composition attributes are relevant:

- Can an object of a template class refer to exactly one object of the corresponding hook class or to any number of objects of its hook class?

- Is the template class a descendant of the hook class? Are both classes unified?

The composition metapatterns presented below result from combining the corresponding relevant composition attribute values.

Unification

A special case is where the template class and the hook class are unified in one class. Figure 4.16 depicts the class diagram of the Unification metapattern. TH indicates the Unification metapattern. The name Unification is derived from the fact that template and hook classes and thus their corresponding objects are not separated.

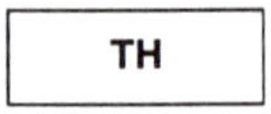

```
┌──────────┐
│    TH    │
└──────────┘
```

Figure 4.16   Unification metapattern.

1:1 Connection

In the 1:1 Connection metapattern an object of a template class refers to exactly one object of its hook class. There is no inheritance relationship between template class and hook class. Figure 4.17(a) depicts the class diagram of this composition metapattern. T◇— H indicates the 1:1 Connection metapattern.

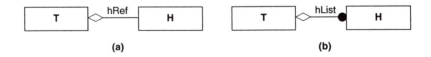

(a)   (b)

Figure 4.17   (a) 1:1 Connection and (b) 1:N Connection metapatterns.

1:N Connection
In the 1:N Connection metapattern an object of a template class refers to any number of objects of its hook class. There is no inheritance relationship between template class and hook class. Figure 4.17(b) depicts the class diagram of this composition metapattern. T◇——● H indicates the 1:N Connection metapattern.

Some authors (for example, Keene 1988) propose using multiple inheritance with mix-in classes in order to gain a degree of flexibility similar to that made possible by the 1:1 and 1:N Connection patterns. A mix-in hook class MixInH defines the appropriate additional or modified behavior in its HookMethod(), like a hook class in the connection patterns. The difference is that T objects do not refer to objects of MixInH. Instead, the behavior defined in MixInH is mixed into a class TWithMixedInH, which inherits from both MixInH and T (see Figure 4.18). Thus HookMethod() of class T is overridden in TWithMixedInH by mixing in HookMethod() of class MixInH via multiple inheritance mechanisms. Instead of coupling T objects and H objects, objects of class TWithMixedInH are used.

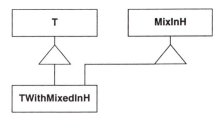

Figure 4.18 Multiple inheritance with mix-in class MixInH.

Without discussing details of multiple inheritance and the exact realization of mixing in specific behavior, we can already recognize that the solution with multiple inheritance has two disadvantages compared to the 1:1 and 1:N Connection patterns. Mix-in classes imply additional class definitions for all required combinations of objects of the template and hook (sub)classes. In the example above, the class TWithMixedInH has to be defined. Moreover, the multiple inheritance solution lacks the flexibility of changing H objects dynamically since most object-oriented programming languages do not support dynamic changes of the inheritance hierarchy at run time.

1:1 Recursive Connection and 1:1 Recursive Unification
In the 1:1 Recursive Connection metapattern an object of a template class refers to exactly one object of its hook class. The template class is a descendant of its hook class. Figure 4.19(a) depicts the class diagram of this

composition metapattern. T◇—▷— H indicates the 1:1 Recursive Connection metapattern.

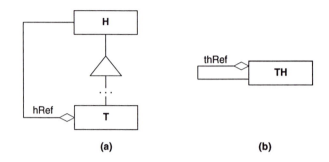

(a)   (b)

Figure 4.19 (a) 1:1 Recursive Connection and (b) 1:1 Recursive Unification metapatterns.

In the degenerated version of this metapattern, classes T and H are unified in one class, resulting in the 1:1 Recursive Unification metapattern. Figure 4.19(b) depicts the class diagram of this composition metapattern. ◻—◇ TH indicates the 1:1 Recursive Unification metapattern.

1:N Recursive Connection and 1:N Recursive Unification
In the 1:N Recursive Connection metapattern an object of a template class refers to any number of objects of its hook class. The template class is a descendant of its hook class. Figure 4.20(a) depicts the class diagram of this composition metapattern. T◇—▷—● H indicates the 1:N Recursive Connection metapattern.

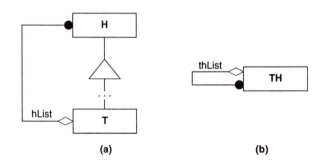

(a)   (b)

Figure 4.20 (a) 1:N Recursive Connection and (b) 1:N Recursive Unification metapatterns.

In the degenerated version of this metapattern, classes T and H are unified in one class, resulting in the 1:N Recursive Unification metapattern. Figure 4.20(b) depicts the class diagram of this composition metapattern. ⬠TH indicates the 1:N Recursive Unification metapattern.

4.4 Impact of composition metapatterns on template methods

All composition metapatterns except for the 1:1 Connection and the Unification pattern imply a typical structure of the template methods. As demonstrated below, the various structures of template methods result directly from the composition attributes.

4.4.1 Template methods in the Unification pattern and the 1:1 Connection pattern

TH and T◇—— H: In the case of the 1:1 Connection pattern the template method simply refers to an object of the hook class H and sends messages to that object. Nothing can be said about the structure of template methods. The same is true for the Unification pattern. A template method in the Unification pattern differs from a template method in the 1:1 Connection pattern in that no reference to the object of the hook class is maintained since the hook method is in the same class.

4.4.2 Template methods in the 1:N Connection pattern

T◇——● H: A template method in the 1:N Connection pattern typically iterates over the H objects and sends a certain message to each of these objects. Sending a message to a hook class object might depend on certain conditions. Example 4.1 illustrates these two typical core structures of a template method in the 1:N Connection pattern.

Example 4.1 Structure of template methods in the 1:N Connection Pattern.

```
... T::TemplateMethod(...) {
        . . .
        for each hookObject: <H *> in hList
                hookObject->HookMethod(...);
        . . .
    }
```

```
... T::TemplateMethod(...) {
        . . .
        for each hookObject: <H *> in hList
                if (Condition(hookObject))
                        hookObject->HookMethod(...);
        . . .
}
```

Besides the structure of template methods, class T itself typically offers the following methods in order to manage the collection of H objects:

- a method to add H objects to hList
- a method to remove H objects from hList
- a method to gain access to each of the grouped H objects.

4.4.3 Template methods in the 1:1 and 1:N Recursive Connection patterns

T◇—▷— H and T◇—▷—● H: In the case of the Recursive Connection patterns, template methods and hook methods typically have the same name, for example, TH(). The template method T::TH() overrides the hook method H::TH(). Example 4.2 shows the structure of TH() in the 1:1 Recursive Connection pattern.

Example 4.2 Structure of template methods in the 1:1 Recursive Connection pattern.

```
... T::TH(...) {
        . . .
        if (hRef)
                hRef->TH();        // hRef is of static type H *
        . . .
}
```

Template methods in the 1:N Recursive Connection pattern are structured analogously (see Example 4.3).

Example 4.3 Structure of template methods in the 1:N Recursive Connection pattern.

```
... T::TH(...) {
        . . .
        for each hookObject: <H *> in hList     // hookObject is of
```

// static type H *
```
                    hookObject->TH(...);
        . . .
}
```

Since hRef and hookObject are of static type pointer to H, objects of any subclass of H, that is, also recursively T objects, can be handled. This allows directed graphs of T objects and H objects to be built up.

For example, the 1:1 Recursive Connection pattern allows building up a directed chain of T objects ending with an H object as the last link in the chain (see Figure 4.21). The reason for this is that only T objects can maintain a reference to another object of static type pointer to H. Thus T and H objects cannot be mixed. An H object—if H is not an abstract class—or a descendant of H has to be the last link of such a chain.

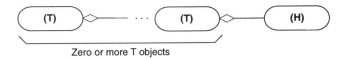

Figure 4.21 Chain of T objects ending with an H object.

Since T is a descendant of H, the last object in the chain can also be a T object. This is why an if-statement has to check in T::TH() whether hRef refers to an object (see Example 4.2).

Any directed graph consisting of T and H objects can be composed. Figure 4.22 shows another sample graph.

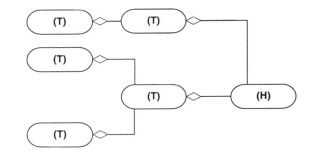

Figure 4.22 Several chains of T objects ending with an H object.

In an analogous way the 1:N Recursive Connection pattern allows building up a directed tree hierarchy with T objects as (sub)roots. Figure 4.23 shows an example of such a tree. Note that leaves of the tree can also be T objects: T objects may refer to zero or more H objects. On the other hand, H objects can never be (sub)roots of the tree.

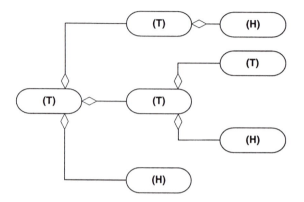

Figure 4.23 Tree hierarchy of T objects and H objects.

What is the purpose of the template methods in the realm of the 1:1 and 1:N Recursive Connection patterns?

Due to the structure of the template methods shown in Examples 4.2 and 4.3, messages are automatically forwarded along the objects in a directed graph. In general, a T object can be viewed as a place holder for all objects following that T object in the directed graph. Instead of sending a message to all these objects, it is sufficient to send the message to the particular T object. This message is then automatically forwarded to the other objects that are located behind that T object in the directed graph.

Due to this forwarding property of typical template methods in recursive connection patterns, a hierarchy of objects built by means of the 1:N Recursive Connection pattern can be treated as a single object.

In order to avoid endless loops of template methods, the directed graphs must not contain cycles. For example, according to the template method structure shown in Example 4.2 the message TH would be forever forwarded in the cyclic composition shown in Figure 4.24.

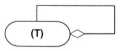

Figure 4.24 Cyclic directed graph consisting of one T object.

4.4.4 Template methods in the 1:1 and 1:N Recursive Unification patterns

⬡ TH and ⬡ TH: In the case of the Recursive Unification patterns, not only are the template class and the hook class unified, but also the corresponding template method and hook method! There is only one method, let us call it UnifiedTH(), that is, template *and* hook method. The typical structure of the method UnifiedTH() in the 1:1 Recursive Unification pattern (see Example 4.4) is analogous to the template method T::TH() in the 1:1 Recursive Connection pattern.

> **Example 4.4** Structure of a template-hook method in the 1:1 Recursive Unification pattern.

```
... TH::UnifiedTH(...) {

        . . .
        if (thRef)
                    thRef->UnifiedTH(...);      // thRef is of static
                                                // type TH *
        . . .
}
```

Analogously, UnifiedTH() in the 1:N Recursive Unification pattern (see Example 4.5) looks like T::TH() in the 1:N Recursive Connection pattern. Note the difference with respect to template methods in Recursive Connection patterns, where the template methods have the same name as hook methods but are distinct.

> **Example 4.5** Structure of a template-hook method in the 1:N Recursive Unification pattern.

```
... TH::UnifiedTH(...) {

        . . .
        for each thObject: <TH *> in thList
                    thObject->UnifiedTH(...);
        . . .
}
```

Analogously to the 1:1 and 1:N Recursive Connection patterns, a directed graph of TH objects can be built. Messages are forwarded along the objects in these directed graphs. Figure 4.25 shows a sample chain of TH objects based on the 1:1 Recursive Unification pattern.

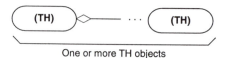

One or more TH objects

Figure 4.25 Chain of TH objects.

Note the difference between the 1:1 Recursive Unification pattern and the 1:1 Recursive Connection pattern. In the former, TH objects can be viewed as equally ranked in the sense that each TH object can refer to another TH object. In the latter, only T objects refer to H objects and not vice versa.

An interesting question in connection with the 1:1 and 1:N Recursive Unification patterns is the following: which properties of UnifiedTH() can be viewed as template method-specific and which as hook method-specific? UnifiedTH() acquires a template flavor in that it preimplements the message forwarding in a directed graph of TH objects. In many examples where this pattern is applied, nothing else is implemented in such template methods; that is, there are no statements replacing "..." before and after the forwarding statements in Examples 4.4 and 4.5. This implies that UnifiedTH() has to be overridden in at least some subclasses. This can be viewed as giving UnifiedTH() a hook flavor. If UnifiedTH() is not overridden in any of the subclasses of TH, only the message UnifiedTH is passed along a directed graph of TH objects and nothing else happens.

Subclasses that override method UnifiedTH() typically call the superclass method at the beginning or end (see Example 4.6). Otherwise the traversal of the directed graph is interrupted.

Example 4.6 Structure of overridden template-hook methods.

```
... THSubclass::UnifiedTH(...) {
        TH::UnifiedTH(...);
        . . .
}
... THSubclass::UnifiedTH(...) {
        . . .
        TH::UnifiedTH(...);
}
```

4.5   When to choose a certain composition metapattern

This section points out relevant criteria and rules of thumb for when to apply which composition patterns and illustrates them by examples.

4.5.1 Unification versus the other six composition metapatterns

Unifying template and hook methods in one class has the following consequence: in order to change the template method by providing a different hook method, a subclass of the unified template-hook class TH has to be defined. Thus the template method cannot be changed dynamically at run time. For example, the Flexible Object Creation framework example presented in Section 4.2.3 applies the Unification pattern. A subclass of the template-hook class A has to be defined in order to change its object creation behavior.

More flexibility is provided if template and hook classes are separated. This means that the behavior of a T object, that is, its template method, can be changed by associating a different H object with the T object. Creating H objects and assigning references to T objects can, of course, be done at run time. The other six composition metapatterns provide this degree of flexibility.

1:1 and 1:N Connection patterns
For example, the State framework example presented in Section 3.6.1 applies the 1:1 Connection pattern T◇—— H. Class T corresponds to class Player, class H to class Role. The run-time behavior of the template method Request() of Player objects depends on the object of hook class Role to which a Player object refers. In order to change the behavior of a Player object, another Role object has to be associated with the Player object. This typically happens at run time.

The 1:1 Connection pattern T◇—— H and the 1:N Connection pattern T◇—● H provide the same degree of flexibility. Both allow changes of the template methods at run time. Which pattern is chosen depends solely on the domain-specific semantic aspects. For example, in the State framework example a Player object can only play one role at a time; thus the 1:1 Connection pattern is adequate. In the Publisher/Subscriber framework example a Publisher object can refer to zero or more subscribers; thus the 1:N Connection pattern is applied.

The subsequent sections focus on recursive composition patterns and typical situations where these composition patterns are suitable.

4.5.2 1:N Recursive Connection and 1:N Recursive Unification patterns

The 1:N Recursive Connection pattern T◇—▷—● H and the 1:N Recursive Unification pattern ⬚—◇● TH are typically applied in order to:

- build a tree hierarchy of objects
- forward messages in the hierarchy.

1:N Recursive Connection pattern

The DesktopItem-Folder example introduced in Chapter 2 represents a typical example of the 1:N Recursive Connection pattern T⬦—▷—● H, with Folder as the template class and DesktopItem as the hook class. Figure 4.26 illustrates the relevant aspects of this framework example.

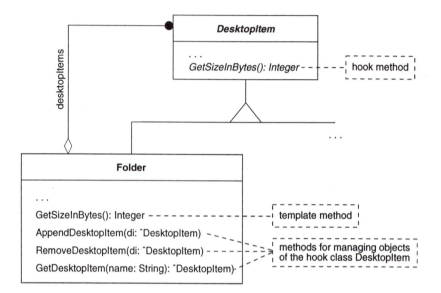

Figure 4.26 1:N Recursive Connection pattern in the DesktopItem-Folder framework.

As described in a general way in Section 4.4.3 we observe the following:

- The hook method DesktopItem::GetSizeInBytes() has the same name as the template method Folder::GetSizeInBytes().

- The implementation of the template method Folder::GetSizeInBytes() iterates over all contained DesktopItem objects and forwards the message GetSizeInBytes to these objects.

- A tree hierarchy can be built. The (sub)roots of the tree are Folder objects. Due to the hierarchical structure and the message forwarding property of Folder's template method GetSizeInItems(), a Folder object can be treated like a single object though it represents a group of DesktopItem objects.

- Template class Folder offers the methods AppendDesktopItem(...) and RemoveDesktopItem(...) in order to add and remove objects of the hook class DesktopItem to/from Folder objects.

Method GetDesktopItem(...) provides access to the contained DesktopItem objects by means of their names.

Access to these objects could also be provided in a more flexible way. Methods called GetNextDesktopItem() and ResetIterator() could be offered to iterate over the contained DesktopItem objects. For example, every time the message GetNextDesktopItem is sent to a Folder object, a reference to the next contained DesktopItem object is returned. After completing the iteration 0 is returned. A method ResetIterator() restarts the iteration.

- Defining a cyclic directed graph, that is, adding a Folder object to its contained DesktopItem objects as exemplified in Example 4.7, implies an endless loop in GetSizeInItems().

Example 4.7 Defining a directed graph with a cycle.

```
Folder *aFolder= new Folder(...);
aFolder->AppendDesktopItem(aFolder);
. . .
aFolder->GetSizeInItems();        // endless loop
```

1:N Recursive Unification pattern
As mentioned at the beginning of this section, both the 1:N Recursive Connection pattern T◇─▷─● H and the 1:N Recursive Unification pattern ◻◇● TH are applied in order to reach the same goals:

- to build a tree hierarchy of objects
- to forward messages in the hierarchy.

What are the differences between these two patterns? Figure 4.27 shows how the 1:N Recursive Unification pattern can be applied to the DesktopItem-Folder example.

Let us first discuss some implementation details. The original template class Folder and its hook class DesktopItem are unified in one class called GroupedDItem, for grouped desktop item. The collection of GroupedDItem instances represented by the instance variable groupedDItems is managed by the methods AppendGroupedDItem(...) and RemoveGroupedDItem(...) analogously to the corresponding methods in class Folder. The same is true for GetGroupedDItem(...).

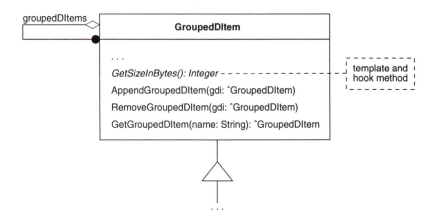

Figure 4.27 DesktopItem-Folder example based on the 1:N Recursive Unification pattern.

A possible implementation of GetSizeInBytes() in class GroupedDItem is shown in Example 4.8. The method implementation is not significantly different from the implementation in the original class Folder. Only the reference variables have other static types and names.

Example 4.8 Sample template-hook method in a 1:N Recursive Unification pattern.

```
int GroupedDItem::GetSizeInBytes()
{
        int size= 0;        // Folder sizes are not taken into account.
        for each gdi: <GroupedDItem *> in groupedDItems
                size= size + gdi->GetSizeInBytes();
        return size;
}
```

The difference is that each descendant class of GroupedDItem has to call the superclass method in the overridden method. Example 4.9 shows a sample implementation of method GetSizeInBytes() for class TextDocument.

Example 4.9 Example demonstrating how to override a template-hook method.

```
int TextDocument::GetSizeInBytes()
{
        int sizeOfGroupedItems= GroupedDItem::GetSizeInBytes();
                // The size of the items grouped under my
                // supervision, that is, by means of my instance
```

```
                    // variable groupedDItems, is calculated.
          if (text != 0)
                    return sizeOfGroupedItems + strlen(text);
          return sizeOfGroupedItems;
}
```

Not calling GroupedDItem::GetSizeInBytes() in TextDocument::GetSizeIn-Bytes() would mean an interruption of the tree traversal and, of course, a wrong result: the size of the subobjects of each TextDocument object would simply be ignored. This implies a source of errors caused by the 1:N Recursive Unification pattern. In most cases descendants must not forget to call the superclass method when overriding a method. In the 1:N Recursive Connection pattern this is usually not required.

Besides these implementation issues we have to discuss the implications of the 1:N Recursive Unification pattern on the way object hierarchies can be composed.

The principal difference is that in the 1:N Recursive Connection pattern there is a special subroot object, in the DesktopItem-Folder example an object of class Folder. Only these special objects can contain other objects. In the 1:N Recursive Unification pattern any object provides this behavior. The reason for this difference is obvious: both the instance variable and methods required for managing a group of objects are defined in the specific template class in the 1:N Recursive Connection pattern. Other descendants of the hook class do not inherit this behavior. In the 1:N Recursive Unification pattern template class and hook class are unified. All descendants of this template-hook class inherit the behavior to manage the corresponding objects.

If the special objects in the 1:N Recursive Connection pattern that manage other objects are called managers, and the instances of other descendants of the hook class are called workers, hierarchies typically look like the example depicted in Figure 4.28(a). In the 1:N Recursive Unification pattern instances of descendants of the unified template and hook classes are both workers and managers, so we call them manager-workers as in the object diagram in Figure 4.28(b).

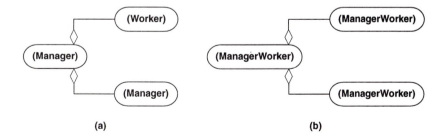

(a)   (b)

Figure 4.28 Composing hierarchies (a) with and (b) without special managers.

The pros and cons of both approaches are apparent. If special manager objects are used, objects become leaner. Workers do not provide the additional behavior required for grouping objects. The disadvantage is that special managers and workers cannot be treated uniformly. This is the advantage of manager-workers: in the process of composing the hierarchy one does not have to decide whether a node will be a leaf node or a subroot. Furthermore, the overall hierarchy contains fewer objects if manager-workers are used—separate managers become redundant.

Some semantic aspects have to be considered, too. For example, we want to put a TextDocument object and a DrawDocument object into a Folder object. Figure 4.29 shows the corresponding object diagram if the original design based on the 1:N Recursive Connection pattern is applied.

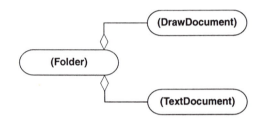

Figure 4.29 Two desktop items in the special manager Folder.

In the case of the design based on the 1:N Recursive Unification pattern, we face the problem that there is no special manager. Should the DrawDocument object contain the TextDocument object or vice versa? Figures 4.30(a) and 4.30(b) illustrate these two alternatives.

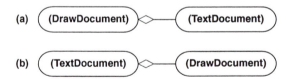

Figure 4.30 Alternative management of two desktop items without a special manager.

As a consequence, class design based on the 1:N Unification pattern emphasizes the *unification* aspect. In the realm of desktop items the 1:N Unification pattern would be appropriate to express document embedding. For example, the object diagram in Figure 4.30(a) expresses that a TextDocument object is embedded into a DrawDocument object. In order to express the semantics of having special managers, we have to base class design on the

1:N Recursive Connection pattern, the right choice for desktop items organized in folders.

4.5.3 1:1 Recursive Connection pattern

The 1:1 Recursive Connection pattern T◇—▷— H is often applied in order to selectively add behavior to instances of H and possibly to objects of all descendants of H without changing H. Imagine that you have a class (sub)hierarchy with class H as its root class, as shown in Figure 4.31.

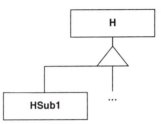

Figure 4.31 Sample class hierarchy with H as root.

Usually, behavior defined in classes is adapted by defining subclasses that specify the delta (difference). This becomes a problem if numerous classes are to be changed. For example, if a certain instance variable is to be added and a method inherited from H is to be changed in all descendants of H, as many subclasses as descendants would have to be defined.

At first glance a convenient solution would be simply to change H and add the behavior there. Such a solution has to be considered carefully. Reusing software components often implies that behavior has to be added to branches of class hierarchies which have not been developed in-house. Changing the root classes of the corresponding class hierarchy branches directly cannot be recommended. Unrecognized interdependencies within class H could be disregarded so that errors could be introduced. Furthermore, in a future release of the class library the adaptations have to be applied again to the source code of the particular class (sub)hierarchy. Finally, the source code might not be available, making such changes impossible.

Another situation might cause a similar problem: sometimes certain behavior is only required in specific situations. From a class designer's point of view, such behavior should not be put into H and inherited by all its descendants. Instead, it would be better to be able to attach behavior temporarily to instances of H and descendants of H in situations where the particular behavior is required.

So a mechansim that allows behavior to be attached to instances of H and its descendants without having to define that behavior in H itself would solve both problems. The 1:1 Recursive Connection pattern forms the basis of such a mechanism. Figure 4.32 illustrates the extended class hierarchy with template class T.

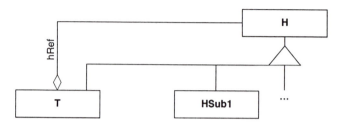

Figure 4.32 Template class T as an additional subclass of H.

The idea behind this extension is that T overrides all methods of H. Each template method simply forwards the call to the object referred to by hRef as illustrated in Example 4.10.

Example 4.10 Sample method implementation in template class T.

```
void T::MethodOfH()
{
        if (hRef)
                hRef->MethodOfH();
}
```

If all template methods forward the call to the object referred to by hRef we can wrap an instance of any descendant of H in a T object and use either the T object or the unwrapped original—either object can be used wherever an object of static type H is required and both have the same behavior.

Of course, class T is superfluous if all methods are forwarded to H objects without any modifications. The trick behind this design is that T can modify the behavior of methods by doing more than just forwarding a request. Furthermore, instance variables and methods can be added. This means that a modified behavior implemented in a T class can be attached to instances of H and of all descendants, for example, HSub1. The following object composition has to be formed: instead of using HSub1 objects directly, these objects are wrapped in a T object; that is, T objects refer to HSub1 objects. Thus HSub1 objects have the additional or modified behavior defined in T.

As outlined above, methods of template class T are implemented according to the general considerations in connection with the 1:1 Recursive Connection pattern as presented in Section 4.4.3. Each method in class H becomes a hook method of the corresponding template method in class T. A template method has the same name and parameters as its corresponding hook method.

The advantages of design based on the 1:1 Recursive Connection pattern are the following:

- Any number of template classes can be defined as subclasses of H. These template classes can define additional/modified behavior. Any number and combination of instances of template classes can be attached to instances of H descendants. Figure 4.33 depicts a sample object diagram with an object of template class T1 and an object of template class T2 attached to an HSub1 instance.

Figure 4.33 Sample chain of instances of T1 and T2 wrapping an HSub1 instance.

Note that according to Section 4.4.3 any number of objects of template classes can be put in front of any instance of H or its descendants. The first object in this chain can be used wherever an object of static type H is required. Messages sent to objects of template classes are automatically forwarded along the chain due to the typical structure of template methods.

- The attached T objects can be changed at run time; that is, the associated special behavior can simply be modified by
   - removing an attached T object
   - attaching additional T objects
   - replacing an attached T object with an instance of another template class.
- Objects of template classes can cooperate with any future descendants of H; that is, classes that are defined as descendants of H after a particular template class has been defined.

Contrast these advantages with the problematic solution of changing H directly. In addition to the other problems, such a direct change cannot provide the run-time flexibility made possible by the solution based on the 1:1 Recursive Connection pattern.

Example: modification of class **DesktopItem**

DesktopItem in the DesktopItem-Folder framework offers a method SetItemName(name: String) which allows the instance variable itemName in DesktopItem objects to be set. Class Folder overrides SetItemName(...) in order to restrict the name length to 30 characters. To define this feature just in Folder was an arbitrary decision in Chapter 2 in order to demonstrate how behavior can be changed in subclasses. Usually, the name length should be restricted either in all DesktopItem objects or in none.

The decision to restrict the name length in all DesktopItem objects might be appropriate in certain situations but not in general. So an improved design of the set name behavior would not restrict the name length in DesktopItem::SetItemName(...) or in DesktopItem's descendants.

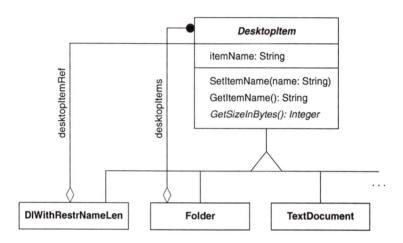

Figure 4.34 Integration of DIWithRestrNameLen in the DesktopItem-Folder framework.

Instead, a template class is to be designed according to the 1:1 Recursive Connection pattern discussed above. Let us call this template class DIWithRestrNameLen. Figure 4.34 shows how DIWithRestrNameLen is integrated into the class hierarchy of the DesktopItem-Folder framework.

An alternative solution would be to add an instance variable to class DesktopItem that stores the maximum name length. Without discussing details of this solution we can identify the disadvantage of an additional instance variable: each instance of a descendant allocates additional storage whether a name length restriction is required or not.

The class interface of DIWithRestrNameLen is shown in Example 4.11. The constructor of class DIWithRestrNameLen has two parameters: the reference to the DesktopItem object to which the name length check behavior has to be added and the maximum length of names in characters.

Example 4.11 Class definition of DIWithRestrNameLen in file
DIWithRestrNameLen.h.

```
class DIWithRestrNameLen : public DesktopItem {
public:
        DIWithRestrNameLen(DesktopItem *diToWrap,
                            int maxNLen= 30);
        void SetItemName(char *name);
        char *GetItemName();
        int GetSizeInBytes();
protected:
        DesktopItem *desktopItemRef;
        int maxNameLen;
};
```

Class DIWithRestrNameLen can be implemented as shown in Example 4.12.
Messages of unchanged methods are forwarded to objects referred to by the
instance variable desktopItemRef.

Example 4.12 Class implementation of DIWithRestrNameLen.

```
#include "DIWithRestrNameLen.h"

DIWithRestrNameLen::DIWithRestrNameLen(
                DesktopItem *diToWrap, int maxNLen)
{
        desktopItemRef= diToWrap;
        maxNameLen= maxNLen;
        SetItemName(desktopItemRef->GetItemName());
}
void DIWithRestrNameLen::SetItemName(char *name)
{
        if (strlen(name) <= maxNameLen)
                desktopItemRef->SetItemName(name);
        else     report error;
}
char *DIWithRestrNameLen::GetItemName()
{
        return desktopItemRef->GetItemName();
}
int DIWithRestrNameLen::GetSizeInBytes()
{
        return desktopItemRef->GetSizeInBytes();
}
```

This class can be used, for example, in order to restrict names of all DesktopItem objects to 20 characters, as demonstrated in Example 4.13. In this code example a method CreateInitialHierarchy() of a class called DIClient has to return a reference to a newly created DesktopItem object. Since the length of the names has to be restricted to 20 characters for each DesktopItem object, instances of class DIWithRestrNameLen are used. The plain Folder object and the plain TextDocument object are wrapped by an object of class DIWithRestrNameLen, which is initialized to accept a maximum name length of 20 characters.

Example 4.13 Sample usage of class DIWithRestrNameLen.

```
. . .
const int maxNameLength= 20;
. . .
DesktopItem *DIClient::CreateInitialHierarchy()
{
        Folder *rootFolder;
        rootFolder= new Folder("Root");        // A plain Folder is
                                                // generated.

        DIWithRestrNameLen *restrDI;
        restrDI= new DIWithRestrNameLen(
                        // A plain TextDocument is generated:
                        new TextDocument("...", "..."),
                        maxNameLength
                );
        rootFolder->AppendDesktopItem(restrDI);

        return    new DIWithRestrNameLen(
                        rootFolder,
                        maxNameLength
                );
}

. . .
```

Figure 4.35 shows the object diagram of the objects generated in CreateInitialHierarchy(). Note that the Folder object does not refer to the TextDocument object but to an instance of class DIWithRestrNameLen which adds the name length check behavior to the TextDocument object. Analogously, the Folder object itself is not returned in CreateInitialHierarchy(), instead the DIWithRestrNameLen object which attaches the name length check behavior to the Folder object is returned.

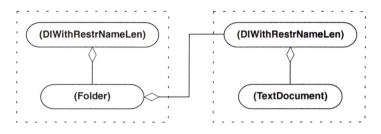

Figure 4.35 Sample object diagram with instances of DIWithRestrNameLen.

The example presented above reveals some problems with this solution. Wrapped objects often provide more behavior than defined in DesktopItem. Folder, for example, provides methods for DesktopItem object management. We cannot simply send a DIWithRestrNameLen object that wraps a Folder object the message AppendDesktopItem(...). Instead we have to keep track of the wrapped instance.

This necessity would cause serious trouble in class DIClient, where CreateInitialHierarchy() is invoked. It is not possible to access the wrapped object(s). So only the messages already defined in class DesktopItem can be sent to a DIWithRestrNameLen object whose reference is returned from CreateInitialHierarchy().

In order to solve this problem, class DIWithRestrNameLen would have to offer a method GetDesktopItemRef() which returns the reference to the wrapped DesktopItem object by means of the statement return desktopItemRef. A client would have to check the dynamic type of the returned reference and cast that reference accordingly.

Besides the access problem sketched above, inherited instance variables often constitute redundant attributes in instances of template classes like DIWithRestrNameLen. The instance variable itemName, for example, is not used in DIWithRestrNameLen objects since SetItemName(...) is overridden so that this message is forwarded to the wrapped DesktopItem instance. We conclude from this problem that all instance variables should only be accessible via methods. For example, if instance variable itemName were defined as public, a client of class DIWithRestrNameLen could erroneously access itemName of a DIWithRestrNameLen object instead of itemName of the wrapped DesktopItem object. (Remark: defining itemName as public would, of course, also make class DIWithRestrNameLen itself superfluous since the setting of this instance variable could then be done directly without invoking SetItemName(...).)

Alternative solution with multiple inheritance?
As discussed in Section 4.3.3 in the realm of the 1:1 Connection and 1:N Connection patterns, multiple inheritance with so-called mix-in classes has

also been proposed to solve the problems stated at the beginning of this section.

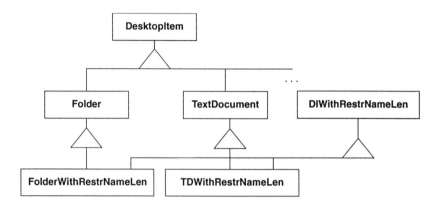

Figure 4.36 Applying multiple inheritance with the mix-in class
DlWithRestrNameLen.

Figure 4.36 sketches this solution for the example of adding name length check behavior to DesktopItem objects. Note that the mix-in class DlWithRestrNameLen has to be defined in a different way than shown in Examples 4.11 and 4.12. Implementation details related to multiple inheritance are not discussed.

The use of mix-in classes again implies class definitions for all descendants whose instances require the additional and/or modified behavior. In the example above the classes FolderWithRestrNameLen and TDWithRestr-NameLen have to be added.

Moreover, the multiple inheritance solution lacks the flexibility of attaching additional or modified behavior dynamically, since most object-oriented programming languages do not support dynamic changes of the inheritance hierarchy at run time.

4.5.4 1:1 Recursive Unification pattern

Though all recursive patterns forward messages along a directed graph, the 1:1 Recursive Unification pattern ⬡ TH is tailor-made for message forwarding. Since a TH object can only refer to one other TH object these objects form chains within a directed graph.

Due to the structure of a template-hook method UnifiedTH() in class TH (see Example 4.14), a message UnifiedTH sent to a TH instance is forwarded by this object to the subsequent TH objects until the end of the chain is reached.

Example 4.14 Structure of unified template and hook method.

```
... TH::UnifiedTH()
{
        if (thRef)
                thRef->UnifiedTH();
}
```

Subclasses of TH can override UnifiedTH() in order to react to the message UnifiedTH in a specific way.

In general, this allows flexible message propagation since the message handling chain can be composed and changed dynamically. Furthermore, an object in such a chain does not have to know which specific object is next.

Example: converting text formats

In order to illustrate the use of the 1:1 Recursive Unification pattern, we enhance the TextDocument class introduced in the realm of the DesktopItem-Folder framework. Example 4.15 shows the original header file of this class. Like all other descendants of DesktopItem, class TextDocument inherits the management of desktop item names from DesktopItem.

The text stored in a TextDocument object can only be set by SetText(...), which requires a string as its parameter value. Class Text-Document can be enhanced by offering a method ReadTextFromFile(...) which requires a file name as its parameter value. The implementation of ReadText-FromFile(...) must check whether the corresponding file can be read, that is, converted to a character string. If this is possible, the conversion should be done and the contents of the file should be stored as a character string in text.

Example 4.15 Definition of class TextDocument in file TextDocument.h.

```
class TextDocument: public DesktopItem {
public:
        TextDocument(char *name, char *contents);
        void SetText(char *otherText);
        char *GetText();

        // TextDocument-specific implementation of the protocol
        // defined in DesktopItem
        int GetSizeInBytes();
protected:
        char *text;
};
```

In order to keep such format conversions flexible, we define a class Converter. Class Converter demonstrates the use of the 1:1 Connection pattern and the 1:1 Recursive Unification pattern.

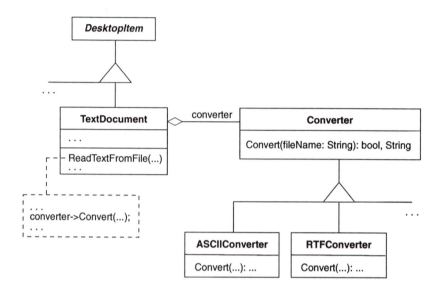

Figure 4.37 1:1 Connection pattern between TextDocument and Converter.

Let us first discuss the 1:1 Connection pattern depicted in Figure 4.37: class Converter is the hook class of the template class TextDocument. The template method ReadTextFromFile(...) uses the hook method Convert(fileName: String), which returns whether a conversion is possible and, if so, the converted string. Thus any conversion strategy can be implemented by overriding Convert(...) in subclasses of hook class Converter. The behavior of ReadTextFromFile(...) can be modified at run time without changing it directly. Instead, only the Converter object referred to by the instance variable converter of a TextDocument object has to be changed at run time.

The 1:1 Recursive Unification pattern can be applied in the realm of class Converter as depicted in Figure 4.38. In this context, class Converter is a unified template and hook class with the unified template and hook method Convert(...). In order to adhere to the 1:1 Recursive Unification pattern, message forwarding has to be implemented accordingly in class Converter and its subclasses. The core parts of these implementation issues are sketched below.

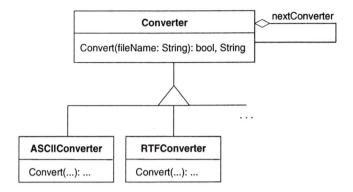

Figure 4.38 Template-hook class Converter based on the 1:1 Recursive Unification pattern.

Based on these two composition patterns, an object composition as shown in Figure 4.39 can be formed. It means that ReadTextFromFile(...) delegates the file conversion to the chain of Converter objects. The first object in the chain is an ASCIIConverter object. It checks whether the file's contents are plain ASCII characters. If so, the characters are read, and a character string is built and returned. If the first converter in the chain cannot handle the file format, it is the next converter's turn. Analogously, the RTFConverter object checks whether the file format adheres to Microsoft's Rich Text Format. If so, the conversion is done. Otherwise control is passed on to the next converter in the chain, which converts Extended PostScript format into a plain character string. If none of the conversion strategies is successful, the file cannot be converted. The TextDocument object is informed about this via the corresponding return parameter from the hook method Convert(...).

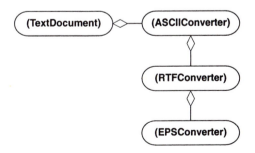

Figure 4.39 Sample composition of Converter objects referred to by a TextDocument object.

Note that the TextDocument object just asks the first object in the chain of converters to do the conversion. This request is forwarded automatically in the chain of converter objects.

Now we take a closer look at implementation issues. Example 4.16 shows a possible definition of the interface of class Converter. Method Convert(...) has two return parameters. One is the character string that results from a successful conversion. The other parameter is called conversionPossible. We define this parameter as call-by-reference by using the C convention to define its type as pointer to bool instead of bool.

Example 4.16 Class definition of Converter in file Converter.h.

```
class Converter {
public:
        Converter(Converter *nextC);
        virtual char *Convert(char *fileName,
                                bool *conversionPossible);
        virtual void SetNextConverter(Converter *nextC);
        virtual Converter *GetNextConverter();
protected:
        Converter *nextConverter;
};
```

A typical implementation of class Converter according to the 1:1 Recursive Unification pattern is shown in Example 4.17. Note that Convert(...) simply forwards the convert request to the next converter in the chain, if there is one. Note also that class Converter has no abstract methods and is not an abstract class.

Example 4.17 Implementation of Converter.

```
#include "Converter.h"

Converter::Converter(Converter *nextC)
{
        SetNextConverter(nextC);
}
char *Converter::Convert(char *fileName, bool *conversionPossible)
{
        *conversionPossible= FALSE;
        if (nextConverter)
                return nextConverter->Convert(fileName,
                                        conversionPossible);
        return " ";
}
```

```
void Converter::SetNextConverter(Converter *nextC)
{
        nextConverter= nextC;
}
Converter *Converter::GetNextConverter()
{
        return nextConverter;
}
```

Example 4.18 outlines how ASCIIConverter as a subclass of Converter could implement Convert(...). The other subclasses of Converter will implement Convert(...) analogously. Note that the message passing along the chain of converters is interrupted as soon as conversion by a specific Converter object becomes possible.

Example 4.18 Sample implementation of Convert() in a subclass of Converter.

```
char *ASCIIConverter::Convert(char *fileName,
                                    bool *conversionPossible)
{
        if ('fileName' contains ASCII characters) {
                char *fileAsString;
                *conversionPossible= TRUE;
                allocate 'fileAsString' and put characters contained
                in 'fileName' into that string
                return fileAsString;
        } else
                return Converter::Convert(fileName,
                                        conversionPossible);
}
```

Example 4.19 illustrates how the instance variable converter could be initialized in the constructor of TextDocument. GetChainOfConverters() is supposed to be a plain C function that composes a chain of converters. The static variable converterChain is used to guarantee that this chain is only allocated once. (Variables that are declared static in C are only accessible within the file where they are declared.)

Example 4.19 Initialization of instance variable converter.

```
. . .
static Converter *converterChain= 0;
Converter *GetChainOfConverters()
{
        if (!converterChain) {
```

```
                        Converter *conv3= new EPSConverter(0);
                                    // 0 <=> end of chain
                        Converter *conv2= new RTFConverter(conv3);
                        converterChain= new ASCIIConverter(conv2);
                }
                return converterChain;
        }
        . . .
        TextDocument::TextDocument(char *name, char *contents)
        {
                SetItemName(name);
                SetText(contents);
                converter= GetChainOfConverters();
        }
```

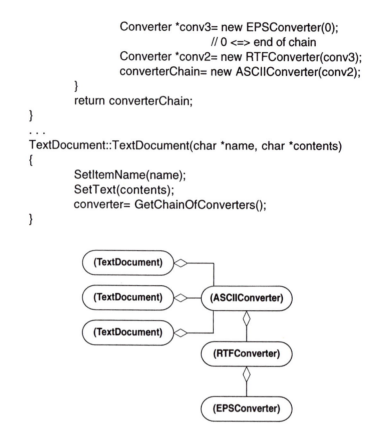

Figure 4.40   One chain of converters for all TextDocument objects.

Thus all TextDocument objects refer to the same chain of converters as exemplified in Figure 4.40 for three TextDocument objects.

Based on a proper initialization of converter as shown in Example 4.19, method ReadTextFromFile(...) could be implemented as demonstrated in Example 4.20.

Example 4.20   Implementation of ReadTextFromFile(...) in class TextDocument.

```
        void TextDocument::ReadTextFromFile(char *fileName)
        {
                bool conversionPossible= FALSE;
                char *textFromFile;
                textFromFile= converter->Convert(fileName,
                                                &conversionPossible);
                if (conversionPossible)
                        SetText(textFromFile);
                else
```

SetText("File could not be converted");

}

Based on the 1:1 Recursive Unification pattern, the ASCIIConverter object is always activated first, then the RTFConverter object, and finally the EPSConverter object, according to the initialization of the converter chain in GetChainOfConverters() shown in Example 4.19. Of course, the chain could be rearranged at run time. This could be useful, for example, if it turns out that most conversions are from RTF files. The application could gather statistics about conversions and use them to decide whether to rearrange the chain. If significantly more RTF files are converted than ASCII files, then it would be better to put the RTFConverter object in front of the ASCIIConverter object. In order to accomplish such a change, the corresponding converters simply have to be switched. In order to notify all TextDocument objects of such a change, two things have to be done:

- Class TextDocument has to define and implement a method SetConverter(Converter *otherConverter) that assigns otherConverter to the instance variable converter.
- SetConverter(...) has to be called for all TextDocument objects. The parameter value passed to SetConverter(...) is the reference to the Converter object that has become first in the chain.

1:1 Recursive Connection pattern as alternative?
The implementation details discussed above are based on the 1:1 Recursive Unification pattern underlying the Converter class (see Figure 4.41(a)). Instead, the 1:1 Recursive Connection pattern could be applied, as depicted in Figure 4.41(b). What are the differences?

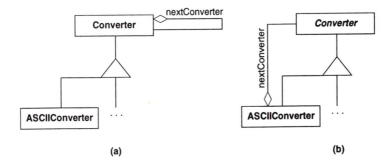

Figure 4.41 (a) 1:1 Recursive Unification pattern versus (b) 1:1 Recursive Connection pattern.

In the case of the 1:1 Recursive Connection pattern, class Converter has no instance variable nextConverter to keep track of the next Converter object in the chain. There are two main possibilities for implementing Converter:

(1)   Converter offers the *abstract* methods SetNextConverter(...) and GetNextConverter(). (Recall that in the case of the 1:1 Recursive Unification pattern these methods could be implemented in class Converter, as shown in Example 4.17.) Each subclass has to override these abstract methods based on the instance variable that maintains the reference to the next Converter object. Example 4.21 demonstrates how method Convert(...) could be implemented in class Converter. The only difference with respect to the original solution is that the reference to the next Converter object is obtained by calling GetNextConverter(), which has to be overridden accordingly in subclasses.

Example 4.21   Implementation of Converter::Convert().

```
char *Converter::Convert(char *fileName, bool *conversionPossible)
{
        *conversionPossible= FALSE;
        Converter *nextConv= GetNextConverter();
        if (nextConv)
                return nextConv->Convert(fileName,
                                        conversionPossible);
        return " ";
}
```

No changes are necessary in the implementation of method Convert(...) in descendants of Converter. For example, the implementation of ASCIIConverter::Convert(...) as shown in Example 4.18 requires no changes. But instead of having to override only method Convert(...), the methods SetNextConverter(...) and GetNextConverter() have to be overridden, too. Example 4.22 shows the resulting class interface of ASCIIConverter.

Example 4.22   Class definition of ASCIIConverter.

```
class ASCIIConverter: public Converter {
public:
        ASCIIConverter(Converter *nextC);
        char *Convert(char *fileName, bool *conversionPossible);
        void SetNextConverter(Converter *nextC);
        Converter *GetNextConverter();
```

```
protected:
        Converter *nextConverter;
};
```

Example 4.23 lists the implementation of the constructor and the methods SetNextConverter(...) and GetNextConverter(). (The constructor of class Converter is changed and requires no parameter. Thus the constructor of ASCIIConverter passes no parameter to its superclass constructor.)

Example 4.23 Implementation of specific methods in ASCIIConverter.

```
#include "ASCIIConverter.h"

ASCIIConverter::ASCIIConverter(Converter *nextC)
{
        SetNextConverter(nextC);
}
. . .
void ASCIIConverter::SetNextConverter(Converter *nextC)
{
        nextConverter= nextC;
}
Converter *ASCIIConverter::GetNextConverter()
{
        return nextConverter;
}
```

The advantage of the solution based on the 1:1 Recursive Connection pattern is that Converter becomes an abstract class. So converter chains can contain only specific converters and not dummy converters, that is, instances of class Converter that do nothing but forward conversion requests. The disadvantage is that each subclass of Converter has to override the abstract methods SetNextConverter(...) and GetNext-Converter() and define a corresponding instance variable.

(2)   Converter only defines the protocol; that is, the methods SetNext-Converter(...), GetNextConverter() and Convert(...) are abstract methods in class Converter. Subclasses have to override these methods. In addition to conversion algorithms, the forwarding of conversion requests in method Convert(...) also has to be implemented. Example 4.24 shows how Convert(...) could be implemented in ASCIIConverter.

Example 4.24 Sample implementation of Convert in class ASCIIConverter.

```
char *ASCIIConverter::Convert(char *fileName,
                              bool *conversionPossible)
{
        *conversionPossible= FALSE;
        if ('fileName' contains ASCII characters) {
                . . .     // unchanged conversion
        }
        else
                if (nextConverter)
                        return nextConverter->Convert(fileName,
                                                      conversionPossible);
                else
                        return " ";
}
```

The advantages and disadvantages are analogous to solution (1). In addition to the methods SetNextConverter(...) and GetNextConverter(), the forwarding of conversion requests has to be implemented in each subclass of Converter.

To sum up, in the text conversion example the 1:1 Recursive Unification pattern seems to be better suited for implementing the forwarding of conversion requests. In general, one has to weigh the pros and cons of these two alternatives. For example, if only a few subclasses of a hook class have to be implemented, the 1:1 Recursive Connection pattern may be preferred to the 1:1 Recursive Unification pattern.

1:N Connection pattern as alternative?
The original solution depicted in Figure 4.42(a) is based on the 1:1 Connection pattern between a TextDocument object and a Converter object. A TextDocument object refers to exactly one Converter object. That Converter object might be first in a chain of Converter objects. Due to the forwarding property of the 1:1 Recursive Unification pattern, a TextDocument object does not have to refer to all converters in the chain.

Instead of applying the 1:1 Recursive Unification pattern or the 1:1 Recursive Connection pattern as outlined above, TextDocument objects could refer to all Converter objects as expressed in the class diagram in Figure 4.42(b). What are the implications of such a solution?

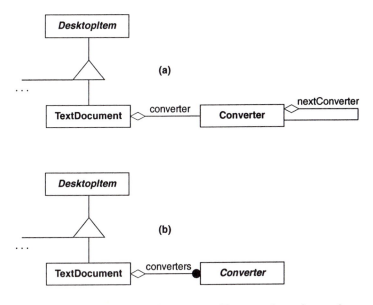

Figure 4.42   1:N Connection pattern (b) as an alternative to the original solution (a).

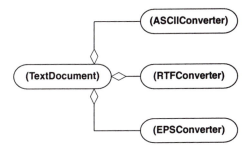

Figure 4.43   Sample composition of Converter objects based on the 1:N Connection pattern.

Figure 4.43 exemplifies an object composition in case where the 1:N Connection pattern underlies the composition of TextDocument and Converter objects. Compare this object diagram to Figure 4.39. Converter objects are not chained in Figure 4.43. A TextDocument object has to manage all its Converter objects.

According to the typical properties of a template class in the realm of the 1:N Connection pattern, class TextDocument should offer methods to add Converter objects to the data structure referred to by instance variable converters and remove Converter objects from it. Example 4.25 shows a possible implementation of ReadTextFromFile(...) in class TextDocument.

Example 4.25 Implementation of ReadTextFromFile(...) according to the 1:N Connection pattern.

```
void TextDocument::ReadTextFromFile(char *fileName)
{
        bool conversionPossible= FALSE;
        char *textFromFile;

        for each converter: <Converter *> in converters
                if (!conversionPossible)
                        textFromFile= converter->Convert(fileName,
                                                &conversionPossible);
        if (conversionPossible)
                SetText(textFromFile);
        else
                SetText("File could not be converted");
}
```

As a consequence, the methods SetNextConverter(...) and GetNextConverter() become superfluous in Converter and its subclasses. Furthermore, method Convert(...) only implements the file conversion. Forwarding conversion requests becomes superfluous since no reference to the next converter is maintained. So class Converter is an abstract class as depicted in Figure 4.42(b). It offers the abstract method Convert(...).

The advantage of this solution is that each TextDocument object can attach and arrange its converters individually. This would also be possible in the original solution. The difference is that in the original solution a separate chain of converters would be required for each individual ordering of converters. In the alternative solution based on the 1:N Connection pattern, Converter objects do not store references to their next converter. Thus only one instance of each specific Converter subclass has to be generated. TextDocument objects build up their individual converter chains by storing Converter object references in the data structure referred to by their instance variable converters.

This advantage is also the disadvantage of this solution: rearranging converter chains has to be done for each TextDocument object.

As a consequence, the solution based on the 1:N Connection pattern should not be chosen if conversion requests are to be handled uniformly for all TextDocument objects. In this case the original solution applying the 1:1 Connection pattern and the 1:1 Recursive Unification pattern has to be preferred. Uniform treatment of text conversions is more appropriate for the problem at hand.

4.6   Capturing object-oriented design with metapatterns

Recall the core characteristic of frameworks, that various aspects have to be kept flexible while others are standardized. Metapatterns permit different levels of flexibility by combining basic object-oriented concepts.

Framework example catalogs try to select frameworks that are not too domain-specific in order to demonstrate how to achieve flexibility. As these framework examples are almost domain-independent, they can also be reused in the development of new frameworks. The Flexible Object Creation sample framework presented in Section 4.2.3 constitutes an example that is reusable in many frameworks since object creation occurs in all frameworks and often has to be kept flexible.

Nevertheless, the approach pursued by state-of-the-art design pattern catalogs has its limits. First of all, few framework examples are not too domain-specific. Furthermore, there should be a means of capturing the design of frameworks in such a way that it can be reused in the development process of new frameworks. Design pattern catalogs list framework *examples*, that is, describe the design of specific frameworks on an abstraction level higher than the underlying programming language. Since the examples are chosen carefully, these framework sample design patterns can be reused in other frameworks. However, they provide no means of capturing the design independently of a more or less specific framework example.

Metapatterns presented in this chapter are suitable for documenting the design of any (application) framework. This section outlines the principal idea of how metapatterns can be attached to frameworks. In this way metapatterns express how the required flexibility—represented by the hot spots—is gained in a particular framework. These design hints are often necessary in order to adapt frameworks. Programmers who develop new frameworks might benefit from studying the design of existing frameworks and applying it to frameworks under development.

Chapter 5 demonstrates how to use metapatterns to capture framework design in the realm of the GUI application framework ET++.

4.6.1   Attaching metapatterns to frameworks

The seven composition metapatterns presented in Section 4.3.3 repeatedly occur in frameworks. Of course, each framework uses specific names for the template and hook classes and the corresponding methods. The core characteristics of the composition metapatterns discussed in Section 4.5 are independent of their particular application. Below we show how metapatterns can be attached to specific frameworks in order to document their design. The sample frameworks used for this purpose have been introduced in this chapter and the previous chapters.

Unification metapattern

The Unification metapattern can be linked, for example, to a sample framework that keeps object creation flexible. Figure 4.44 depicts such an attachment schematically by means of arrows. The class name TH in the metapattern corresponds to class Application. The template method T() in class TH corresponds to NewManager(); the hook method H() in class TH corresponds to DoMakeManager().

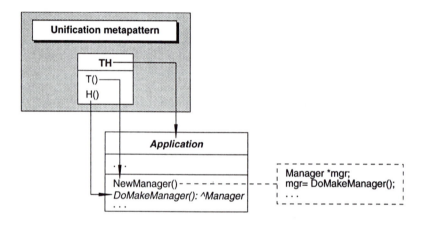

Figure 4.44 Attaching the Unification metapattern to a sample framework.

The essential aspects of attaching the Unification metapattern to the sample framework shown in Figure 4.44 are expressed textually as follows:

Metapattern: TH

TH -> Application

T() -> NewManager()

H() -> DoMakeManager() : ^Manager

Hot spot: the creation of Manager objects

Note that writing the hook method *DoMakeManager()* in *italic style* expresses that this method is an abstract method.

Due to the characteristics of the Unification pattern, a subclass has to be specified in order to adapt the object creation behavior. That behavior cannot be adapted at run time.

1:1 Connection metapattern

The 1:1 Connection pattern is applied in the State framework and in one solution of the text conversion presented in Section 4.5.4. Figure 4.45 illustrates how the components of the 1:1 Connection metapattern correspond to the classes and methods of the State framework.

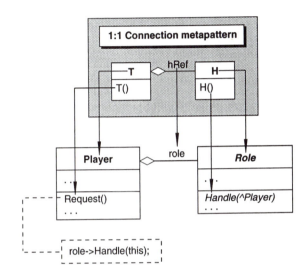

Figure 4.45 Attaching the 1:1 Connection metapattern to a sample framework.

The essential aspects of attaching the 1:1 Connection metapattern to the State framework are expressed textually as follows:

Metapattern:	T<>——H
T ->	Player
H ->	*Role*
T() ->	Request()
H() ->	*Handle(^Player)*
hRef ->	role
Hot spot:	how requests are handled by a **Player** object

Due to the characteristics of the 1:1 Connection pattern, the behavior that is kept flexible by means of this pattern can be adapted at run time.

1:N Connection metapattern

The 1:N Connection pattern is applied in the Publisher/Subscriber framework. Figure 4.46 illustrates how the components of the 1:N Connection metapattern correspond to the classes and methods of this framework.

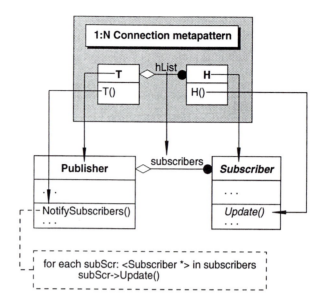

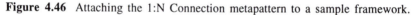

Figure 4.46 Attaching the 1:N Connection metapattern to a sample framework.

The essential aspects of attaching the 1:N Connection metapattern to the Publisher/Subscriber framework are expressed textually as follows:

Metapattern:	T◇——●H
T ->	Publisher
H ->	*Subscriber*
T() ->	NotifySubscribers()
H() ->	*Update()*
hList ->	subscribers
Hot spot:	how Subscriber objects are updated

Due to the characteristics of the 1:N Connection pattern, the behavior that is kept flexible by means of this pattern can be adapted at run time.

1:N Recursive Connection and 1:N Recursive Unification metapatterns

The 1:N Recursive Connection pattern is applied in the DesktopItem-Folder framework. Figure 4.47 illustrates how the components of the 1:N Recursive Connection metapattern correspond to the classes and methods of the DesktopItem-Folder framework.

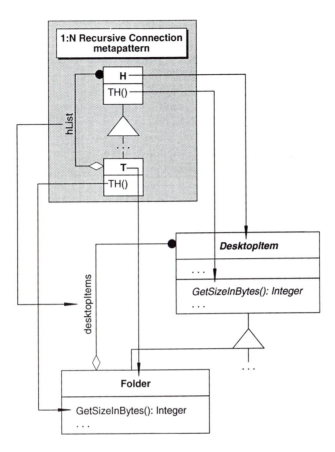

Figure 4.47 Attaching the 1:N Recursive Connection metapattern to a sample framework.

The essential aspects of attaching the 1:N Recursive Connection metapattern to the DesktopItem-Folder framework are expressed textually as follows:

Metapattern: T◇—▷—●H

T ->   Folder

H ->   *DesktopItem*

T::TH() ->   GetSizeInBytes()

H::TH() ->   *GetSizeInBytes()*

hList ->   desktopItems

Hot spot: how DesktopItem objects calculate their size

Due to the characteristics of the 1:N Recursive Connection pattern, Folder objects can be treated as single DesktopItem objects so that hierarchies can be composed. Requests like GetSizeInBytes are automatically forwarded within these object hierarchies since the template method GetSizeInBytes() adheres to the typical structure of template methods in the 1:N Recursive Connection pattern. Furthermore, the behavior that is kept flexible by means of this pattern, that is, the size calculation, can be adapted at run time—Folder objects calculate their size correctly if the contained items are changed.

In the realm of recursive composition metapatterns, the template and hook methods are sometimes not relevant. Recursive metapatterns imply that certain object structures can be composed as discussed in Section 4.4. As a consequence, template and hook methods can be ignored if only the object composition aspect counts. Figure 4.48 illustrates this for the 1:N Recursive Unification pattern attached to the GroupedDItem framework. Details of that framework are presented in Section 4.5.2.

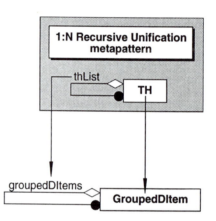

Figure 4.48   Attaching the 1:N Recursive Unification metapattern to a sample framework.

1:1 Recursive Connection metapattern

The 1:1 Recursive Connection pattern is applied in the realm of the DesktopItem-Folder framework in order to restrict the name length of DesktopItem objects. Figure 4.49 illustrates how the components of the 1:1 Recursive Connection metapattern correspond to the classes of the DesktopItem-Folder framework. Note that not all template and hook methods are shown in Figure 4.49. The 1:1 Recursive Connection pattern is applied in class DIWithRestrNameLen in order to change the behavior of SetItemName(...). The other requests are forwarded without changes to the wrapped DesktopItem object. So the SetItemName(...) method is a template and hook method and worth examining in this example framework.

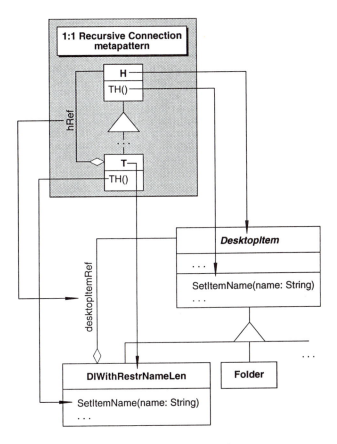

Figure 4.49 Attaching the 1:1 Recursive Connection metapattern to a sample framework.

The essential aspects of attaching the 1:1 Recursive Connection metapattern to the DesktopItem-Folder framework are expressed textually as follows:

Metapattern:	T◇─▷─H
T ->	DIWithRestrNameLen
H ->	*DesktopItem*
T::TH() ->	SetItemName()
	(other methods of T are also template methods but irrelevant in the realm of this pattern's hot spot)
H::TH() ->	SetItemName()
	(corresponding relevant hook method)
hRef ->	desktopItemRef
Hot spot:	how DesktopItem objects handle name changes

The 1:1 Recursive Connection pattern is used in this context to selectively modify behavior of class DesktopItem and all its descendants without changing DesktopItem itself. All requests—except SetItemName, whose behavior is to be changed—are forwarded to the wrapped DesktopItem object according to the description of this sample framework in Section 4.5.3. Changes of the name setting behavior are possible at run time by wrapping DesktopItem objects in DIWithRestrNameLen objects.

1:1 Recursive Unification metapattern

The 1:1 Recursive Unification pattern is applied in order to forward text file conversion requests within a chain of converters. Figure 4.50 illustrates how the components of the 1:1 Recursive Unification metapattern correspond to the Converter framework.

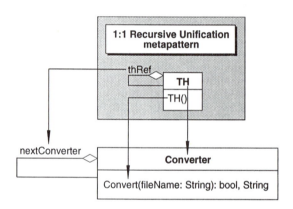

Figure 4.50 Attaching the 1:1 Recursive Unification metapattern to a sample framework.

The essential aspects of attaching the 1:1 Recursive Unification metapattern to the Converter framework are expressed textually as follows:

Metapattern:	⬭ TH
TH ->	Converter
TH() ->	Convert()
thRef ->	converter
Hot spot:	how Converter objects convert files to text strings

The 1:1 Recursive Unification pattern is used in this context to forward file conversion requests within a chain of Converter objects based on the typical structure of template-hook methods described in Section 4.4.4. Besides this

forwarding task, how the file conversion is handled by a particular Converter object is kept flexible.

4.6.2 Proposed tool support

Figures 4.44–50 show that the particular components of metapatterns are linked to framework examples. This is also expressed textually by the sign ->. As a consequence, hypertext appears to be well suited to annotating frameworks with metapatterns.

In a sample (application) framework each of the seven metapatterns might be linked to numerous components of the framework; that is, the components of a composition metapattern are linked to domain-specific template and hook classes and the corresponding methods. Each metapattern probably occurs several times in a framework. So metapatterns might be viewed as a means of capturing and categorizing the design incorporated in a framework.

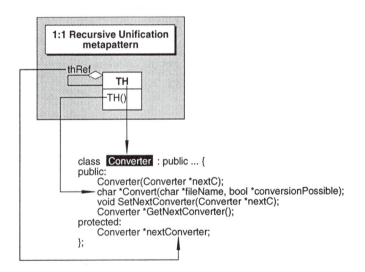

Figure 4.51 Linking the 1:1 Recursive Unification metapattern to source code.

Assuming that a framework is properly annotated, that is, metapatterns are linked to relevant framework components, a user of a suitable hypertext tool can browse through the design incorporated in a framework. For example, clicking in the 1:1 Recursive Unification metapattern (see Figure 4.50) on the class name TH would cause the component Converter to be shown if this sample framework is linked to the metapattern. A sample framework can either be depicted graphically as in Figure 4.50, or the links can be attached directly to source code. Figure 4.51 exemplifies this for class Converter, demonstrating that the effect of clicking on the class name TH in the metapattern could be that the corresponding class definition with the highlighted class name is displayed. Analogously, method Convert(...) and instance variable nextConverter would be highlighted if the user clicks on the corresponding components in the metapattern.

The characteristics of the 1:1 Unification metapattern suggest further design information that could be provided, for example:

- how the forwarding is implemented in the template-hook method TH() in class TH and its descendants;

- where in the overall framework the chain of Converter objects is built;

- which components of the overall framework use the chain of Converter objects.

The user interface of an appropriate tool supporting the metapattern approach could provide corresponding menu entries tailored to the specific needs of each metapattern. If a user of such a tool selects the corresponding questions, hypertext links again constitute a suitable means of answering these questions in the realm of a particular framework. Analogously, the characteristics of each metapattern could be explained.

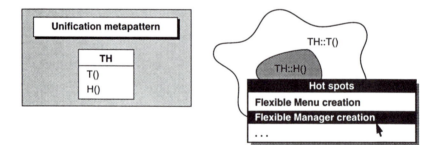

Figure 4.52   Choosing a hot spot of a particular framework.

Besides metapattern-specific differences discussed in Sections 4.4 and 4.5, frameworks attached to each metapattern differ in their hot spots, that is, the semantic aspects that are kept flexible. This is true for all metapatterns. It can be utilized in the user interface as sketched in Figure 4.52. For example, in the realm of ET++ the Unification metapattern is used to keep object creation flexible in various components. If a user clicks in the right-hand cloud on the gray spot symbolizing the flexible aspect of a framework, a menu listing the hot spots of all sample frameworks to which the metapattern is attached could pop up.

Assuming that the user chooses the menu entry "Flexible **Manager** creation" as shown in Figure 4.52, the corresponding framework would be linked to the Unification metapattern as demonstrated in Figure 4.53. Here it is assumed that the components of the cloud representing the framework are also linked to the corresponding framework components. In order to provide feedback to the user on which framework example is linked to a metapattern, the chosen hot spot could be displayed beneath the metapattern name as demonstrated in Figure 4.53.

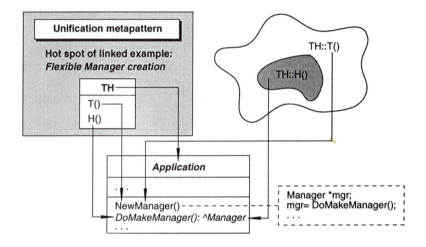

Figure 4.53 Sample framework linked to a metapattern after choosing the hot spot semantics.

We term the environment outlined above a *metapattern browser*. A metapattern browser allows the user to browse through the design of a particular framework. Any framework can be instrumented by a metapattern browser. Analogous to a cookbook, a metapattern browser for a specific framework should be authored by somebody with an in-depth knowledge of the framework, ideally the framework developer(s). Below we outline the required tools to define a metapattern browser for a specific framework.

Tools for defining metapattern browsers

A hypertext system tailored to the needs of metapatterns forms the precondition for defining metapattern browsers for any framework. The base nodes from which users follow links are the seven metapatterns. A metapattern browser author has to be able to define links between the components of each metapattern and nodes which are class/object diagrams and/or source code fragments. Supposing that a user interface like the one outlined above is chosen for the metapattern browser, the flexible aspect of each framework sample linked to a metapattern has to be provided by the metapattern browser author and inserted in the hypertext system in a corresponding pop-up menu associated with the hook method in the framework cloud.

In order to draw class or object diagrams efficiently, an editor that supports drawing diagrams in a particular notation such as the Object Model Notation is required. An advanced version of such an editor could automatically draw diagrams after the user points out which classes and methods are relevant by selecting them in the source code.

4.6.3 Summarizing remarks

In general, frameworks, especially application frameworks, constitute a bonanza of object-oriented design that can be captured by metapatterns. The idea of attaching metapatterns to components of frameworks presented in this chapter should be applied only to mature frameworks. It does not make sense to define metapattern browsers for frameworks that are in their early development stages, that is, where it is still not clear whether template and hook classes are defined and implemented according to the needs of the framework domain.

Metapattern browsers for mature (application) frameworks can be viewed as advanced design pattern catalogs. Some aspects of a specific framework might be domain-independent to a large degree, so that this design can be applied in the development of new frameworks. In these cases metapattern browsers serve the same purpose as design pattern catalogs. Actually, design pattern catalogs can be viewed as carefully chosen subsets of the design examples that can be captured and categorized in metapattern browsers.

Compared to design pattern catalogs, metapattern browsers can in addition instrument any domain-specific framework and document its design. The fact that metapattern browsers allow efficient design documentation of frameworks can help in adapting the hot spots of a framework to specific needs.

The fact that *myriads of metapattern annotations* are possible in (application) frameworks might be considered a disadvantage: practically every method calls other methods and thus becomes a template method that is based on hook methods. For example, in the framework depicted in Figure 4.53 method NewManager() calls not only DoMakeManager() but also other methods. Metapatterns could be attached to all these calls in which NewManager() is the template method and the invoked methods are hook methods. As already mentioned, the people who developed the framework or know it well usually comprehend the relevant aspects that should be put into a metapattern documentation. As a consequence, a metapattern documentation might never be complete, analogously to a framework cookbook.

In order to demonstrate how to apply the metapattern approach in the realm of complex application frameworks, we chose the GUI application framework ET++. Chapter 5 shows how useful metapattern annotations attached to a framework can help in grasping its design.

Chapter 5

Sample application of the metapattern approach

This chapter demonstrates the usefulness of attaching metapatterns to a complex, mature application framework. We chose the GUI application framework ET++ (Weinand *et al.* 1988, Weinand *et al.* 1989, Eggenschwiler and Gamma 1992, Gamma 1992, Weinand 1992) for this purpose. ET++ is a GUI application framework that builds especially on the lessons learned from the MacApp (Apple 1989, Wilson *et al.* 1990) application framework for implementing Macintosh applications. ET++ was developed by André Weinand and Erich Gamma in Prof. Marty's group at the University of Zurich. The same team was responsible for the evolution of ET++ at the Union Bank of Switzerland's Informatics Laboratory (UBILAB) in Zurich. ET++ was implemented in C++ and runs on common UNIX platforms supporting various window systems such as X11.

For the following reasons ET++ represents an application framework well suited to demonstrating the metapattern approach:

- ET++ constitutes an application framework with *outstanding design*. One of the principal goals in the development of ET++ was to find and refine appropriate abstractions, that is, abstract classes, for the GUI domain. A small number of basic mechanisms are based on these abstractions which have evolved since 1987. Its design has reached a satisfactory maturity level.

- The source code of ET++, sample applications built with ET++, and basic tools for object-oriented programming such as class and object structure browsers are *available for free*. Furthermore, ET++ can be compiled with the likewise free gnu C++ compiler. (Appendix C explains how to obtain ET++ and the source code of the sample application discussed in this chapter.)

This chapter uses metapatterns to describe the design of some of ET++'s core mechanisms and a few other aspects that are required in order to adapt the application framework to the needs of a simple hypertext system. Note that it is explicitly not our intention to provide a detailed description of the ET++ application framework.

The first section of this chapter outlines ET++'s domain both in a general way and by presenting the features of the hypertext system application from a user's point of view.

Some of the design aspects presented might be applied in the development of other (application) frameworks. A discussion of this issue concludes the chapter.

5.1   Overview of ET++'s domain

A team at the Xerox Palo Alto Research Center (PARC) started to investigate effective human/computer interaction in the early 1970s. Smalltalk was developed in order to realize these concepts. Smalltalk's interactive programming environment provided the foundation for GUIs which utilize not only a keyboard but also a mouse as input devices. The GUIs available today on most computing platforms resulted from adaptation and enhancement of the original ideas incorporated in the Smalltalk environment. Here we focus on some core concepts underlying GUIs.

A GUI can be viewed as an example of a visualized object-oriented system. Objects such as file icons, windows, a trash can, and so on are displayed. Each object understands certain messages. In order to perform actions via such an interface, a desktop object has to be selected and then told what it has to do by sending a message to it.

To simplify the selection of desktop objects, GUIs provide a *pointing device* such as a mouse. The concept of *menus* is often used in order to prevent the user having to recall the full range of potential messages defined for an object. The user simply selects an object and then chooses the required message from a menu. This causes a corresponding action by the object.

Menus are not the only way of sending messages to objects. Some actions can be specified by directly manipulating objects. Issuing commands in this way is called *direct manipulation*. Some examples are:

- copying a document from one device to another by dragging its iconic representation between the iconic representations of the devices;
- double-clicking on icons to open them, a shortcut for choosing the Open command from a menu;
- compiling a program text by dragging its iconic representation over the iconic representation of a suitable compiler.

In addition, the following properties of GUIs are considered crucial.

It is important that each user action effects a commensurate change in the user interface, that is, gives the user *appropriate feedback*. Examples of feedback in user interfaces are highlighting selected objects or indicating that a time-consuming operation is being carried out. The latter can be accomplished, for example, by displaying a meter or an hourglass while an action is going on.

Furthermore, a GUI should be *consistent*, that is, free of exceptions and special conditions. This should be true not only for a particular application but for all activities on the computer. As a consequence, once familiar with the user interface, the user can transfer skills between applications. New applications can be explored with minimal effort. *Undoable commands* also encourage users to experiment with applications.

GUIs that make use of two-and-a-half dimensional effects make user interface elements look more attractive. The appearance of the user interface elements on the screen is often termed a GUI's *look*. Guidelines such as Apple's Human Interface Guidelines (Apple 1987) describe how to keep a particular GUI consistent and conform to the GUI characteristics outlined above. Applications that adhere to such guidelines have a certain standard *feel* from a user's point of view. For example, working with an Apple Macintosh GUI feels different than working with a Microsoft Windows GUI, though both apply comparable user interface elements.

5.1.1 ET++'s support of GUI concepts

The application framework ET++ provides elementary user interface building blocks (for example, buttons and menus), basic data structures (for example, the classes ObjList, ObjArray) and high-level application components such as the classes Application, Document, View, Command, and Window. Together with the elementary building blocks the high-level application components predefine as far as possible the look and feel of ET++ applications.

In the example used in this chapter, ET++ classes are adapted in order to provide the functionality of a simple hypertext system. Figure 5.1 shows a screenshot of this ET++ application. In the course of editing a hypertext document the Find/Change menu item was chosen from the Edit menu, opening the corresponding dialog. This hypertext system could be used as an editor for simple cookbook recipes. A more advanced hypertext system was used to produce the cookbook recipes in Section 3.4.2. In the simple hypertext system discussed in this chapter, only links to other hypertext documents can be defined. It is not possible to define code-example links. Furthermore, there is no special hypertext graph presenter to list the available recipes and manage the visited hypertext documents in a request history.

If the user of the simple hypertext system activates a particular button in the text, the document that is associated with that button is opened. For example, the hypertext document entitled "Data in documents" is opened if the button with that label is pressed in the hypertext document entitled "Creating Documents" (see Figure 5.1). If the corresponding document is already open, its window is brought to the front.

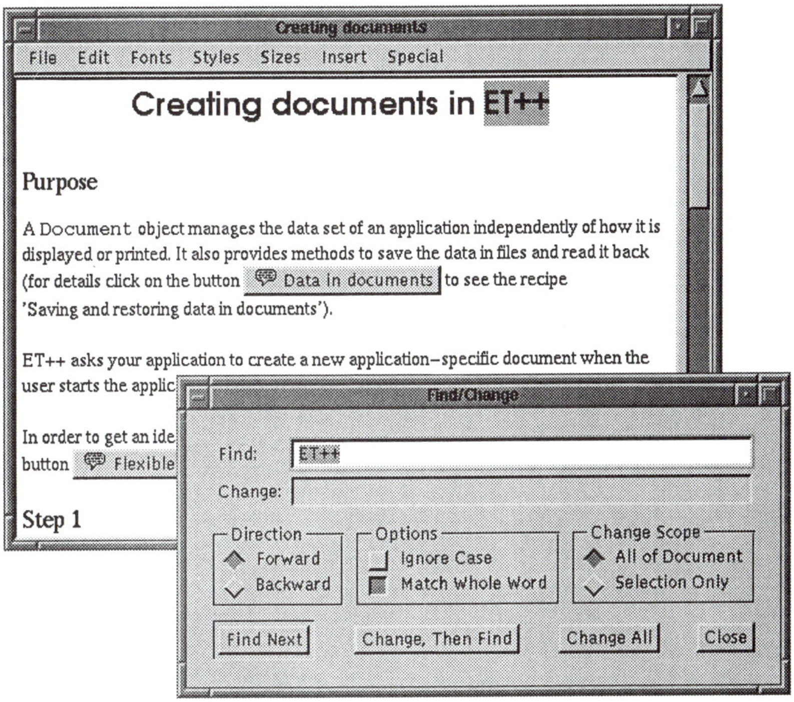

Figure 5.1 Screenshot of a hypertext system built with ET++.

The hypertext system whose functionality is described in detail in Section 5.1.2 could also be used in the realm of the mailing framework outlined in Chapter 2. This would allow mailing of hypertext documents in addition to plain text documents.

Hypertext systems are useful for various domains. For example, the World-Wide Web, a powerful information system on the Internet, combines the ease of use of hypertext GUIs with the information source Internet.

ET++ handles the following aspects of GUIs almost automatically:

- ET++ applications take care of windows (moving, resizing, activation on clicking, and so on) and their contents (for example, scrolling).

- Uniform handling of file and dialog management for loading, saving, and printing documents helps to maintain consistency across applications.

- ET++ automatically supports hardcopy output in various formats such as PostScript.

- Flicker-free screen update based on double buffering and support of the Macintosh and Motif look contribute to attractive visual design and consistent user interfaces.

For the features listed above, programmers have simply to use ET++ components and put them together accordingly. For example, in order to support scrolling, an instance of class Scroller has to be generated and composed with the contents that have to be scrolled. This is described in Section 5.2.4 and applied in Section 5.3.2.

Supporting the following features of GUI applications usually requires adaptations of ET++ classes:

- In order to make the selection of objects by means of the mouse possible, ET++ provides sophisticated, yet easy-to-adapt mechanisms for handling events (mouse movements, mouse clicks, menu selection, keyboard input, and so on) and providing proper feedback. Some building blocks, for example, text views, already handle events such as text selection, cut/copy/paste commands, dragging and dropping of selected text, and so on properly without additional programming effort.

- Subclasses of the ET++ class Command have to be defined and implemented in order to support single-level or multilevel undo commands. Specific Command subclasses are predefined for some ET++ components such as text views.

- Data can be transferred within an application and across applications via a clipboard. The text view components of ET++ already support the exchange of cut/copied text via the clipboard.

5.1.2 An ET++ hypertext system

Recall the characteristics of a hypertext system outlined in Section 3.4.2: a hypertext system allows the *creation of and navigation through* a directed graph. The nodes of such a graph are different parts of documents such as texts and drawings. The edges are unidirectional and link these nodes.

In the sample application that we build by adapting ET++, we restrict ourselves to text document nodes. A text document is represented by a window that contains the typical menus required for text editing and the area in which to display and edit text (see Figure 5.1). The difference compared to a plain text editor is that hypertext link buttons can be contained as characters.

Since the hypertext system should allow creation of *and* navigation through a directed graph of text documents, activating a button in a text may cause one of the following actions: in *creation mode* the user can specify the text document to which a particular button is linked; in *navigation mode* the user can follow the link, that is, the text document associated with the activated button is opened.

In order to toggle between these two modes the menu item Navigation Mode is chosen from the Special menu (see Figure 5.2). Each time this menu item is chosen, the mode is toggled between creation and navigation mode. This is indicated by means of a check box. If there is a check box in front of the text Navigation Mode, the text document is in navigation mode. In creation mode there is no check box in front of this menu item.

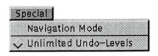

Figure 5.2   Changing the mode of the hypertext system.

Creating a hypertext graph
When the hypertext system starts up, an empty text document is opened in creation mode. The user can then enter and delete text, cut/copy/paste portions of text, define fonts, sizes, styles, and so on by means of the commands offered in the corresponding menus. Additional text documents can be created by choosing the New command from the File menu.

In order to insert a hypertext link button, the command Link Button is chosen from the Insert menu as shown in Figure 5.3. This command causes the insertion of a button at the position of the caret in the text.

Figure 5.3   Inserting a hypertext link button.

If the text document is in creation mode, a click on a link button causes a Link Dialog window to pop up as shown in Figure 5.4. This dialog lists all text documents created so far in the application. In order to associate a text document with a button, the name of the text document is selected from the list and the button labeled Define Link clicked. In Figure 5.4 the text document "Sample method DoMakeManager" is associated with the link button for which the dialog was opened. The text shown inside a link button is always the name of the associated text document.

The Rename Dialog window (see Figure 5.4) is opened if the menu item Rename is chosen from the File menu. This dialog allows the names of text documents to be changed. The names are displayed in the window title bar. For example, the text document shown in Figure 5.1 has the name "Creating Documents". In order to define the name of a text document, the corresponding text document is selected from the list of text documents. The name of the selected document is shown in the text edit field beneath the list of text documents. When the Define Name button is clicked, the name of the selected document is set to the name displayed in the text edit field.

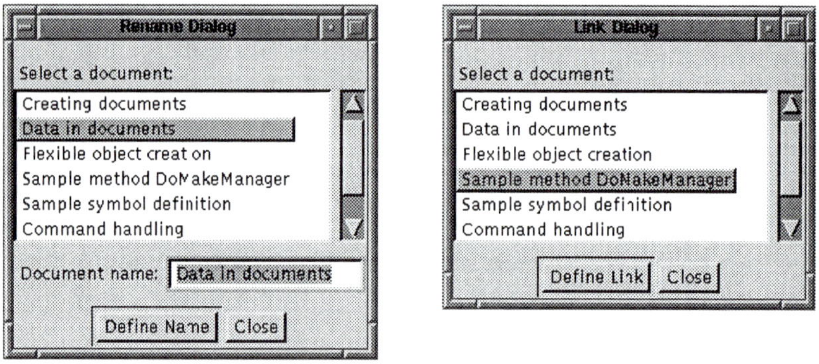

Figure 5.4 Rename and link dialogs.

Navigating through a hypertext graph
If a text document is in navigation mode, a click on a link button causes the text document associated with that link to be opened. If that text document is already open, its window is put in front of the other windows. In the case that no text document is associated with a link button, the button can still be activated, but no further action will be taken.

Note that each text document can be either in creation or navigation mode. In navigation mode text cannot be edited. When testing a newly created hypertext graph, all text documents should be in navigation mode.

Other features
A hypertext document can be edited in ways familiar from common text editor applications, for example:

- Text including hypertext link buttons can be cut/copied/pasted within a text document and between text documents. Text is put into the clipboard by selecting a text portion and choosing Cut or Copy from the Edit menu. The Paste command pastes the clipboard contents into the text. As a shortcut, selected text can be dragged and dropped within a text document by means of the mouse.

- Choosing the Find/Change command from the Edit menu opens a dialog that provides text find-and-replace functionality as illustrated in Figure 5.1.

- Text fonts, styles and sizes can be changed.

- All text edit operations are undoable. The number of undo levels can be switched between one and unlimited in the Special menu (see Figure 5.2).

- The contents of a text document can be printed and previewed by choosing the Print command from the File menu.

As the goal of this chapter is to demonstrate the usefulness of attaching metapatterns to a complex application framework, we refrain from the implementation of the following features:

- Saving hypertext graphs: The created hypertext graph cannot be saved as a file. Though ET++ would almost automatically support storing/restoring the hypertext graph created by that application, we refrain from presenting the design and implementation of this feature. This ET++ adaptation would require the explanation of C++ details that are irrelevant in the context of this chapter.

- Removing documents: Text documents can only be created, not removed from the hypertext graph. Closing a text document, for example, by choosing the Close command from the File menu, does not remove the document from the hypertext graph. So a closed text document is opened again if a link button associated with that text document is activated in navigation mode. Closed text documents are also listed in the link and rename dialogs.

5.2   Capturing ET++'s core design with metapatterns

This section focuses on the main mechanisms and concepts of ET++. The corresponding components of the application framework are annotated by means of metapatterns. This demonstrates the suitability of the metapattern approach for communicating the design of a complex framework in an efficient way.

Figure 5.5 shows the inheritance relationships of those ET++ classes that are relevant in the context of this chapter. The cornerstones of ET++ discussed in Section 5.2.1 are written in boldface. Abstract classes are written in *italics*.

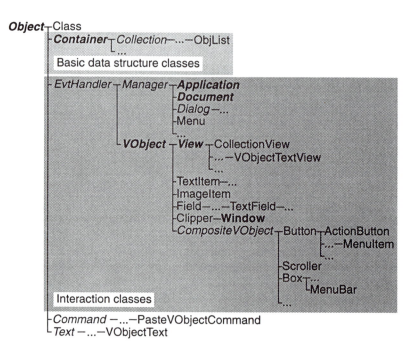

Figure 5.5 Parts of the ET++ class hierarchy.

5.2.1 ET++'s cornerstones

This section outlines the properties of what we consider ET++'s cornerstones, that is, the root class Object, the basic data structure classes, and the classes Application, Document, VObject, View, and Window. A basic understanding of these classes and their relationships is necessary in order to grasp the advanced ET++ design issues presented in the subsequent sections.

ET++'s root class
Almost all ET++ classes are derived from class Object and so share its behavior. The abstract class Object defines and partially implements the protocol of various services. For example, class Object allows inquiries about meta-information and implements the Publisher/Subscriber pattern. We select these two sample services since both are required in the realm of the hypertext system implementation. Weinand *et al.* (1989), among others, describe the other services offered by class Object.

   Meta-information: Meta-information is a generic term for information about objects and classes. An example situation where meta-information is required is discussed in Section 2.1.2. C++ does not allow inquiries about an object (for example, its instance variables, its class, class hierarchy information).

Due to this C++ deficiency, many advanced C++ class libraries implement a mechanism to provide meta-information. In any case, the programmer has to obey some coding patterns. In ET++ the powerful C macros MetaDef and MetaImpl extract the necessary information from the class definitions in header and implementation files (see Appendix A). ET++ applies a mechanism that is modeled on Smalltalk's metaclass concept. A special object, an instance of class Class, containing information about a class, corresponds to each class in the framework. Class objects store, for example, the name of a class, its associated superclass, the size of a class instance in bytes, and the types of its instance variables.

Meta-information can be accessed via methods offered in the root class Object. Thus meta-information can be retrieved from all instances of Object descendants. Class Object offers the following methods which allow access to meta-information:

bool IsKindOf(*className*): This method returns TRUE if the object whose method IsKindOf(...) is called is an instance of the class *className* or a descendant of *className*.

Class *IsA() returns a pointer to that instance of class Class which contains the meta-information about the particular object as described above.

char *ClassName() returns the class name.

Example 5.1 illustrates the use of these methods. The macro Guard is a short-cut for checking the dynamic type of an object and casting the corresponding reference variable.

Example 5.1 Sample use of Object's methods relying on meta-information.

```
#include "SampleDoc.h"        // Defines class SampleDoc as
                              // a subclass of the ET++ class
                              // Document.

. . .
Object *op= new SampleDoc(...);
bool tmp= op->IsKindOf(Object);      // => tmp == TRUE
tmp= op->IsKindOf(Document);         // => tmp == TRUE
tmp= op->IsKindOf(SampleDoc);        // => tmp == TRUE
tmp= op->IsKindOf(DrawDoc);          // => tmp == FALSE

cout << op->ClassName();             // SampleDoc is written to
                                     // the output stream.

cout << op->IsA()->Size();           // The size in bytes of a
                                     // SampleDoc instance is
                                     // written to the output
```

```
                                          // stream. (Method
                                          // Size() is offered by
                                          // class Class.)

     if (op->IsKindOf(Document) )         // Both lines are
                                          // equivalent to:
            ((Document *)op)->...         // Guard(op,
                                          //          Document)-> ...
     . . .
```

Publisher/Subscriber pattern: In ET++ class Object corresponds to both publisher and subscriber. By means of dashed lines Figure 5.6 shows how the Publisher/Subscriber sample framework corresponds conceptually to class Object in ET++.

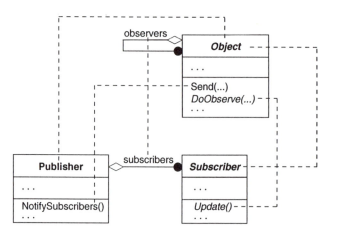

Figure 5.6 Publisher/Subscriber pattern in class Object.

In the realm of ET++ the term *change propagation mechanism* is preferred to Publisher/Subscriber pattern. The term *observer* is used instead of subscriber. As a consequence, the objects *observing* a particular Object object are managed by the methods named

    void AddObserver(Object *op)

    Object *RemoveObserver(Object *op)

which add/remove an object to/from the data structure represented by observers. In the implementation of class Object the references to the observing objects that should be notified about changes to an Object object are not stored explicitly in that object; that is, the instance variable observers exists only conceptually, not in the implementation. In order to avoid unnecessary storage overhead—many objects don't have observing objects—the implementation is based on hash-linking as outlined in Section 3.6.1.

The methods

void Send(int id, int part, void *data)

void DoObserve(int id, int part, void *data, Object *op)

comprise the interaction protocol. In order to notify observing objects of changes, an object invokes Send with appropriate arguments. Users may define identifiers for objects and certain changes which might be sufficient for observing objects to know what to do when the observed object has changed. In order to keep the change propagation mechanism flexible, a void * reference, that is, a reference to any data type, can be used to pass specific parameters. Send is implemented in Object so that these arguments and a reference to the changed object (that is, this as the last parameter value of DoObserve) are passed to the observing objects by calling DoObserve for all objects conceptually contained in the data structure represented by the instance variable observers. DoObserve is an abstract hook method which has to be overridden.

The 1:N Recursive Unification pattern underlies the change propagation mechanism (see Figure 5.7). The fact that this pattern is used implies that a hierarchy of dependent objects can be defined: objects that observe a particular object can in turn be observed by other objects. Circular dependencies cause an endless loop.

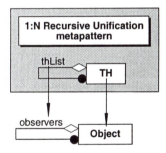

Figure 5.7 Change propagation based on the 1:N Recursive Unification metapattern.

An interesting aspect of the design of the change propagation mechanism is the fact that it deviates a bit from the 1:N Recursive Unification pattern. The template method (the notification of observing objects) and the hook method (the way an update is accomplished) are not unified in one method but separated in the two methods Send and DoObserve. This makes overriding DoObserve more convenient. If template and hook method were unified, an overriding method would always have to call the corresponding method of its superclass.

The semantic aspect of the 1:N Recursive Unification pattern is still valid: observing objects can be viewed as objects tightly coupled with the observed object.

Basic data structure classes

The container classes implement basic data structures such as list, array and set. They are typically used without any modifications. All container classes manage objects of static type pointer to Object. For example, all elements contained in an ObjList instance have the static type pointer to Object. This makes heterogeneous data structures possible: instances of any descendant of Object can be put in a data structure, although this freedom requires some means for checking dynamic object types. So class Object's methods for accessing meta-information become crucial. Since ET++ provides meta-information, this approach to implementing containers does without parameterized types as offered in recent C++ versions.

Besides the elementary operations of adding and removing objects from a data structure it is important to iterate over the objects contained in a data structure. How to code these operations is demonstrated in Appendix A.

Classes defining a generic ET++ application

GUI applications are *event-driven* and try to avoid modes. As a consequence, a user of an event-driven application can enter commands ideally in any order via input devices such as mouse and keyboard. A GUI application has to process incoming events accordingly. For example, clicking with the mouse on the title bar of a window should be handled by a GUI application in such a way that the window can then be moved by the mouse. Clicking on the menu bar should cause the opening of the corresponding menu from which the user can select an item by moving the mouse over the menu and releasing the mouse button over the selected menu item. While the mouse is being moved over a menu, the corresponding menu items should be highlighted.

In ET++ and similar application frameworks such as MacApp, an Application object gathers incoming events and dispatches them to the various components of the application. Each running ET++ application has exactly one Application object. Creating an Application object and sending the message Run to it is always the initial step of an ET++ application, usually coded in the main() function. This starts the *event loop*, that is, a loop that constantly processes the incoming events. After starting the event loop, ET++ automatically calls DoMakeManager(), an abstract method defined in class Application. A specific subclass of Application has to override DoMakeManager() and generate an appropriate Manager object (see below). Then the message Show is sent to the Manager object, which usually causes a window which is specific to the Manager object to be opened. The same steps, that is, creation and showing of a Manager object, are repeated every time the user chooses the New command from the File menu.

Many GUI applications manage documents. For example, any number of spreadsheets can be handled by a spreadsheet application. The data constituting one spreadsheet (its numbers, formulas and text contained in the cells) are handled by a subclass of the abstract class Document. Analogously, the hypertext system application deals with any number of text documents.

An object of a specific View subclass handles displaying the data of a Document object. Usually a View object is contained in a Window object that offers all the operations that characterize a window, such as moving and resizing.

So another property of class Application is that an Application object manages any number of Document objects. As not all GUI applications have to manage documents—for example, a desktop calculator needs no documents at all—the abstract class Manager was introduced in ET++. A Manager object manages zero or more Manager objects based on the 1:N Recursive Unification pattern (see Figure 5.8(a)). Since Application and Document are subclasses of Manager, the situation where an Application object might have to manage an arbitrary number of Document objects is a special case that is incorporated in that design (see Figure 5.8(b)). This design does not restrict an Application object to managing Document objects. Instances of any descendant of Manager can be handled.

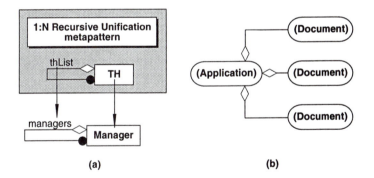

(a)   (b)

Figure 5.8 (a) The design of class Manager and (b) a resulting sample object composition.

The most important aspect of a GUI application is to render the data stored in a specific Manager object on the screen. Class VObject (for *visual object*) is the abstract superclass of all visual objects that are displayed on the screen. VObject objects offer a high-level protocol related to graphic objects. That protocol consists of numerous abstract and concrete methods, for example, methods for drawing on the screen.

According to Weinand *et al.* (1989) it was a design goal to keep instances of VObject small and efficient, so that it is possible to use a great number of them (for example, as cells of spreadsheets) without performance penalties. As a consequence, VObject instances have no built-in coordinate transformation and establish no clipping boundary. So any inefficient internal implementation based on the clipping mechanism of the underlying window system becomes superfluous. The clipping property can be added selectively to VObject objects based on the 1:1 Recursive Connection pattern. This is discussed in Section 5.2.4.

The general mechanisms of VObject and EvtHandler (discussed in Section 5.2.2) together with other concrete and abstract interaction classes, such as View, Window, MenuBar, and ActionButton, are used to build every visible component of the user interface with which the user interacts by means of the keyboard or mouse.

VObject greatly contributes to the overall outstanding design of ET++ since it allows a flexible combination of components. For example, a menu item can be any visual object. Typically, TextItem objects are used in menus. In some situations the generality of menu items is helpful. For example, in a graphic editor application the fill color of shapes can be defined in a menu that contains the appropriate visual objects representing the fill colors.

The predefined components VObjectText and VObjectTextView allow storing, rendering and editing text containing visual objects as single characters. For example, in the hypertext system application we can use these components in order to insert action buttons as single characters into a text. Other core mechanisms of ET++ such as event handling also work with any visual object inserted into a text. For example, handling a mouse click on a button inserted in the text is almost preimplemented in ET++.

Window is yet another example of a component that is based on VObject. The contents of a window is a VObject object. Hierarchical composition of VObject objects based on the 1:N Recursive Connection pattern together with alignment settings allow definition of any layout of composed visual objects in an elegant and uniform way. These aspects are discussed in Section 5.2.3.

MVC-related issues

The abstract class View conceptually represents a rectangular drawing area that defines and partially implements a protocol to forward input events to contained interaction objects, to print them, and to maintain a current selection. The fact that a Document instance can have several View objects to display its data (= *model*) closely resembles the MVC concept.

View objects are both controller and view components in the sense of the MVC concept since they inherit controller properties from class Evthandler. Nevertheless, a strict separation of model and view components is still considered to be very important. Let us discuss, for example, the ready-to-use View subclasses. The data structure necessary to store a text that contains arbitrary VObject objects as single characters is provided by class VObjectText. Instances of class VObjectTextView display data represented by a VObjectText object—model and view components are separated. VObjectTextView also offers the usual text editing capabilities.

A specific Document that should be used in the hypertext system—let us call it HypertextDoc—could define an instance variable of type pointer to VObjectText in order to represent the data. Another property of class Document is that it handles the display of its data by generating and managing the appropriate objects, that is, Window objects and View objects. Of course, the abstract class Document cannot know in advance which specific View object(s) handle(s) the data. This has to be defined in a specific Document subclass. In the case of HypertextDoc we assume that the text with VObject objects should be displayed and edited in one View object. Thus the predefined class VObjectTextView is tailor-made to do the job. A HypertextDoc object has to have the corresponding instance variable and initialize it by generating a VObjectTextView object that handles the data represented by the instance variable that refers to a VObjectText instance.

CollectionView is another example of a predefined View subclass that adheres to the separation of model and view components. A CollectionView object lists items of any Collection object containing VObject objects. Items displayed in a CollectionView object can also be selected.

In this case the benefits of the separation of model and view components become obvious. A CollectionView object can display the data stored in any specific Collection object, no matter whether it is, for example, an ObjList, a Set object, or an instance of any future descendant of the abstract class Collection.

5.2.2 Event handling (1:1 Recursive Unification pattern)

The 1:1 Recursive Unification pattern underlying class EvtHandler forms the basis of event handling in ET++ (see Figure 5.9). Class EvtHandler does not define an instance variable to allow its objects to refer to the next EvtHandler object in the chain. Instead, an abstract method GetNextHandler() is defined, which its descendants have to override.

The other methods of EvtHandler adhere to the typical structure of template-hook methods in the 1:1 Recursive Unification pattern as demonstrated for method DoMenuCommand() in Figure 5.9.

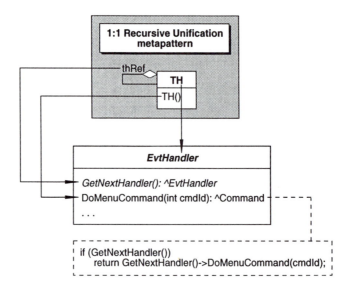

Figure 5.9 Class EvtHandler based on the 1:1 Recursive Connection metapattern.

Recall that the 1:1 Recursive Unification pattern is designed to build a directed graph of objects and to forward messages along that graph. An EvtHandler object can only refer to one other EvtHandler object. Thus EvtHandler objects form a chain within the directed graph. The message handling chain can be composed and changed dynamically. A particular object in an EvtHandler object chain does not have to know which specific object is next.

ET++ builds up the EvtHandler object chain almost automatically. In an application with Document objects the Document objects have the Application object as their next event handler. The View objects which display and edit the data of Document objects have the corresponding Document objects as their next event handler. A Window object showing the data of a particular Document object has that Document object as its next handler. Figure 5.10 illustrates the event handler chains that are built in a running hypertext system application with two documents. We assume that the specific Application subclass is called HypertextApp and that the specific Document subclass is called HypertextDoc. A HypertextDoc object uses a VObjectTextView object to display and edit its data. Details of the code that has to be written by the programmer who adapts ET++ are presented in Section 5.3.2.

How does the fact that an Application object implements the event loop match the concept of event handler chains? An Application object receives all input events and dispatches them to the appropriate event handler chain. The mouse position is the primary criterion for deciding which EvtHandler object chain gets the chance to handle the event first. By means of method

SetFirstHandler, a programmer defines which object in a particular chain gets the event first. In the example shown in Figure 5.10 each **VObjectTextView** object should be set as the first event handler of the particular chain.

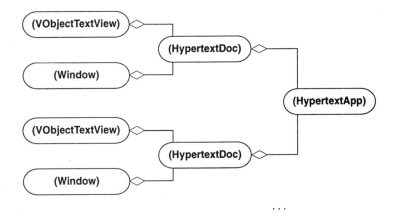

Figure 5.10 Event handler chains in the hypertext system application.

In order to react to specific events, the corresponding methods have to be overridden. For example, if a specific menu is defined in a **HypertextDoc** object we want to react to the selection of menu items in that menu. The menu Insert with the entry Link Button constitutes a **HypertextDoc**-specific menu. In order to react to menu selections, method **DoMenuCommand** could be overridden in HypertextDoc as shown in Example 5.2.

Example 5.2 Reacting to a menu selection event in class **HypertextDoc**.

```
. . .
Command *HypertextDoc::DoMenuCommand(int cmdId)
{
        switch (cmdId) {

                . . .

                case cIdInsertLinkButton:
                    return new
                                PasteVObjectCommand(
                                    vobTxtView,
                                    new LinkButton(...)
                        );

        . . .
```

```
                              default:
                                  return Document::DoMenuCommand(cmdId);
                          }
                          . . .

                      }
                      . . .
```

Each menu item has an integer identifier which is assigned when the menu item is created. The menu item Link Button is assumed to have the constant cldInsertLinkButton as its identifier. After a menu item has been selected from a menu, the message DoMenuCommand is sent to the first event handler in the chain of event handlers that corresponds to the window where the menu selection occurred. The parameter value passed to DoMenuCommand is the identifier of the selected menu item.

Since method DoMenuCommand is implemented according to the 1:1 Recursive Connection pattern, that is, the superclass method is called so that the message forwarding is not interrupted, the message DoMenuCommand is passed on from the first event handler, the particular VObjectTextView object, to the next event handler in the chain, that is, a HypertextDoc object.

If the passed parameter value is cldInsertLinkButton, the appropriate Command object is generated and returned (see below). In that case the message passing along the event handler chain is interrupted.

The concept of building event handler chains can be viewed as an elegant solution of event handling adhering to the object-oriented philosophy of avoiding centralized control. Each event handler in the chain is responsible for handling events that affect it. Event handlers do not have to know about each other. The Application object just passes incoming events to the first handler in the appropriate chain.

This principle that each event handler does its share of the overall task that has to be accomplished is the important principle underlying class EvtHandler. The methods offered by EvtHandler only differ in the semantic meaning of the task they represent. DoMenuCommand is the method for reacting to menu selections. Other examples are:

> void DoSetupMenu(Menu *m): to define which menu items are enabled/ disabled in the Menu object referred to by m. This task has to be accomplished every time a menu is opened.

> void Control(...): to react to incoming events such as mouse clicks.

Descendants of EvtHandler that override methods of EvtHandler do this in order to contribute to the particular task. For example, VObjectTextView overrides the methods DoSetupMenu and DoMenuCommand so that typical edit menu commands such as Cut, Copy and Paste are handled properly by its instances. The various font and style menu commands are also handled by VObjectTextView instances. Analogously, corresponding methods are overridden in order to handle keyboard and mouse events. For example, double-clicking inside a VObjectTextView instance selects the word at the mouse position where the double-click occurs (if there is a word).

Menu items such as New, Save, Save as... are handled by Document objects. An Application object handles the Quit command.

Undoable commands

The abstract class Command forms the basis for supporting the implementation of a framework for undoable commands. This framework relies on Command's abstract methods DoIt() and UndoIt().

A programmer has to define subclasses of Command in order to store the information necessary for undoing operations in instance variables. ET++ already provides some subclasses of Command, for example, PasteVObject-Command. A PasteVObjectCommand object allows pasting a visual object into a VObjectTextView object. A PasteVObjectCommand instance has to store a reference to the visual object to be inserted, a reference to the VObjectTextView instance where the insertion should take place, and the current caret position in the VObjectTextView object. DoIt is overridden in PasteVObjectCommand, so that the visual object is inserted in the VObjetTextView object as the character at the caret position. UndoIt is overridden so that the inserted visual object is removed.

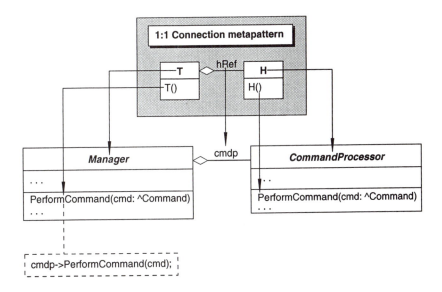

Figure 5.11 Manager handing Command objects over to a command processor.

The simple protocol offered by Command is sufficient for the implementation of an undo/redo framework in ET++ classes. A Manager object passes

Command objects to its associated CommandProcessor object. The 1:1 Connection pattern keeps the command-handling strategy flexible (see Figure 5.11). Manager is the template class, CommandProcessor the abstract hook class. Due to the characteristics of the 1:1 Connection pattern the command processing strategy can be changed at run time. How this is accomplished in the realm of the hypertext system example is presented in Section 5.3.3.

Note that the semantic aspect that is kept flexible in class **Manager** by means of the 1:1 Connection pattern to class CommandProcessor is similar to the State framework example. Class Manager corresponds to class **Player**, class CommandProcessor to class Role. By means of the 1:1 Connection pattern, how a Manager object handles Command objects is kept flexible—it plays different roles depending on the associated CommandProcessor object.

Objects of subclasses of CommandProcessor are composed with Command objects based on the 1:1 Connection pattern and the 1:N Connection pattern. In both cases class Command becomes the hook class with DoIt and UndoIt as hook methods; the way a command is executed and reverted is kept flexible.

CommandProcessor1 implements a single-level undo command-handling strategy and thus is based on the 1:1 Connection pattern—a CommandProcessor1 object refers to only one Command object. Since this can be viewed as special case of the other command processing strategy, we do not explain it further.

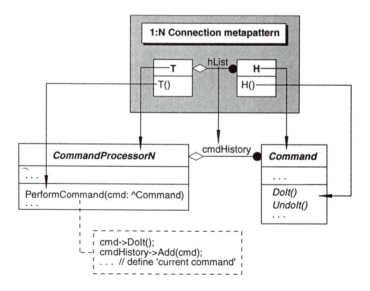

Figure 5.12   Processing commands.

CommandProcessorN implements a command handling strategy that does not restrict the number of undo levels at all. Figure 5.12 illustrates conceptually how the 1:N Connection pattern underlies the template class CommandProcessorN and the hook class Command. The actual implementation of CommandProcessor::PerformCommand in ET++ deviates slightly from the illustration in Figure 5.12. Discussing these implementation details would not reveal further insights into the design of the command handling framework, so the subsequent discussion is based on the conceptual design of this ET++ aspect.

The concept behind the undo/redo framework implemented in CommandProcessor subclasses is based on managing a reference to the current Command object. Figures 5.13(a) and 5.13(b) exemplify this concept. We assume that three Command objects have already been handed over from a Manager object to its CommandProcessorN object. The Command objects are ordered from left to right depending on when they were handed over by the corresponding Manager object. The leftmost Command object was handed over first, and so on. The rightmost Command object was handed over most recently and became the current Command object (see Figure 5.13(a)). So the CommandProcessorN object has already sent the message DoIt to that Command object.

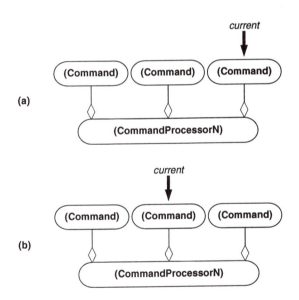

Figure 5.13 Processing gathered Command objects.

Since the current Command object is the rightmost in the list of Command objects, the CommandProcessorN object takes care that only the Undo menu item is enabled in the Edit menu. The Redo menu item is disabled. If the user chooses to undo the last command, the CommandProcessorN object sends the message UndoIt to the current Command object and the Command object to the left of the current Command object becomes the new current Command object (see Figure 5.13(b)). This is done in the case of each undo request until the end of the Command object list is reached; then the menu item Undo is disabled.

If the user chooses Redo from the Edit menu, the CommandProcessorN object defines the Command object to the right of the current Command object as the new current Command object and sends DoIt to that Command object.

To sum up, the abstract class Command forms the basis of a command handling framework, that is, a generic implementation of handling undo/redo requests. Based on the 1:1 Connection pattern and the 1:N Connection pattern, both the processing strategy (Manager-CommandProcessor) and how commands are executed and reverted (CommandProcessor-Command) are kept flexible. Due to the characteristics of the 1:1 Connection pattern underlying Manager-CommandProcessor, the command processing strategy can also be changed at run time.

5.2.3 Visual object hierarchies (1:N Recursive Connection pattern)

The 1:N Recursive Connection pattern underlies the classes VObject and CompositeVObject (see Figure 5.14). Thus any hierarchy of VObject objects that can be treated as a single VObject object can be composed.

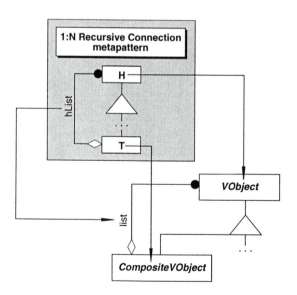

Figure 5.14 Classes VObject and CompositeVObject based on the 1:N Recursive Connection metapattern.

The property that a hierarchy of objects can be built and treated as a single object is required in many components of ET++. For example, a Window object contains one visual object. Based on the composition property of CompositeVObject objects, it is no problem to build any hierarchy of visual objects and hand that hierarchy over to a Window object as a single VObject object.

Layout specification
Descendants of CompositeVObject handle the proper layout management of visual object hierarchies. Weinand *et al.* (1989) motivate the ET++-specific layout management: "Dialog items most often come in groups. .... if the size of a single item changes, the overall layout of the dialog has to be redone."

The basic idea is that only the relative position of grouped VObject instances is specified for an instance of a descendant of CompositeVObject. For example, it could be specified that the grouped visual objects are placed one below another with a left alignment and a certain gap between each VObject instance. Based on these specifications, the respective CompositeVObject object calculates the positions of all grouped items.

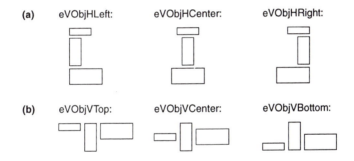

Figure 5.15 Alignment specification of grouped visual objects.

Class Box as a subclass of CompositeVObject constitutes the root of classes that handle layout. The primary parameter for alignment is an indication of whether items are arranged one below another or side by side. If items are arranged one below another, the alignment has to be chosen from left, center and right alignment (see Figure 5.15(a)). ET++ defines the enumeration constants eVObjHLeft, eVObjHCenter and eVObjHRight for these ways of positioning visual objects. The H (for horizontally) seems confusing at first glance since the items are arranged one below another. It expresses that the horizontal width of a VObject instance is essential for alignment.

Analogously, the relative position of items that are grouped side by side is specified as shown in Figure 5.15(b). The gap between grouped visual objects is specified by a Point instance. Depending on the arrangement of grouped objects, either the x or y point coordinate defines the size of the gap.

Due to the 1:N Recursive Connection pattern, any hierarchy of visual objects can be composed. At each level in the hierarchy different layout attributes can be used. For example, the layout of the dialog items in the rename dialog (see Figure 5.16) is defined in the following way: the single visual objects in this dialog are the TextItem object "Select a document:", the CollectionView object listing the names of the already defined text documents, the TextItem object "Document name:", a TextField object, and the ActionButton objects Define Name and Close.

The TextItem object "Select a document:" and the CollectionView object are grouped in a Box object with the layout attribute eVObjHLeft. The TextItem object "Document name:" and the TextField object are grouped in a Box object with the layout attribute eVObjVCenter. The ActionButton objects Define Name and Close are grouped in a Box object with the layout attribute eVObjVCenter. These three Box objects are themselves visual objects and are grouped in a Box object with the layout attribute eVObjHCenter.

Figure 5.16 Rename dialog.

Other descendants of Box allow the definition of different stretching behaviors of grouped visual objects. For example, if visual object hierarchies are put in a window that can be resized, some visual objects should not change their size while others should be resized accordingly. We refrain from discussing these details and other special layout classes since they reveal no further insights into how layout specification can be based on the 1:N Recursive Connection pattern.

To sum up, ET++'s layout classes demonstrate how the grouping pattern can be used in order to elegantly support any layout of visual objects required in the realm of GUIs. This way of defining the layout of visual objects is also what makes run-time changes between different GUI looks feasible. The size of visual objects differs in existing GUI looks. For example, action buttons in the Motif GUI standard look have a different size than those in the Macintosh standard look. Only an automatic layout (re)calculation offered by the classes discussed above allows keeping visual objects nicely aligned when the GUI look is changed.

5.2.4 Attaching special behavior (1:1 Recursive Connection pattern)

ET++ uses the 1:1 Recursive Connection pattern several times in order to allow the flexible attachment of special behavior to objects. We pick out two examples where this metapattern is applied.

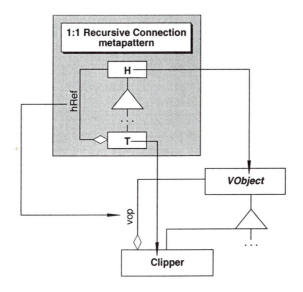

Figure 5.17 Clipper based on the 1:1 Recursive Connection pattern.

Recall that one goal in the definition of VObject was to keep its objects small and efficient, so that it is possible to use a great number of VObject objects without performance penalties. Thus visual objects do not establish a clipping boundary. Instead, the clipping property can be added selectively when needed by means of a Clipper instance. Clipper is a typical example where the 1:1 Recursive Connection pattern is applied (see Figure 5.17). Methods except those that have to be changed for clipping are directly forwarded to the wrapped VObject object.

Clipping is often necessary in connection with View objects. Recall that View objects represent a drawing area where visual objects can be placed. If a View object were put directly in a Window object, the size of the window would have to be exactly adjusted to the size of the View object and could not be changed. Thus clipping is often used in this context. A View object is clipped by a Clipper object. Since a Clipper object is also a VObject object, the Clipper object is put into the window (or as part of the visual object hierarchy constituting the window contents) instead of the plain View object.

Figure 5.18 exemplifies the clipping property of a Clipper object attached to a View object that contains some visual objects. The size of the View object is larger than that of the Clipper object so that it is clipped by the Clipper object.

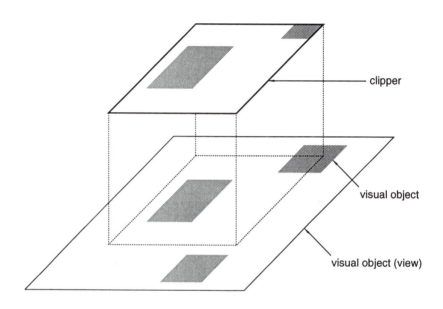

clipper

visual object

visual object (view)

Figure 5.18 Clipping a visual object (a View object).

The displayed portion of the clipped visual object can be scrolled by pressing the left mouse button and dragging the mouse across one of the borders of the Clipper instance.

Most GUIs do not only support this primitive way of scrolling. Scrollbars should be attached to a Clipper instance for a more convenient way of scrolling, as illustrated in Figure 5.19. The hierarchical composition capability of CompositeVObject objects discussed in the previous section is applied in ET++ to compose ScrollBar objects and a Clipper object. This is accomplished by a Scroller object. A Scroller object adds scroll bars to a Clipper instance if necessary, that is, if the visual object shown by the Clipper instance exceeds the size of the Clipper instance in one direction.

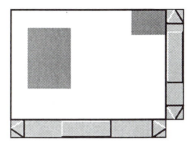

Figure 5.19 Clipper object with scroll bars.

BorderItem is another typical example where the 1:1 Recursive Connection pattern is applied. A BorderItem instance puts a border (possibly with a title integrated into that border) around a VObject object. So this framing behavior can be selectively added to any VObject instance by means of a BorderItem object. Since BorderItem is itself a descendant of VObject, multi-bordered VObject objects can be composed—a BorderItem object can wrap another BorderItem object, and so on.

5.2.5 Flexible object creation (Unification pattern)

The Unification metapattern is applied in many ET++ classes in order to keep object creation flexible. ET++ applies the naming convention that a hook method that keeps the object creation behavior flexible contains the word Make in its name. Methods that start with Do are abstract methods that have to be overridden. For example, DoMakeManager is an example of an abstract hook method that keeps the creation of Manager objects flexible. In this section the methods DoMakeManager, DoMakeContent, DoMakeMenuBar and MakeCmdProcessor are chosen in order to illustrate that object creation is a behavior that has to be kept flexible in various different situations.

Flexible creation of managers
An Application object calls method NewManager, for example, every time a New command is chosen from the File menu. Which specific Manager object is created has to be kept flexible. Thus NewManager does not create a Manager object, but calls DoMakeManager in order to accomplish this task. In a specific application such as the hypertext system, method DoMakeManager has to be overridden in a subclass of Application. In the case of the hypertext system, a HypertextDoc object is created and a reference to that object is returned in HypertextApp::DoMakeManager. Below we express textually how the Unification metapattern is attached to class Application with the hook method DoMakeManager.

Metapattern:	TH
TH->	*Application*
T()->	NewManager()
H()->	*DoMakeManager(): ^Manager*
Hot spot:	the creation of Manager objects

Flexible creation of the window content
A Manager object uses a Window object in order to display its data. The inside of a window has to be a VObject object. This inner visual object is composed of a menu bar and another visual object termed *content* in ET++ terminology. The content is defined in method DoMakeContent, which has to be overridden in descendants of Manager that display their data in a window. For example, in the hypertext system the content of a window associated with a HypertextDoc object is a Scroller object. The visual object that can be scrolled is a VObjectTextView object that displays the data of a HypertextDoc object, that is, the corresponding VObjectText instance. Below we express textually how the Unification metapattern is attached to class Manager with the hook method DoMakeContent.

Metapattern:	TH
TH->	*Manager*
T()->	DoMakeWindows()
H()->	*DoMakeContent(): ^VObject*
Hot spot:	the creation of the visual object representing the content of the associated window

The window content can, of course, be any visual object. For example, in the case of the link and rename dialogs, method DoMakeContent is overridden so that the corresponding composite visual object consisting of several visual objects is returned.

Flexible creation of menu bars
A Manager object uses a Window object in order to display its data. The inside of that window is composed of a menu bar and the content. Method DoMakeMenuBar keeps the creation of the menu bar flexible. Below we express textually how the Unification metapattern is attached to class Manager with DoMakeMenuBar as its hook method.

Metapattern: TH

TH->   *Manager*

T()->   DoMakeWindows()

H()->   DoMakeMenuBar(): ^MenuBar

Hot spot: the creation of the associated window's menu bar

A MenuBar object is composed of several menus. For example, the File and Edit menus are often part of a document window's menu bar. On the other hand, Dialog objects usually have no menu bar at all; that is, DoMakeMenuBar is implemented in class Dialog so that it returns 0. Due to the flexibility that characterizes the underlying Unification pattern, dialogs can have menu bars, too. In this case, DoMakeMenuBar just has to be overridden accordingly in a Dialog subclass.

Flexible creation of command processors
The Unification pattern is also applied in class **Manager** to keep the creation of CommandProcessor objects flexible. Below we express textually how the Unification metapattern is attached to class **Manager** with MakeCmdPro-cessor as hook method.

Metapattern: TH

TH->   Manager

T()->   GetCmdP()

H()->   MakeCmdProcessor(): ^CommandProcessor

Hot spot: the creation of the associated command processor

The default implementation is the creation of a **CommandProcessor1** object whose reference is returned. That allows single-level undo. In order to provide unlimited undo/redo operations, MakeCmdProcessor has to be overridden so that a CommandProcessorN object is created.

5.3   Resulting sample adaptation of ET++

Metapatterns have been applied in Section 5.2 in order to capture and communicate the core design of ET++ components. The adaptation of ET++ to provide the functionality of the hypertext system described in Section 5.1.2 results almost naturally from the design underlying ET++. This section describes the most important implementation issues in that specific application framework adaptation. The design knowledge provided in Section 5.2 should allow understanding of the necessary adaptation steps. The complete source code of the hypertext system is listed in Appendix A for those who are interested in all the adaptation details.

Figure 5.20 gives an overview of the classes that are added in the hypertext system application as descendants of **Manager**. The additional classes are accentuated by a gray background.

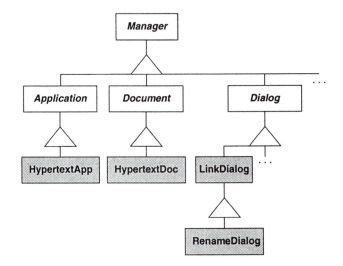

Figure 5.20 Additional descendants of **Manager**.

The additional descendants of **VObject** are depicted in Figure 5.21.

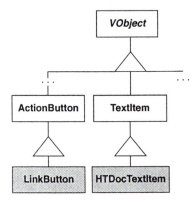

Figure 5.21 Additional descendants of **VObject**.

The hypertext system constitutes an example of an application that is typical of the domain for which ET++ was designed. This sample application corroborates the statement that well-designed application frameworks allow reuse not only of their single building blocks but also of their *architecture*.

The integration of the additional classes requires almost no design expertise. Only the following design issue is specific to the additional classes: defining RenameDialog as a subclass of LinkDialog (see Section 5.3.5 for details) allows reuse of LinkDialog functionality in RenameDialog.

What is actually needed to design the architecture of an application built on the basis of an application framework is to understand the principal architectural design issues of the particular application framework so that the architecture can be reused. Metapatterns can greatly assist in doing this, as exemplified in Section 5.2.

5.3.1 Creation of hypertext documents

In order to adapt the Manager object creation behavior of class Application, a subclass that overrides method DoMakeManagerhas to be specified. Sections 4.2.3 and 5.2.5 discuss the related design issues. The Application subclass is called HypertextApp. Since the hypertext system is document-based, we also have to define and implement a subclass of Document called HypertextDoc. HypertextApp::DoMakeManager creates a HypertextDoc instance as an application-specific Manager object (see Example 5.3).

> **Example 5.3** Creating an application-specific Manager object.
>
> ```
> Manager *HypertextApp::DoMakeManager(Symbol managerType)
> {
>         return new HypertextDoc(managerType);
> }
> ```

The header and implementation files defining and implementing class HypertextApp are listed in Appendix A. Details regarding the adaptation of class Application as shown in these listings adhere to the "Creating documents" recipe presented in Section 3.4.1.

5.3.2 Document adaptations

The abstract class Document has to be adapted in the hypertext system so that the application-specific data (the hypertext) can be stored, displayed and edited. For this purpose the predefined ET++ components MenuBar, Scroller, VObjectText and VObjectTextView are sufficient. We just have to compose the corresponding objects accordingly. No additional classes have to be defined.

Example 5.4 shows the class definition of HypertextDoc with the methods that are relevant in this context. The Boolean instance variables store the corresponding states of a HypertextDoc object which are shown and changed in the Special menu.

Example 5.4 Definition of HypertextDoc in file HypertextDoc.h.

```
class HypertextDoc : public Document {
public:
        MetaDef(HypertextDoc);

        HypertextDoc(Symbol managerType);
        ~HypertextDoc();

        VObject *DoMakeContent();

        MenuBar *DoMakeMenuBar();
        void DoSetupMenu(Menu *menu);
        Command *DoMenuCommand(int cmdId);

        . . .

        CommandProcessor *MakeCmdProcessor();
protected:
        VObjectTextView *vobTxtView;
        VObjectText *vobTxt;
        bool inNavigationMode;
        bool unboundCmdProc;
};
```

Creation of model and view components
The principal components of each HypertextDoc object representing the data and the means to display these data are created in the constructor of HypertextDoc. Example 5.5 shows the creation of these components in boldface. The code also demonstrates that establishing the event handler chains requires almost no programming effort. The first parameter value passed to the constructor of VObjectTextView has to be the reference to the next event handler of the created VObjectTextView instance. By passing a reference to "this" HypertextDoc object, it becomes the next handler of the view.

Example 5.5 Constructor of HypertextDoc.

```
HypertextDoc::HypertextDoc(Symbol managerType)
                                : Document(managerType)
{
        vobTxt= new VObjectText;
```

```
vobTxtView= new VObjectTextView(
                    this,      // This HypertextDoc object
                               // is the next event handler
                               // of the VObjectTextView
                               // object.
                    Point(500, 1000), // initial view size
                    vobTxt);           // the data displayed by
                                       // the view
        inNavigationMode= FALSE;
        unboundCmdProc= TRUE;
}
```

Figure 5.22 illustrates the relationship between a HypertextDoc object and its associated VObjectTextView and VObjectText objects and how these components correspond to the MVC concept.

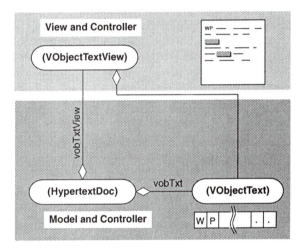

Figure 5.22 Relationship between the components of a document.

According to the design of Manager discussed in Section 5.2.5, method DoMakeContent has to be overridden in order to define the content of the window that shows the data represented by a hypertext document. Example 5.6 lists the corresponding code of that method.

Example 5.6 Specification of the window content.

```
VObject *HypertextDoc::DoMakeContent()
{
        SetFirstHandler(vobTxtView);
```

```
                    return new Scroller(vobTxtView);
            }
```

According to the design discussed in Section 5.2.2, the VObjectTextView
instance referred to by the instance variable vobTxtView in a HypertextDoc
object is defined as the first event handler in an event handler chain consisting
of a VObjectTextView instance followed by the corresponding HypertextDoc
instance and the HypertextApp object.

    This VObjectTextView instance is wrapped in a Scroller object, so that
the view is clipped and the portion of the view that is visible through that
Scroller object can be scrolled.

Menu bar adaptation

The menu bar of a HypertextDoc object should contain the menus File, Edit,
Fonts, Styles, Sizes, Insert, and Special. Some ET++ classes such as class
Manager offer a method MakeMenu that creates a default menu depending on
the value of the passed integer parameter. The menus Edit, Fonts, Styles, and
Sizes used in the hypertext system are ET++ default menus which are created
by calling MakeMenu with the corresponding identification constant (see
Example 5.7). Instead of the default File menu, a customized File menu is
defined in HypertextDoc::DoMakeMenuBar. That File menu does not, for
example, contain menu items such as Save and Save As since the hypertext
system application does not provide this functionality. Analogously, the
menus Insert and Special are created and appended to the menu bar.

Example 5.7 Menu bar adaptation in class HypertextDoc.

```
MenuBar *HypertextDoc::DoMakeMenuBar()
{
        MenuBar *mb= new MenuBar;
        //---- File menu
        Menu *fileMenu= new Menu("File");
        fileMenu->AppendItems(
                "New@N",                 cNEW,
                "Close",                 cCLOSE,
                "-",                     // a line item is inserted
                "Print ...@P",           cPRINT,
                "-",
                "Rename ...@R",          cIdRename,
                "-",
                "Quit@Q",                cQUIT,
                0
        );
        mb->AddMenu(fileMenu);
```

```
// append default ET++ menus
mb->AddMenu(MakeMenu(cEDITMENU));
mb->AddMenu(TextView::MakeMenu(cFONTMENU));
mb->AddMenu(TextView::MakeMenu(cSTYLEMENU));
mb->AddMenu(TextView::MakeMenu(cSIZEMENU));


//---- Insert menu
Menu *insertMenu= new Menu("Insert");
insertMenu->AppendItem("Link Button",
                            cIdInsertLinkButton);
mb->AddMenu(insertMenu);


//---- Special menu
Menu *specialMenu= new Menu("Special",
                        FALSE,          // dim all?
                        FALSE);         // reset all?
                                        // FALSE =>
                                        // menu with
                                        // check boxes
specialMenu->AppendItems(
        "Navigation mode",         cIdMode,
        "-",
        "Unlimited Undo-Levels",   cIdUndoLevels,
        0
);

// Set check boxes depending upon the values of the
// corresponding instance variables that have been set
// in the constructor.
specialMenu->CheckItem(cIdMode, inNavigationMode);

specialMenu->CheckItem(cIdUndoLevels,
                        unboundCmdProc);
mb->AddMenu(specialMenu);


// Allow the VObjectTextView instance to modify the Edit
// menu so that menu items for find/change requests
// can be offered.
FindChange::InstallChange(mb, vobTxtView);

return mb;
}
```

Section 5.3.3 discusses how events related to the defined menus are handled in the methods DoSetupMenu and DoMenuCommand.

Unlimited undo/redo levels

The Command object handling strategy of a HypertextDoc object is defined by associating one instance of the predefined CommandProcessor subclass with a document. The default command processing strategy of a document object is one-level undo/redo, that is, a CommandProcessor1 instance is associated with a document. In order to define a different command processing strategy, method MakeCmdProcessor has to be overridden. Example 5.8 demonstrates this for HypertextDoc. Creating a CommandProcessorN instance and returning a reference to the object implies unlimited undo/redo levels in the corresponding HypertextDoc object.

Example 5.8   Defining the command processing strategy.

```
CommandProcessor *HypertextDoc::MakeCmdProcessor()
{
        if (unboundCmdProc)                    // set in the constructor
                return new CommandProcessorN;
        else
                return new CommandProcessor1;
}
```

Since a Manager object and a CommandProcessor object are composed based on the 1:1 Connection pattern as discussed in Section 5.2.2, the command processing strategy can be switched at run time. The necessary code is discussed in Section 5.3.3. If the flexibility of the command processing strategy was based on the Unification pattern (incorporated in former versions of ET++), this behavior could not be changed at run time.

5.3.3 Event handling

A HypertextDoc object has to handle the events that correspond to its specific menus, that is, the Rename menu item in the File menu, the Link Button menu item in the Insert menu and the menu items Navigation Mode and Unlimited Undo Levels in the Special menu.

Besides handling these menu commands, mouse clicks on the link buttons inserted in the text have to be handled accordingly: if a HypertextDoc object is in navigation mode, the text document associated with a particular button has to be opened when the user clicks on that button. If the HypertextDoc object is not in navigation mode, the link dialog has to be opened.

Hypertext-specific menu items

Recall that for each HypertextDoc object an event handler chain is defined with the corresponding VObjectTextView object as its first handler, followed by the particular HypertextDoc object and the HypertextApp object.

The menu commands defined in the ET++ default menus Edit, Fonts, Styles, and Sizes are handled by the VObjectTextView object. In order to handle the specific menu items defined for a HypertextDoc object, the methods DoSetupMenu and DoMenuCommand have to be defined and implemented in HypertextDoc, adhering to the structure of template-hook methods in the 1:1 Recursive Unification pattern. Method DoSetupMenu (see Example 5.9) calls the superclass method so that the message passing along the event handler chain is not interrupted.

Example 5.9 Implementation of DoSetupMenu in HypertextDoc.

```
void HypertextDoc::DoSetupMenu(Menu *menu)
{
        Document::DoSetupMenu(menu);
        FindChange::DoSetupMenu(menu);
        menu->EnableItems(
                cldRename,       // enable Rename  (File menu)
                cldMode,         // enable Navigation Mode (Special
                                 // menu)
                cldUndoLevels,   // enable Unlimited Undo Levels
                                 // (Special menu)

                0
        );

        // Enable/disable Link Button depending on the current
        // mode.    (Insert menu)
        menu->EnableItem(cldInsertLinkButton,
                        !inNavigationMode);
}
```

Example 5.10 shows the skeleton of method DoMenuCommand. If a HypertextDoc-specific menu item is selected, the DoMenuCommand message is not passed along the event handler chain—no other object can handle the specific menu item selection. Otherwise (default branch of the **switch** statement) the message is passed along the event handler chain.

Some branches of the switch statement might not return a reference to a Command object. Thus gNoChanges is returned after the **switch** statement. For example, in the case of cldRename, the rename dialog is opened. No Command object is used since this action does not need to be undoable, so the action is directly coded in the corresponding case branch (see below).

Example 5.10 Structure of DoMenuCommand in HypertextDoc.

```
Command *HypertextDoc::DoMenuCommand(int cmdId)
{
        switch (cmdId) {
                case cldRename:
                        . . .
                        break;
                case cldInsertLinkButton:
                        . . .
                        break;
                . . .
                default:
                        return
                                Document::DoMenuCommand(cmdId);
        }
        return gNoChanges;        // global variable predefined in
                                  // ET++ that refers to a Command
                                  // object that causes no action

}
```

In the following we discuss how to handle the specific menu items in the case branches of DoMenuCommand. The corresponding code partially relies on the classes LinkButton and RenameDialog. Details regarding these classes are discussed below. We just have to know in advance that **RenameDialog** offers a method ShowUnderMouse that opens that dialog. Instances of class LinkButton represent the buttons inserted into the text as single characters. LinkButton provides a method SetState in order to set the state of a LinkButton object to be in navigation mode (TRUE passed as the parameter value to SetState) or creation mode (FALSE).

If the menu item Rename is selected from the File menu, method DoMenuCommand is called with the parameter value clcRename. Example 5.11 shows how to open the corresponding rename dialog. The implementation demonstrates how to avoid the creation of another RenameDialog instance every time the Rename menu item is selected. A variable gRenameDialog is defined as a static variable so that it can only be accessed within the file where it is declared. If the Rename menu item has been selected for the first time, an instance of RenameDialog is created and its reference assigned to gRenameDialog. The same coding pattern is applied in the link dialog in class LinkButton.

Example 5.11 Handling the menu command Rename.

```
static RenameDialog *gRenameDialog;
. . .
Command *HypertextDoc::DoMenuCommand(int cmdId)
```

```
        {
                switch (cmdId) {
                        . . .
                        case cldRename:
                                if (!gRenameDialog)
                                        gRenameDialog=
                                                new RenameDialog;
                                gRenameDialog->ShowUnderMouse();
                                break;
                        . . .
        }
```

If the menu item Link Button is selected from the Insert menu, method DoMenuCommand is called with the parameter value cldInsertLinkButton. Example 5.12 shows how to insert a LinkButton object into the text as a single character by means of a PasteVObjectCommand object. The predefined class PasteVObjectCommand implements the insertion of a visual object in such a way that the command is undoable.

Example 5.12   Handling the menu command Link Button.

```
                        . . .
                        case cldInsertLinkButton:
                                LinkButton *lb= new LinkButton;
                                lb->SetState(inNavigationMode);
                                return new  PasteVObjectCommand(
                                                vobTxtView, lb
                                );
                        . . .
```

If the menu item Navigation Mode is selected from the Special menu, method DoMenuCommand is called with the parameter value cldMode. In this case the state of all LinkButton objects contained in the text has to be toggled (see Example 5.13). In order to keep the code more readable, we use pseudonotation to represent iteration over the link buttons contained in the text. A VObjectText instance returns a collection of all contained visual objects by sending the message GetVisualMarks. Some further coding is necessary in order to actually get access to the LinkButton objects. The code listed in Appendix A shows these details.

Note that the check box in the menu item Navigation Mode that indicates the mode of a HypertextDoc object is automatically toggled by the Menu object; no further code is required for that. Toggling the instance variable inNavigationMode implies that the menu item Link Button in the Insert menu is either enabled or disabled (see Example 5.9).

If a HypertextDoc object is in navigation mode, no text editing should be possible. As a consequence, the message SetReadOnly with the current value of inNavigationMode is sent to the associated VObjectTextView instance.

Example 5.13   Handling the menu command Navigation Mode.

```
. . .
case cldMode:
        inNavigationMode = !inNavigationMode;
        vobTxtView->SetReadOnly(
                        inNavigationMode
        );
        for each lb: <LinkButton *> in
                        vobTxt->GetVisualMarks()
                        lb->SetState(inNavigationMode);
        break;
. . .
```

If the menu item Unlimited Undo Levels is selected from the Special menu, method DoMenuCommand is called with the parameter value cldUndoLevels. The CommandProcessor object associated with a HypertextDoc object is switched as shown in Example 5.14 by calling SetCmdProcessor, a method that is defined and implemented in class Manager.

Example 5.14   Handling the menu command Unlimited Undo Levels.

```
. . .
case cldUndoLevels:
        unboundCmdProc = !unboundCmdProc;
        if (unboundCmdProc)
                SetCmdProcessor(
                        new CommandProcessorN);
        else
                SetCmdProcessor(
                        new CommandProcessor1);
        break;
. . .
```

Mouse clicks on link buttons
Recall the ET++ event handling principle that each event handler does its share of the overall task to be accomplished. DoSetupMenu and DoMenuCommand are the corresponding methods for dealing with menus. Class EvtHandler offers the method Control in order to react to events such as mouse clicks. For example, if a user clicks on an ActionButton object

displayed in a VObjectTextView instance, the Control method of that button is called automatically. If a specific action should be caused by the mouse click event, the Control method has to be overridden accordingly.

For this purpose we define class LinkButton as a subclass of ActionButton. The implementation of Control depends on the state of a LinkButton object. In accordance with HypertextDoc, the corresponding instance variable that stores the state is called inNavigationMode. Furthermore, we must define an instance variable that refers to the HypertextDoc object that should be opened if the link button is pressed in navigation mode. That instance variable is called targetHTDoc. The instance variable targetHTDoc is set to the hypertext document selected in the collection view of the link dialog when the user presses the Define Link button in that dialog (see Section 5.3.5).

Example 5.15 shows the aspects of the definition of class LinkButton that are relevant in the context of handling mouse clicks.

Example 5.15 Definition of class LinkButton.

```
class LinkButton : public ActionButton {
public:
          MetaDef(LinkButton);
          LinkButton();

          void SetTargetHTDoc(HypertextDoc *htDoc);
          HypertextDoc *GetTargetHTDoc();

          void SetState(bool state);          // state == TRUE
                                               // => navigation mode
          bool GetState();

          void Control(int id, int part, void *val);
          . . .

protected:
          HypertextDoc *targetHTDoc;           // target hypertext
                                               // document
          bool inNavigationMode;     // TRUE =>
                                     // The linked hypertext
                                     // document is presented when
                                     // I'm activated.
                                     // FALSE =>
                                     // The hypertext document I
                                     // should be linked to can be
                                     // specified in the link dialog.

          . . .
};
```

Example 5.16 shows the corresponding implementation of Control in class LinkButton. LinkButton::Control calls Control of its superclass first. The superclass method implements the usual visual feedback when an action button is clicked.

Note that the parameters are simply passed to the superclass method. The parameters would allow the exact identification of the event that caused the invocation of the Control method. In the case of an action button, a mouse click is the only event that causes a call of Control. No detailed checks are necessary. For example, a single click and a double click should not be distinguished.

Example 5.16 Event handling in LinkButton.

```
static LinkDialog *gLinkDialog;
. . .
void LinkButton::Control(int id, int part, void *val)
{
        ActionButton::Control(id, part, val);

        if (inNavigationMode) {
                if (targetHTDoc)  // Check whether the reference
                                  // is already set.
                        targetHTDoc->Open();
                } else {
                        if (!gLinkDialog)  // Generate the dialog
                                           // exactly once when it is
                                           // needed for the first
                                           // time.
                                gLinkDialog= new LinkDialog;
                        gLinkDialog->SetLinkButton(this);
                        gLinkDialog->ShowUnderMouse();
                }
}
```

A link button behaves differently according to its state as prescribed by the instance variable inNavigationMode. One could argue that the 1:1 Connection metapattern with the semantics of the State framework could be applied in the realm of class LinkButton instead of an instance variable inNavigationMode (see Figure 5.23). A separate class Role that offers a method Control could be defined. LinkButton::Control would just pass the request to handle a mouse click to the associated Role object by sending the message Control to it. Subclasses of Role, that is, NavigationRole and CreationRole, would override the Control method of Role accordingly. This is demonstrated in Figure 5.23 for NavigationRole::Control. The appropriate Role object has to be associated with a LinkButton object in SetState.

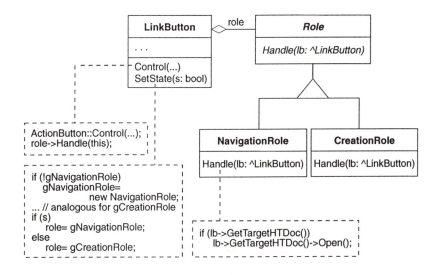

Figure 5.23 Inappropriate use of the 1:1 Connection pattern.

Defining a separate class Role for this purpose would make the design of the event handling mechanism in LinkButton objects unnecessarily complicated. The solution with the instance variable inNavigationMode is lean and elegant. In the example outlined in Figure 5.23, the rule of thumb to define classes for one abstraction is violated. The Role class proposed above is too trivial to be considered as a useful abstraction. Role objects lack critical mass; that is, they offer too little functionality to be considered as an abstraction that is modeled by a class.

Recall class CommandProcessor, whose objects cooperate with Manager objects based on the 1:1 Connection pattern. In that example class CommandProcessor is an adequate abstraction, that is, offers enough functionality to be modeled in a class.

5.3.4 Change propagation

The label of a link button always has to be the name of the HypertextDoc object to which a particular link button refers. Of course, several link buttons (maybe displayed in different HypertextDoc objects) can refer to one HypertextDoc object. Figure 5.24 illustrates this schematically for two LinkButton objects. In Figure 5.24(a) the two LinkButton objects refer to a HypertextDoc object with the name Hello. If the name of the HypertextDoc object is changed to Hi the labels of the link buttons have to be changed, too (see Figure 5.24(b)).

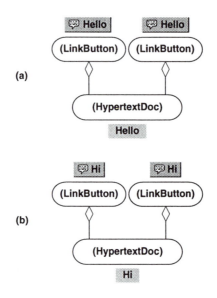

Figure 5.24 Dependencies between link button labels and the name of a document.

The change propagation mechanism offered by the ET++ class **Object** (see Section 5.2.1) is designed to implement the desired behavior (see Example 5.17). Every time a HypertextDoc object is associated as the target document of a LinkButton object, that link button has to become an observing object of the corresponding HypertextDoc object. (Note that these observer relationships are not depicted in Figure 5.24.) If the LinkButton object already refers to a HypertextDoc object, it has to be removed from the corresponding list of observers. Method DoObserve is overridden so that the label of the particular button is changed accordingly.

Example 5.17 Defining a link button as observer of a HypertextDoc object.

```
void LinkButton::SetTargetHTDoc(HypertextDoc *htDoc)
{
        if (targetHTDoc)
                targetHTDoc->RemoveObserver(this);
        targetHTDoc= htDoc;
        if (targetHTDoc)
                targetHTDoc->AddObserver(this);
        AdaptLabelToHTDoc();    // Sets the label of the button to
                                // the name of the target hypertext
                                // document.

}
. . .
```

```
void LinkButton::DoObserve(int, int, void *, Object *)
{
        AdaptLabelToHTDoc();
}
```

A HypertextDoc object has to take care that the message DoObserve is sent to all its observing objects every time its name is changed. For that purpose, HypertextDoc simply overrides SetName as shown in Example 5.18. (The message SetName is sent from the rename dialog to HypertextDoc objects.) The invocation of Send in HypertextDoc::SetName causes the message DoObserve to be sent to all observing objects.

Example 5.18   Informing the observing link buttons.

```
void HypertextDoc::SetName(const char *name)
{
        Document::SetName(name);
        Send();         // Inform the observing link buttons that
                        // I've changed my name.
}
```

Note that a HypertextDoc object does not have to care which LinkButton objects are observing it. It is the task of the LinkButton objects to register/un-register as observers of a HypertextDoc object.

A problem arises if a LinkButton object is deleted. This could happen if a text portion that contains a LinkButton object is deleted. This would cause a dangling pointer—the reference to the deleted LinkButton object is still in the observer list of the last HypertextDoc object it referred to. In order to solve this problem, the destructor of LinkButton has to be implemented as shown in Example 5.19.

Example 5.19   Avoiding dangling pointers.

```
LinkButton::~LinkButton()
{
        if (targetHTDoc)
                targetHTDoc->RemoveObserver(this);
}
```

5.3.5 Dialogs

Dialog is a subclass of Manager that is specifically designed to handle dialogs. We do not discuss all the details offered by this class. Instead, we focus on the two methods DoMakeContent and DoSetup that have to be overridden for the link and rename dialogs.

As already discussed above, DoMakeContent defines the content of the window associated with the Dialog object. Contrary to the Scroller object that forms the content of a window associated with a HypertextDoc object, the content of the link and rename dialog windows is composed of typical dialog items such as buttons, text items and a collection view (see Figure 5.25). Visual object hierarchies with layout attributes are defined in DoMakeContent according to Section 5.2.3.

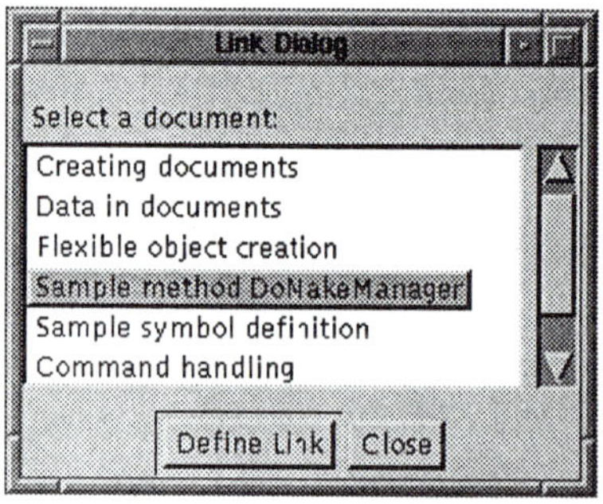

Figure 5.25 Link dialog.

DoSetup is called every time the dialog window is opened by calling ShowUnderMouse. So method DoSetup can be overridden in order to set up a dialog, for example, to enable or disable dialog items. In the link and rename dialogs the contents of the collection view are also set in DoSetup. This collection view lists the names of all HypertextDoc objects that are managed by the application.

Collection of document names

A CollectionView object can handle any Collection object containing visual objects. The contained visual objects are listed in a CollectionView object. A collection view also handles events such as mouse clicks to allow the selection of these visual objects.

In order to reuse class CollectionView, we have to build up a collection of visual objects that represent the document names. Class TextItem is suited for that task.

Since HypertextDoc objects are not uniquely identified by their names—several HypertextDoc objects might have the same name—the reference to the HypertextDoc object represented by a TextItem object has to be stored with that text item. For this purpose we adapt TextItem in a subclass HTDocTextItem so that a relationship between an HTDocTextItem object and a HypertextDoc object can be established as shown in Figure 5.26. For this purpose HTDocTextItem simply has to add an instance variable targetHTDoc of type pointer to HypertextDoc and offer the methods SetTargetHTDoc and GetTargetHTDoc.

Figure 5.26 Relationship between an HTDocTextItem object and a HypertextDoc object.

Based on HTDocTextItem, method LinkDialog::BuildHTDocList first creates an ObjList instance, then creates an HTDocTextItem instance for each Hypertext-Doc object managed by the application and adds each HTDocTextItem object to the list (see Example 5.20). In order to keep the code more readable we use a pseudonotation to represent iteration over the Manager objects managed by the HypertextApp object. The predefined global reference variable gApplication refers to the one and only HypertextApp object. GetManagers is a pseudonym. The actual implementation listed in Appendix A has to use method MakeIterator in order to implement the iteration loop.

Example 5.20 Creation of the document name list.

```
ObjList *LinkDialog::BuildHTDocList()
{
        ObjList *managedDocs= new ObjList;
        for each hd: <HypertextDoc *> in
                        gApplication->GetManagers()
                managedDocs->Add(
                        new HTDocTextItem(hd->GetName(), hd)
                );
        return managedDocs;
}
```

BuildHTDocList is used in the constructor of LinkDialog and in DoSetup to define the visual objects contained in a CollectionView object (see Example 5.21).

Example 5.21 Selected aspects of class LinkDialog.

```
class definition:
        class LinkDialog: public Dialog {
        public:
                MetaDef(LinkDialog);
```

```
                    LinkDialog();
                    VObject *DoMakeContent();
                    void DoSetup();
                    . . .
        protected:
                    HypertextDoc *targetHTDoc;        // target hypertext
                                                      // document defined
                                                      // for link button

                    CollectionView *htDocsView;
                    ObjList *BuildHTDocList();
                    . . .

        };
```

class implementation:
```
        LinkDialog::LinkDialog() : Dialog("Link Dialog")
        {
                    htDocsView= new CollectionView(
                                        this,           // I'm the next
                                                        // event handler
                                        BuildHTDocList()
                                );
                    htDocsView->SetId(cldHTDocsView);
                    . . .

        }
        . . .

        void LinkDialog::DoSetup()
        {
                    htDocsView->SetCollection(BuildHTDocList());
                                        // The collection
                                        // originally displayed by
                                        // htDocsView is freed.
                    targetHTDoc= 0;     // No document name is selected
                                        // yet.

                    . . .

        }
```

Event handling

Method Control is also overridden in order to handle events. Nevertheless, a more fine-grained implementation of Control is necessary (see Example 5.22) than LinkButton::Control. In LinkDialog::Control the first parameter is used to identify which dialog item was activated. If the user selects an item in the collection view, Control is invoked with the parameter value cldHTDocsView. Based on the selected document name the instance variable targetHTDoc is set accordingly. (This is done by sending the selected HTDocTextItem object the message GetTargetHTDoc.)

If the user presses the Define Link button, the target hypertext document associated with a LinkButton object is set by sending the message SetTargetHTDoc to the LinkButton object for which the dialog was opened.

Example 5.22 Event handling in a link dialog.

```
void LinkDialog::Control(int id, int part, void *v)
{
        switch (id) {
                case cldHTDocsView: {
                        . . .      // Enable the Define Link button.
                        targetHTDoc=    hypertext document that
                                        corresponds to the item
                                        selected in the collection
                                        view
                        break;
                case cldDefineLink:
                        if (targetHTDoc) {
                                linkButton->SetTargetHTDoc(
                                                targetHTDoc);
                                // close the dialog:
                                Dialog::Control(id, part, v);
                        }
                        break;
                        . . .

                }
        }
```

Rename dialog
Defining RenameDialog as a subclass of LinkDialog allows reuse of LinkDialog's behavior for handling the collection view of document names. The implementation of RenameDialog listed in Appendix A is analogous to LinkDialog and self-explanatory.

5.4   Summarizing remarks

Recall that the main purpose of design patterns is to capture the design of a framework and its individual classes without revealing implementation details. Such abstract design descriptions should allow communication of mature designs in an efficient way. As a consequence, design patterns can help to adapt a framework to specific needs and to construct new frameworks which incorporate mature and proven designs.

This chapter demonstrates that metapatterns are suited for attachment to a complex application framework. Contrary to design pattern catalogs that contain more or less domain-independent framework examples, metapatterns prove to be suited to annotating a complex, domain-specific framework in an efficient way.

The core characteristic of any framework is that various aspects have to be kept flexible while others are standardized. The essential design that has to be communicated includes the hot spots of a framework and the degree of flexibility inherent in these hot spots. Metapatterns point out exactly this design information. The hook methods and hook classes show the hot spots of a framework. The characteristics of a particular metapattern describe the degree of flexibility. For example, the Unification metapattern that has object creation behavior as a hot spot does not allow adaptations at run time. Other metapatterns such as the 1:1 Connection metapattern allow run-time adaptations. We demonstrated this for the hot spot "command processing strategy" in the realm of the components **Manager** and **CommandProcessor**.

Understanding ET++'s principal design implies that adaptation steps become quite natural. Section 5.2 just pointed out those design aspects that are relevant for the ET++ adaptation in the realm of the hypertext system application. Of course, metapatterns could be attached analogously to other components of ET++ in order to capture their design.

So metapatterns represent an excellent means of communicating a framework's design in an efficient way on an abstraction level significantly higher than the underlying implementation language. They can be attached to any (application) framework.

Nevertheless, framework cookbooks are still considered useful in the realm of framework adaptations since they can describe all implementation details required for an adaptation. For example, many language-specific details have to be considered in successfully adapting a framework.

Metapatterns can stimulate the design of new (application) frameworks. A software engineer who grasps the design of a domain-specific framework might find some aspects that are domain-independent and that can be applied in other frameworks. In ET++ the layout specification and (re)calculation of hierarchically grouped visual objects is such an example. For instance, this design idea might be reused in the development of a framework for virtual reality applications.

Furthermore, studying the design of an application framework with near perfect abstractions might motivate finding such abstractions in frameworks for other domains. For example, the abstract class **VObject** gives an impression of how the overall design of the application framework benefits from such an abstraction—the flexibility offered by ET++ to combine almost freely any visual objects stems from that abstraction. The reader should imagine the effort that would be required to implement a hypertext system with a GUI application framework that does not offer the visual object abstraction and building blocks like **VObjectText** and **VObjectTextView** that are based on this abstraction. Without the well-designed abstract class **VObject** it would be impossible to offer such powerful yet flexible building blocks.

Chapter 6

Implications for software development

Metapatterns capture and communicate the design of frameworks, thus supporting the adaptation of frameworks and the development of new frameworks. This chapter focuses on the latter aspect of metapatterns.

The previous chapters have already demonstrated the benefits of frameworks. Since metapatterns and the proposed enhancement of existing object-oriented analysis and design (OOAD) methodologies are based on frameworks, we briefly summarize the characteristics of object-oriented frameworks in the following section.

Design patterns are viewed by many authors (for instance, Gamma 1992) as a complement to OOAD methodologies. We think that design pattern catalogs complementing existing OOAD methodologies are insufficient to actively support the development of frameworks. Based on an outline of typical OOAD methodologies we propose an enhancement of these methodologies called the *hot-spot-driven approach*. We point out how metapatterns can actively support this approach.

6.1 Framework-centered software development

The principal characteristic of a framework is that it consists of ready-to-use and semifinished building blocks. Well-designed (application) frameworks also predefine most of the overall architecture, that is, the composition and interaction of its components. (Well-designed means that a framework offers the domain-specific hot spots and the desired flexibility to adapt those hot spots.) So not only source code but also architecture design—which might be considered as an even more important characteristic of frameworks—is reused in applications built on top of a framework.

The GUI application framework ET++ discussed in Chapter 5 gives an impressive example of the degree of reusability that can be achieved in well-designed frameworks. Besides allowing reuse of the architecture of the framework (as demonstrated in the hypertext system application), Weinand *et al.* (1989) state that writing an application with a complex GUI by adapting ET++ can result in a reduction in source code size (that is, the source code that has to be written by the programmer who adapts the framework) of *80% percent or more* compared to software written with the support of a conventional graphic toolbox.

Frameworks and metapatterns

The previous chapter demonstrated how metapatterns can capture the design of a complex yet mature application framework. The question is how frameworks for any domain can be developed based on the experience gained in the development of already existing frameworks.

Metapatterns can assist in this process as soon as the domain-specific hot spots have been identified. By means of metapatterns the degree of flexibility can be fine-tuned. Nevertheless, the initial step has to be the identification of these hot spots. Domain-specific knowledge is required to find them. In order to make a more efficient development of frameworks possible, we propose a hot-spot-driven approach as a necessary enhancement of existing OOAD methodologies. Metapatterns can then actively support the development of well-designed frameworks that accommodate the hot spots. This vision is outlined in Section 6.3.

Framework development process

Once the initial hot spots have been identified, the actual framework development process starts. This software development process differs radically from conventional software development. The well-known software life-cycle models are barely useful for describing the development of frameworks. Meyer's cluster model of the software life cycle (Meyer 1990) is a general characterization of the flavor of framework development; a cluster, in this context, is a group of related classes constituting one life cycle.

An interesting aspect of the framework development process is that design and implementation are typically intertwined. For example, the design of class VObject in ET++ evolved during the implementation of other ET++ components. The implementation of other components that use VObject revealed design deficiencies in class VObject. So some components were in the implementation phase while others were being (re)designed at the same time. Also, the migration of VObject up the class hierarchy evolved during the implementation and (re)design of ET++ components. In general, a framework development team has to be prepared and willing to radically redesign and reimplement components if new and/or better abstractions are found.

The hot-spot-driven approach proposed in this chapter might contribute to finding appropriate abstractions faster so that the number of redesign cycles might be reduced. In order to demonstrate the complementary nature of a hot-spot-driven approach with regard to existing OOAD methodologies, we outline some representative methodologies in the following section.

6.2   Limits of state-of-the-art OOAD methodologies

Conventional (as opposed to object-oriented) software engineering methodologies mainly use data flow diagrams. One of the most widespread representations of the data flow approach is Structured Analysis/Structured Design (SA/SD), a well-documented methodology which can be applied to many problems. This methodology is described in detail by, for instance, Yourdon (1979, 1989) and DeMarco (1979).

SA/SD does not only use data flow diagrams for specifying software systems. Process specifications, a data dictionary, state transition diagrams, and entity/relationship diagrams are applied in the analysis phase to describe a system. The design phase adds various details to the analysis model. Many of the object-oriented methodologies, such as the Object Model Technique (OMT) (Rumbaugh *et al.* 1991) and Booch's method (Booch 1991) evolved from SA/SD.

We selected OMT as a representative example with which to sketch the core characteristics of an object-oriented methodology. Class-Responsibility-Collaboration (CRC) cards proposed by Beck and Cunningham (1989) are a simple yet powerful noncomputerized object-oriented analysis/design vehicle. Our brief outline of OMT and CRC cards is intended to point out the limits of state-of-the-art OOAD methodologies as far as frameworks are concerned.

Object Modeling Technique
OMT belongs to the category of full-fledged OOAD methodologies like those proposed by Booch (1991), Coad and Yourdon (1990), Jacobson (1992), and Wirfs-Brock *et al.* (1990). Rumbaugh *et al.* (1991) confirm our point of view that these full-fledged object-oriented methodologies are conceptually quite similar despite significant differences in their notations: "All of the object-oriented methodologies, including ours, have much in common, and should be contrasted more with non-object-oriented methodologies than with each other."

OMT consists of two major components: a set of notations to express modeling concepts and the actual design methodology.

The *object model notation* depicts the static structure of objects/classes and their relationships. We used this notation throughout this book. We do not discuss the other two notations applied to describe the dynamic model and the function model. OMT uses notations almost identical to SA/SD for that purpose. The object model notation evolved from the entity/relationship notation, too. That notation was enhanced to allow the expression of object-oriented concepts such as inheritance. Compared to SA/SD, where data flow diagrams dominate, the object model is regarded as a first-class citizen in OMT.

The proposed design methodology tries to give hints and to describe how to formulate the object, dynamic, and functional models. OMT's methodology covers the software life-cycle phases analysis, design and implementation, though the emphasis is put on analysis and design.

Details of how to accomplish certain tasks in the various phases are described in a vague manner. For identifying object classes, for example, OMT suggests a vague method already known from Abbott (1983): candidate classes are found in a verbal description of the problem that has to be solved by a software system.

We selected some proposed steps for object design from Rumbaugh *et al.* (1991):

- Operations for the object model can be obtained from the other models, for example, an operation could correspond to an event in the dynamic model.

- Algorithms that implement operations have to be designed. For example, algorithms that minimize the cost of implementing operations should be chosen.

- Software control should be implemented by fleshing out the approach chosen during system design.

- The class structure has to be adjusted to increase inheritance. For example, common behavior should be abstracted out of groups of classes.

To sum up, OMT is limited in that the development and adaptation of frameworks are not primarily addressed in that methodology. A statement by Rumbaugh *et al.* (1991) corroborates that point of view: how to formulate a model "is language-independent and applies *equally well* to object-oriented languages, traditional procedural languages, and databases."

The general rules of thumb might assist in the development of well-structured object-oriented systems, but barely in the development of advanced object-oriented frameworks as discussed in this book. The same is true for other full-fledged state-of-the-art OOAD methodologies.

CRC cards

The CRC card approach was presented by Kent Beck and Ward Cunningham (1989) at the OOPSLA'89 conference. CRC cards are especially helpful in finding objects/classes. Thus they can be viewed as a complement to the method proposed by Abbott (1983). Finding classes in a verbal description according to Abbott would be the first step. The classes found and their collaborations can be refined by means of CRC cards.

So CRC cards are a basic vehicle for object-oriented analysis and design. They are not and were never intended to be a full-fledged OOAD methodology. But the CRC card method can be part of an OOAD methodology. For example, the full-fledged OOAD methodology proposed by Wirfs-Brock *et al.* (1990) incorporates the CRC card approach.

CRC cards are plain index cards as used in offices. Figure 6.1 exemplifies the scheme of an index card for describing the ET++ class View.

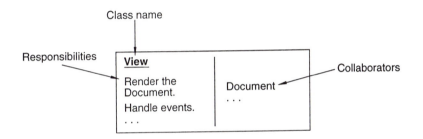

Figure 6.1 Sample CRC card.

The collaborator Document listed in the card for class View expresses the relationship between these two classes. The responsibilities are described informally in a concise manner, ignoring implementation-specific details.

CRC cards are primarily intended to help in understanding the relationships between classes/objects based on scenarios. For this purpose designers have to handle real cards and arrange cards so that strongly related cards are closer to each other. Real cards are viewed as better suited for this purpose than computerized ones. Beck and Cunningham (1989) stress the value of physically moving the cards around: "When learners/designers pick up an object, they seem to more readily identify with it, and are prepared to deal with the remainder of the design from its perspective."

Conclusion

Of course, finding classes is an initial activity in the development process of any object-oriented system, especially of frameworks. The various methods proposed by OOAD methodologies, such as a combination of Abbott's method and CRC cards, are useful for that initial step. Nevertheless, state-of-the-art OOAD methodologies offer no appropriate means to assist in the development of frameworks. The hot-spot-driven approach envisioned in the following section as a complementary enhancement of state-of-the-art OOAD methodologies is a first step in that direction.

6.3   Vision of a hot-spot-driven approach

Successful framework development requires the identification of domain-specific hot spots (see Figure 6.2). The various aspects of a framework that cannot be anticipated for all adaptations have to be implemented in a generic way.

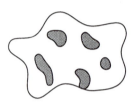

Figure 6.2   Framework with flexible hot spots.

As a consequence, domain experts have to be asked: Which aspects differ from application to application? What is the desired degree of flexibility? Must the flexible behavior be changeable at run time?

For example, in the domain of reservation systems the initial *hot-spot-driven analysis* might reveal that the rate calculation has to become one of the hot spots of an application framework for that domain. If how rental rates are calculated for a rental item has to be kept flexible, the Unification metapattern could be chosen in the framework design as shown in Figure 6.3.

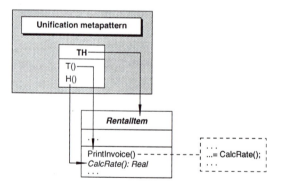

Figure 6.3   A hot spot based on the Unification metapattern.

So reservation systems built by adapting this framework have to specify the rate calculation in a subclass of RentalItem. For example, a class HotelRoom in a hotel reservation system will override CalcRate differently than a class Vehicle in a car rental reservation system.

If the rate calculation must be kept flexible at run time, the 1:1 Connection metapattern would be appropriate as shown in Figure 6.4.

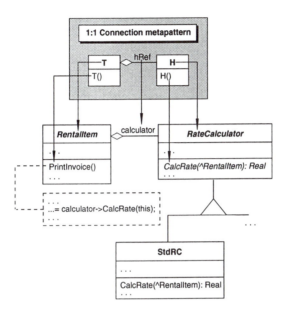

Figure 6.4 A hot spot based on the 1:1 Connection metapattern.

In the event that several, flexibly combinable rate calculators should cooperate to accomplish the rate calculation task, the 1:1 Recursive Unification metapattern could be chosen, as shown in Figure 6.5, for passing rate calculation messages along a chain of rate calculators.

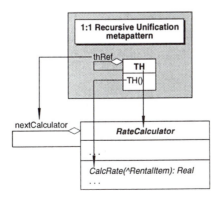

Figure 6.5 A hot spot based additionally on the 1:1 Recursive Unification metapattern.

So the hot-spot-driven approach can be depicted schematically as shown in Figure 6.6.

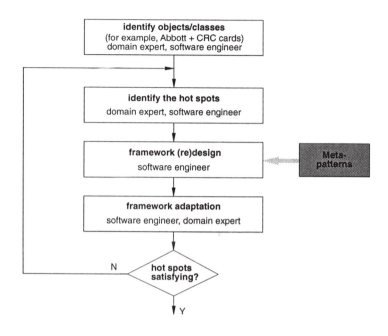

Figure 6.6 Hot-spot-driven approach.

Once the desired hot spots are identified, the characteristics of metapatterns detailed in Section 4.5 assist in supporting the appropriate level of flexibility.

Envisioned tool support

The hot-spot-driven design approach could be actively supported by what might be called a *hot-spot tool*. Based on the characteristics of metapatterns, a certain metapattern (combination) is chosen for a hot spot. The semantic aspects of the template and hook components are defined by providing the appropriate names. Based on these specifications the class skeletons could be generated.

Of course, it will often be necessary to integrate additional tasks into already existing components. For example, consider Figure 6.3: in a class RentalItem the rate calculation might be just one aspect among many. In other words, a class will participate in many metapatterns.

A hot-spot tool has to be aware of this and support its user in finding the appropriate names for the abstractions. For example, it should be possible to view the semantic aspects associated with one class. If they are quite different, splitting a class into several classes might be recommended. If a class represents an abstraction that does not have critical mass, that class should be unified with another class.

An adequate hot-spot tool could be viewed as a means of supporting the (re)design of a framework and the design documentation both at once. Such advanced support for developing frameworks would definitely have the potential to make the dream of having well-designed frameworks for numerous domains come true earlier. The fundamental object-oriented concepts already represent the few steps that make a gigantic leap in the software industry possible—the leap from *manu*factured[1] artifacts towards software produced from adaptable semifinished frameworks. Let's go on to make this vision become reality!

---

[1] From Latin *manus*, hand—hence by hand

Appendix A

`

Hypertext system sources

This appendix lists the source files of the classes adapting ET++ to a hypertext system application as presented in Chapter 5. In order to understand the coding details of these source files the relevant coding patterns are presented first.

A.1 Coding conventions for structuring source code

The structuring of source code in C++ and C is mainly based on coding conventions derived from analogous conventions already applied in C. A class definition is put in a header file which has the name of the class and the suffix .h. The corresponding implementation is stored in an implementation file which has the name of the class and the suffix .C. If classes form a logical unit, their class definitions are collected in a single header file and their implementations in a corresponding single implementation file.

In order to avoid multiple inclusions and thus compilations of a header file, the preprocessor statements #ifndef, #define and #endif form a bracket around the definitions contained in a header file. Example A.1 illustrates the use of these preprocessor statements. The preprocessor is C-specific and reads source code before it is passed to the compiler. Preprocessor statements start with a '#' sign. The statement include, for example, means that a preprocessor inserts the text stored in the file named in the include statement. The statement define defines a preprocessor constant. The define statement in Example A.1 means that the preprocessor constant HypertextDoc_First is defined as an empty string. The preprocessor statement #define MAX 100 would define the preprocessor constant MAX to have the value 100. The statement pair ifndef-endif expresses that the text in between is only passed to the compiler if the preprocessor constant associated with the ifndef statement is not already defined. As a consequence, the contents of a header file can only be included in a file once even if there are multiple include statements including the same header file. After the first preprocessor scan of the text between the ifndef and endif statements, the preprocessor constant **Hypertext-Doc_First** is defined in the define statement. This prevents the textual expansion of the header file in all subsequent inclusions of the header file within one compilation unit.

Example A.1 Avoidance of multiple header file inclusions in header file HypertextDoc.h.

```
#ifndef  HypertextDoc_First
#define  HypertextDoc_First

#include "Document.h"

class VObjectTextView;
. . .
class HypertextDoc: public Document {
public:
        . . .
protected:
        VObjectTextView *vobTxtView;
        . . .
};

#endif  HypertextDoc_First
```

In order to avoid extensive inclusion of files that might significantly slow down the compilation speed, the number of included files should be kept to a minimum. In a header file in which a new class is defined, it is sufficient to include only the header file in which the superclass of the new class is defined. For example, only Document.h is included in the example shown in Example A.1.

Pointers to other classes are defined in a forward declaration as demonstrated for class VObjectTextView in the example above. The header files of these classes need to be included only in the implementation files.

A.2 Meta-information

Meta-information can be accessed as discussed in Section 5.2.1. In order to get access to meta-information a programmer has to adhere to some coding patterns. The developers of ET++ try to "bother the programmer as little as possible" (Weinand *et al.* 1989). Powerful C macros **MetaDef** in the class definition part and MetaImpl in the class implementation part extract the necessary information out of a class definition. The programmer just has to specify the class name in the MetaDef macro. The list of instance variables with their types has to be given in the **MetaImpl** macro. The other information is extracted automatically. Example A.2 demonstrates this ET++ coding pattern in a class definition.

Example A.2 ET++ macro MetaDef in a class definition (file HypertextDoc.h).

```
class HypertextDoc: public Document {
public:
        MetaDef(HypertextDoc);
        HypertextDoc(...);
        . . .
protected:
        VObjectTextView *vobTxtView;
        . . .
};
```

Example A.3 shows how to use MetaImpl. If no information about instance variables is required or if there are no instance variables, the macro call NewMetaImpl0(HypertextDoc, Document) suffices.

Example A.3 ET++ macro MetaImpl in a class implementation (file HypertextDoc.C).

```
#include  "HypertextDoc.h"

NewMetaImpl(HypertextDoc,  Document,
               (TP(vobTxtView),  ...)  );

HypertextDoc::HypertextDoc(...) :  . . .
{       . . .
```

Some symbols used to describe the types of instance variables are listed below:

- T: any simple type such as int, char, and so on, as well as the ET++-defined types Point and Rectangle
- TP: instance variables that are pointers to any type
- TS: instance variables that are character strings, that is, of type char *
- TE: instance variables of an enumeration type.

A.3   Basic data structure operations

Recall the provisional vehicles used in Chapter 2 to handle data structures in C++. Example A.4 shows the use of these vehicles in the realm of class Folder so that Folder objects can manage a list of DesktopItem objects.

Example A.4 Managing a list of DesktopItem objects in class Folder.

header file 'Folder.h':
```
class Folder: public DesktopItem {
public:
        Folder(char *name);
        . . .
        int GetSizeInBytes();
        // management of contained desktop items
        void AppendDesktopItem(DesktopItem *additionalItem);
        void RemoveDesktopItem(DesktopItem*
                                        itemToBeRemoved);
        . . .
protected:
        List <DesktopItem *> *desktopItems;
};
```

implementation file 'Folder.C':
```
#include "Folder.h"
Folder::Folder(char *name) : DesktopItem(name)
{
        desktopItems= new List <DesktopItem *>;
}
...
int Folder::GetSizeInBytes()
{
        int size= 0;       // a folder itself is supposed to have size 0
        for each di: <DesktopItem *> in desktopItems
                size= size + di->GetSizeInBytes();
        return size;
}
void AppendDesktopItem(DesktopItem *additionalItem)
{
        desktopItems->Add(additionalItem);
}
void RemoveDesktopItem(DesktopItem *itemToBeRemoved);
{
        desktopItems->Remove(itemToBeRemoved);
}
```

Supposing that DesktopItem is a descendant of the ET++ class Object, the ET++ class ObjList could be used in order to manage DesktopItem objects in class Folder. This is demonstrated in Example A.5.

Example A.5 Using the ET++ class ObjList for managing DesktopItem objects.

header file 'Folder.h':
```
class Folder: public DesktopItem {
public:
        . . .
protected:
        ObjList *desktopItems;
};
```

implementation file 'Folder.C':
```
#include "Folder.h"
. . .
Folder::Folder(char *name) : DesktopItem(name)
{
        desktopItems= new ObjList;
}
. . .
int Folder::GetSizeInBytes()
{
        int size= 0;       // a folder itself is supposed to have size 0
        Iterator   *next;
        Object   *op;
        next=   desktopItems->MakeIterator();

        while  (op=  (*next) ()  )

            size= size +
                    Guard(op,DesktopItem)->GetSizeInBytes();
        return size;
}
void AppendDesktopItem(DesktopItem *additionalItem)
{
        desktopItems->Add(additionalItem);
}
void RemoveDesktopItem(DesktopItem *itemToBeRemoved);
{
        desktopItems->Remove(itemToBeRemoved);
}
```

In order to understand syntactically the iteration over a data structure as exemplified in Folder::GetSizeInBytes(), consider the following: an abstract class Iterator provides a method called '()', that is, the operator '()' is overloaded. This method—in Example A.5 the method invocation is marked by a gray rectangle—returns the reference to the next element in a **Container** object. After reaching the end, 0 is returned. Since operator '()' returns a reference of static type pointer to Object, a type-safe cast by means of the Guard macro is necessary. (Simply writing op->GetSizeInBytes() would be reported as error by the compiler since op is of static type **pointer to Object;** method GetSizeInBytes is defined in class **DesktopItem** and not in class Object.)

A.4   ET++ adaptation

File HypertextApp.h
```
#ifndef HypertextApp_First
#define HypertextApp_First

#include "Application.h"

//---- HypertextApp ------------------------------------------------------------------------
class HypertextApp: public Application {
public:
        MetaDef(HypertextApp);
        HypertextApp(int argc, char **argv);

        Manager *DoMakeManager(Symbol managerType);
};

#endif HypertextApp_First
```

File HypertextApp.C
```
#include "HypertextApp.h"
#include "HypertextDoc.h"

#include "Class.h"

//---- HypertextApp ------------------------------------------------------------------------
NewMetaImpl0(HypertextApp,Application);

HypertextApp::HypertextApp(int argc, char **argv) : Application(argc, argv,
                                                         cHTDocType)
{
}


Manager *HypertextApp::DoMakeManager(Symbol managerType)
{
        return new HypertextDoc(managerType);
}
```

File   Main.C

```
#include "HypertextApp.h"

//---- main --------------------------------------------------------------------------------------

main(int argc, char **argv)
{
        HypertextApp *hypertextApp= new HypertextApp(argc, argv);
        hypertextApp->Run();
}
```

File   HypertextDoc.h

```
#ifndef HypertextDoc_First
#define HypertextDoc_First

#include "Document.h"

class TextView;
class VObjectText;
class VObjectTextView;
class MenuBar;
class CommandProcessor;

//---- HypertextDoc --------------------------------------------------------------------------

extern Symbol cHTDocType;

class HypertextDoc : public Document {
public:
        MetaDef(HypertextDoc);

        HypertextDoc(Symbol managerType);
        ~HypertextDoc();

        VObject *DoMakeContent();

        MenuBar *DoMakeMenuBar();
        void DoSetupMenu(Menu *menu);
        Command *DoMenuCommand(int cmdId);

        void SetName(const char *name);
        bool Close();      // overridden so that the user is not asked
                           // whether to save changes

        CommandProcessor *MakeCmdProcessor();
protected:
        VObjectTextView *vobTxtView;
        VObjectText *vobTxt;
        bool inNavigationMode;
        bool unboundCmdProc;
};

#endif HypertextDoc_First
```

File   HypertextDoc.C
```
#include "HypertextDoc.h"
#include "LinkButton.h"
#include "LinkAndRenameDialogs.h"
#include "CmdIds.h"

#include "Class.h"
#include "VObjectText.h"
#include "VObjectTView.h"
#include "StyledText.h"
#include "Dialog.h"
#include "FindChange_e.h"
#include "Scroller.h"
#include "Menu.h"
#include "MenuBar.h"
#include "TextItem.h"
#include "CommandProcessor.h"
#include "TextMarks.h"

static RenameDialog *gRenameDialog;

Symbol cHTDocType("HYPERTEXT");


//---- HypertextDoc ---------------------------------------------------------------------

NewMetaImpl(HypertextDoc,Document, (TP(vobTxt), TP(vobTxtView)));

HypertextDoc::HypertextDoc(Symbol managerType) : Document(managerType)
{
        vobTxt= new VObjectText;
        vobTxtView= new VObjectTextView(
                                this,     // This HypertextDoc object
                                          // is the next event handler
                                          // of the VObjectTextView
                                          // object.
                                Point(500, 1000), // initial view size
                                vobTxt);
        inNavigationMode= FALSE;
        unboundCmdProc= TRUE;
}

HypertextDoc::~HypertextDoc()
{
        SafeDelete(vobTxtView);
        SafeDelete(vobTxt);
}

VObject *HypertextDoc::DoMakeContent()
{
        SetFirstHandler(vobTxtView);
        return new Scroller(vobTxtView);
}
```

```
MenuBar *HypertextDoc::DoMakeMenuBar()
{
        MenuBar *mb= new MenuBar;

        //---- File menu
        Menu *fileMenu= new Menu("File");
        fileMenu->AppendItems(
                "New@N",                cNEW,
                "Close",                cCLOSE,
                "-",                    // a line item is inserted
                "Print ...@P",          cPRINT,
                "-",
                "Rename ...@R",         cIdRename,
                "-",
                "Quit@Q",               cQUIT,
                0
        );
        mb->AddMenu(fileMenu);

        // append default ET++ menus
        mb->AddMenu(MakeMenu(cEDITMENU));
        mb->AddMenu(TextView::MakeMenu(cFONTMENU));
        mb->AddMenu(TextView::MakeMenu(cSTYLEMENU));
        mb->AddMenu(TextView::MakeMenu(cSIZEMENU));

        //---- Insert menu
        Menu *insertMenu= new Menu("Insert");
        insertMenu->AppendItem("Link Button", cIdInsertLinkButton);
        mb->AddMenu(insertMenu);

        //---- Special menu
        Menu *specialMenu= new Menu("Special",
                                FALSE,          // dim all?
                                FALSE);         // reset all? FALSE => menu with
                                                //                   check boxes
        specialMenu->AppendItems(
                "Navigation mode",              cIdMode,
                "-",
                "Unlimited Undo-Levels",        cIdUndoLevels,
                0
        );
        // set check boxes depending on the values of the corresponding
        // instance variables that have been set in the constructor
        specialMenu->CheckItem(cIdMode, inNavigationMode);
        specialMenu->CheckItem(cIdUndoLevels, unboundCmdProc);
        mb->AddMenu(specialMenu);

        // allow the VObjectTextView instance to modify the Edit menu so that
        // menu items for find/change requests can be offered
        FindChange::InstallChange(mb, vobTxtView);

        return mb;
}
```

```
void HypertextDoc::DoSetupMenu(Menu *menu)
{
        Document::DoSetupMenu(menu);
        FindChange::DoSetupMenu(menu);
        menu->EnableItems(
                cIdRename,              // Enable Rename  (File menu).
                cIdMode,                // Enable Navigation Mode (Special menu).
                cIdUndoLevels,          // Enable Unlimited Undo Levels
                                        // (Special menu).
                0
        );
        // Enable/disable Link Button depending on the current mode.
        menu->EnableItem(cIdInsertLinkButton, !inNavigationMode); // (Insert menu)
}

Command *HypertextDoc::DoMenuCommand(int cmdId)
{
        switch (cmdId) {
                case cFIND: {
                        FindChange::ShowChangeDialog(vobTxtView);
                        break;
                }
                case cFINDAGAIN: {
                        FindChange::FindAgain(vobTxtView);
                        break;
                }
                case cCLOSE: {
                        Hide();
                        break;
                }
                case cIdRename: {
                        if (!gRenameDialog)
                                gRenameDialog= new RenameDialog;
                        gRenameDialog->ShowUnderMouse();
                        break;
                }
                case cIdInsertLinkButton: {
                        LinkButton *lb= new LinkButton;
                        lb->SetState(inNavigationMode);
                        return new PasteVObjectCommand(vobTxtView, lb);
                }
                case cIdMode: {
                        inNavigationMode = !inNavigationMode;
                        vobTxtView->SetReadOnly(inNavigationMode);
                        MarkList *ml= vobTxt->GetVisualMarks();
                        Iterator *next= ml->MakeIterator();
                        Object *op;
                        while (op= (*next)()) {
                                VObjectMark *vobM= Guard(op,VObjectMark);
                                LinkButton *lb=
                                        Guard(vobM->GetVObject(),LinkButton);
                                lb->SetState(inNavigationMode);
                        }
                        break;
```

```
                    }
                case cldUndoLevels: {
                        unboundCmdProc = !unboundCmdProc;
                        if (unboundCmdProc)
                                SetCmdProcessor(new CommandProcessorN);
                        else
                                SetCmdProcessor(new CommandProcessor1);
                        break;
                }
                default:
                        return Document::DoMenuCommand(cmdld);
        }

        return gNoChanges;        // global variable referring to a Command object
                                  // that causes no action
}

void HypertextDoc::SetName(const char *name)
{
        Document::SetName(name);
        Send();                        // Inform the observing link buttons that
                                       // I've changed my name.
}

bool HypertextDoc::Close()
{
        return Manager::Close();
}

CommandProcessor *HypertextDoc::MakeCmdProcessor()
{
        if (unboundCmdProc)                // set in the constructor
                return new CommandProcessorN;
        else
                return new CommandProcessor1;
}
```

File   LinkButton.h

```
#ifndef LinkButton_First
#define LinkButton_First

#include "Buttons.h"

class HypertextDoc;

//---- LinkButton ---------------------------------------------------------------------------

class LinkButton : public ActionButton {
public:
        MetaDef(LinkButton);

        LinkButton();

        void SetTargetHTDoc(HypertextDoc *htDoc);
```

```
        HypertextDoc *GetTargetHTDoc();

        void SetState(bool state);          // state == TRUE => navigation mode
        bool GetState();

        void Control(int id, int part, void *val);
        void DoObserve(int id, int part, void *vp, Object *op);
protected:
        HypertextDoc *targetHTDoc;          // target hypertext document
        bool inNavigationMode;              // TRUE  => I present the linked hypertext
                                            //              text document when
                                            //              I'm activated.
                                            // FALSE => The hypertext document I
                                            //              should be linked to can be
                                            //              specified in the link dialog.
        VObject *GenerateInner();           // Generates a composite visual object
                                            // consisting of a balloon image and
                                            // a text item.
        void AdaptLabelToHTDoc();           // Sets the label of the button to the
                                            // name of the target hypertext document.
};

#endif LinkButton_First
```

File   LinkButton.C
```
#include "LinkButton.h"
#include "HypertextDoc.h"
#include "LinkAndRenameDialogs.h"

#include "Class.h"
#include "ImageItem.h"
#include "TextItem.h"
#include "Filler.h"
#include "Box.h"
#include "Bitmap.h"

static u_short BalloonBits[]= {
#         include "images/Balloon.image"
};

static SmartBitmap BalloonImage(Point(16,13), BalloonBits);

static LinkDialog *gLinkDialog;


//---- LinkButton --------------------------------------------------------------------------------------

NewMetaImpl0(LinkButton,ActionButton);

LinkButton::LinkButton() : ActionButton(cIdNone, GenerateInner())
{
        targetHTDoc= 0;
        inNavigationMode= TRUE;
}
```

```
LinkButton::~LinkButton()
{
        // When I'm deleted (e.g., due to edit operations in the text
        // such as hitting the backspace key or cutting a text portion
        // I'm part of), I have to be removed from the observer list
        // of the hypertext document I referred to.
        if (targetHTDoc)
                targetHTDoc->RemoveObserver(this);
}


VObject *LinkButton::GenerateInner()
{
        // The inside of an action button has to be a visual object;
        // in the case of a link button the inner visual object is composed
        // of an image item (a balloon) and a text item that represents
        // the name of the hypertext document to which the link refers.
        // Initially, that is, when the link button refers to no hypertext
        // document, the label is Link. When a hypertext document is defined,
        // the label of the action button has to be changed to the name of
        // the hypertext document. This is done in AdaptLabelToHTDoc().
        // Note that the visual objects contained in a composite visual
        // object such as a box can be accessed via the At('index') method.
        return
                new Box(cIdNone, Point(0,1), gPoint2, eVObjVBase,
                        new Filler(gPoint5),                    // At(0)
                        new ImageItem(BalloonImage),            // At(1)
                        new TextItem("Link"),                   // At(2)
                        0
                );
}


void LinkButton::AdaptLabelToHTDoc()
{
        // An action button is itself a composite visual object with
        // its label as first element (->At(0)). The label is
        // again a composite visual object (see comments in GenerateInner())
        // so that the text item that is part of the label can be
        // accessed by At(2).
        TextItem *innerTextItem;
        CompositeVObject *compVob= Guard(At(0),CompositeVObject);
        innerTextItem= Guard(compVob->At(2),TextItem);

        if (targetHTDoc) {
                innerTextItem->SetString(targetHTDoc->GetName(), TRUE);
                CalcExtent();
                ForceRedraw();
        }
}


void LinkButton::SetTargetHTDoc(HypertextDoc *htDoc)
{
        if (targetHTDoc)
                targetHTDoc->RemoveObserver(this);
        targetHTDoc= htDoc;
```

```
        if (targetHTDoc)
                targetHTDoc->AddObserver(this);
        AdaptLabelToHTDoc();
}

HypertextDoc *LinkButton::GetTargetHTDoc()
{
        return targetHTDoc;
}

void LinkButton::SetState(bool st)
{
        inNavigationMode= st;
}

bool LinkButton::GetState()
{
        return inNavigationMode;
}

void LinkButton::Control(int id, int part, void *val)
{
        ActionButton::Control(id, part, val);

        if (inNavigationMode) {
                if (targetHTDoc)
                        targetHTDoc->Open();
        } else {
                if (!gLinkDialog)  // Generate the dialog exactly once
                                   // when it is needed for the first time.
                        gLinkDialog= new LinkDialog;
                gLinkDialog->SetLinkButton(this);
                gLinkDialog->ShowUnderMouse();
        }
}

void LinkButton::DoObserve(int , int , void *, Object *)
{
        AdaptLabelToHTDoc();
}
```

File LinkAndRenameDialogs.h

```
#ifndef LinkAndRenameDialogs_First
#define LinkAndRenameDialogs_First

#include "Dialog.h"
#include "TextItem.h"

class CollectionView;
class ActionButton;
class ObjList;
class TextField;
class LinkButton;
class HypertextDoc;
```

```
// A collection view can only display visual objects contained in a
// sequencable collection such as an object list. We use text items
// as visual objects in the list.
// In order to store the reference of the hypertext document that
// corresponds to a particular text item, the TextItem subclass
// HTDocTextItem is defined as shown below.


//---- HTDocTextItem -------------------------------------------------------------------
class HTDocTextItem : public TextItem {
public:
        MetaDef(HTDocTextItem);
        HTDocTextItem(char *, HypertextDoc *htDoc);

        void SetTargetHTDoc(HypertextDoc *htDoc);
        HypertextDoc *GetTargetHTDoc();
protected:
        HypertextDoc *targetHTDoc;
};


//---- LinkDialog -------------------------------------------------------------------
class LinkDialog: public Dialog {
public:
        MetaDef(LinkDialog);

        LinkDialog();
        ~LinkDialog();

        VObject *DoMakeContent();

        void DoSetup();
        void SetLinkButton(LinkButton *lb);
protected:
        void Control(int id, int part, void *v);

        LinkButton *linkButton;         // the link button for which I
                                        // edit the attributes
        HypertextDoc *targetHTDoc;      // target hypertext document defined
                                        // for link button
        ActionButton *defineLinkButton;

        CollectionView *htDocsView;
        ObjList *BuildHTDocList();       // Build up list of hypertext document
                                         // names.
};


//---- RenameDialog -------------------------------------------------------------------
class RenameDialog: public LinkDialog {
public:
        MetaDef(RenameDialog);

        RenameDialog();
        ~RenameDialog();
```

```
        VObject *DoMakeContent();

        void DoSetup();
protected:
        void Control(int id, int part, void *v);
        ActionButton *defineNameButton;
        TextField *htDocNameField;
        void UpdateAfterHTDocNameChange();
};

#endif LinkAndRenameDialogs_First
```

File   LinkAndRenameDialogs.C

```
#include "LinkAndRenameDialogs.h"
#include "CmdIds.h"
#include "LinkButton.h"
#include "HypertextDoc.h"

#include "ObjList.h"
#include "CollView.h"
#include "Scroller.h"
#include "Buttons.h"
#include "Box.h"
#include "Fields.h"
#include "Class.h"
#include "Filler.h"
#include "Application.h"


//---- HTDocTextItem -------------------------------------------------------------------------
NewMetaImpl0(HTDocTextItem,TextItem);
HTDocTextItem::HTDocTextItem(char *n, HypertextDoc *htDoc)
                                : TextItem(n)
{
        targetHTDoc= htDoc;
}

void HTDocTextItem::SetTargetHTDoc(HypertextDoc *htDoc)
{
        targetHTDoc= htDoc;
}

HypertextDoc *HTDocTextItem::GetTargetHTDoc()
{
        return targetHTDoc;
}

//---- LinkDialog -------------------------------------------------------------------------
NewMetaImpl0(LinkDialog,Dialog);

LinkDialog::LinkDialog() : Dialog("Link Dialog")
{
        defineLinkButton= new ActionButton(cIdDefineLink, "Define Link",
                        TRUE);  // TRUE => default button
```

```
                // for displaying already created hypertext documents
                htDocsView= new CollectionView(this, BuildHTDocList());
                htDocsView->SetId(cIdHTDocsView);
}

LinkDialog::~LinkDialog()
{
                SafeDelete(defineLinkButton);
                SafeDelete(htDocsView);
}

ObjList *LinkDialog::BuildHTDocList()
{
                ObjList *managedDocs= new ObjList;
                Object *op;
                Iterator *next= gApplication->MakeIterator();
                while (op= (*next)() ) {
                        HypertextDoc *hd;
                        if (op->IsKindOf(HypertextDoc)) {
                                hd= (HypertextDoc*)op;
                                managedDocs->Add(
                                        new HTDocTextItem(hd->GetName(),hd));
                        }
                }
                return managedDocs;
}

VObject *LinkDialog::DoMakeContent()
{
                return
                        new Box(cIdNone, Point(1,0), gPoint10, eVObjHCenter,
                                new Filler(gPoint5),
                                new Box(cIdNone, Point(1,0), gPoint2, eVObjHLeft,
                                        new TextItem("Select a document:"),
                                        new Scroller(htDocsView, Point(230,80)),
                                        0
                                ),
                                new Box(cIdNone, Point(0,1),
                                        gPoint2, eVObjVCenter,
                                        defineLinkButton,
                                        new ActionButton(cIdCancel, "Close"),
                                        0
                                ),
                                0
                        );
}

void LinkDialog::DoSetup()
{
                htDocsView->SetCollection(BuildHTDocList());     // The collection
                                                // originally displayed by htDocsView is freed.
                defineLinkButton->Enable(FALSE);
                targetHTDoc= 0;
}
```

```
void LinkDialog::SetLinkButton(LinkButton *lb)
{
        linkButton= lb;
        if (linkButton)
                targetHTDoc= linkButton->GetTargetHTDoc();
}

void LinkDialog::Control(int id, int part, void *v)
{
        switch (id) {
                case cldHTDocsView: {
                        defineLinkButton->Enable(TRUE);
                        // Get selection rectangle of collection view with
                        // already created hypertext documents.
                        Rectangle selHTDocRect= htDocsView->GetSelection();
                                                           // (== v)
                        HTDocTextItem *selItem=
                          Guard(htDocsView->GetItem(selHTDocRect.origin.x,
                                  selHTDocRect.origin.y),HTDocTextItem);

                        // Which hypertext document corresponds to the selected
                        // item?
                        if (selItem)
                                targetHTDoc= selItem->GetTargetHTDoc();
                        break;
                }
                case cldDefineLink: {
                        if (targetHTDoc) {
                                linkButton->SetTargetHTDoc(targetHTDoc);
                                Dialog::Control(id, part, v);   // close the dialog
                        }
                        break;
                }
                case cldCancel: {
                        Dialog::Control(id, part, v);           // close the dialog
                        break;
                }
        }
}




//---- RenameDialog -------------------------------------------------------------------------------
NewMetaImpl0(RenameDialog,LinkDialog);

RenameDialog::RenameDialog()
{
        SetName("Rename Dialog");
        defineNameButton= new ActionButton(cldDefineName, "Define Name", TRUE);
        htDocNameField= new TextField(cldNone, 12);
}
```

```
RenameDialog::~RenameDialog()
{
        SafeDelete(defineNameButton);
        SafeDelete(htDocNameField);
}

void RenameDialog::UpdateAfterHTDocNameChange()
{
        Rectangle selHTDocRect= htDocsView->GetSelection(); // store the selection
        htDocsView->SetCollection(BuildHTDocList());
        htDocsView->SetSelection(selHTDocRect, TRUE);        // restore the
                                                             // selection
}

VObject *RenameDialog::DoMakeContent()
{
        return
                new Box(cldNone, Point(1,0), gPoint10, eVObjHCenter,
                                new Filler(gPoint5),
                                new Box(cldNone, Point(1,0), gPoint2, eVObjHLeft,
                                        new TextItem("Select a document:"),
                                        new Scroller(htDocsView, Point(233,80)),
                                        0
                                ),
                                new Box(cldNone, Point(0,1),
                                        gPoint2, eVObjVCenter,
                                        new TextItem("Document name:"),
                                        htDocNameField,
                                        0
                                ),
                                new Box(cldNone, Point(0,1),
                                        gPoint2, eVObjVCenter,
                                        defineNameButton,
                                        new ActionButton(cldCancel, "Close"),
                                        0
                                ),
                                0
                        );
}

void RenameDialog::DoSetup()
{
        htDocsView->SetCollection(BuildHTDocList());    // The collection
                                        // originally displayed by htDocsView is freed.
        defineNameButton->Enable(FALSE);
        htDocNameField->SetString("", TRUE);
        targetHTDoc= 0;
}

void RenameDialog::Control(int id, int part, void *v)
{
        switch (id) {
                case cldHTDocsView: {
                        LinkDialog::Control(id, part, v);
```

```
                        defineNameButton->Enable(TRUE);
                        if (targetHTDoc)
                                htDocNameField->SetString(
                                        targetHTDoc->GetName(), TRUE);
                        break;
                }
                case cldDefineName: {
                        if (targetHTDoc) {
                                targetHTDoc->SetName(
                                        htDocNameField->GetString());
                                UpdateAfterHTDocNameChange();
                        }
                        break;
                }
                case cldCancel: {
                        Dialog::Control(id, part, v);          // close the dialog
                        break;
                }
        }
}
```

File CmdIds.h
```
#ifndef HTCmdIds_First
#define HTCmdIds_First

//---- HypertextDoc --------------------------------------------------------------------
const int cldRename                          = cldFirstUser +  0;
const int cldInsertLinkButton                = cldFirstUser +  1;
const int cldMode                            = cldFirstUser +  2;
const int cldUndoLevels                      = cldFirstUser +  3;

//---- Link and Rename Dialogs --------------------------------------------------------
const int cldDefineLink                      = cldFirstUser + 10;
const int cldDefineName                      = cldFirstUser + 11;
const int cldHTDocsView                      = cldFirstUser + 12;

#endif HTCmdIds_First
```

Appendix B

Glossary

abstract class: a class that is not instantiable and that standardizes the interface for subclasses.

abstract coupling: two classes coupled via a reference relationship; at least one of the two classes is an abstract class.

abstract method: a method with a dummy implementation; abstract methods are typically part of abstract classes.

ADS: (abstract data structure) an entity that consists of data and routines.

ADT: (abstract data type) an entity that consists of data and routines and represents a type so that any number of variables can be declared.

application framework: a framework that constitutes a generic application for a domain area.

change propagation mechanism: a framework for informing objects about changes and asking them to update accordingly.

class: an extensible ADT.

cookbook: (for frameworks) a set of recipes.

contract: an alternative term for class interface expressing the standardization property of a class interface for its subclasses.

CRC cards: (Class/Responsibility/Collaboration) a simple yet powerful noncomputerized OOAD vehicle used in some OOAD methodologies.

descendant: a class that inherits from another class, but not necessarily as a direct subclass.

design patterns: a means of capturing and communicating the design of object-oriented systems.

dynamic binding: the run-time determination of the behavior of an operation.

ET: (Editor Toolkit) a C library for the GUI domain developed by Erich Gamma; predecessor of ET++.

ET++: a C++ application framework for the GUI domain developed by Erich Gamma and André Weinand at the University of Zurich and the Union Bank of Switzerland's Informatics Laboratory.

event loop: core part of a GUI application that processes queued events such as mouse clicks.

formal contract: the formal description of how interdependent objects cooperate.

framework: a semifinished software architecture that can be adapted to specific needs by applying object-oriented programming concepts; generic term for application framework and small framework.

frozen spot: aspect of a framework that is not designed for adaptation.

GUI: graphic user interface.

hook method: corresponds to a hot spot in a framework.

hot spot: a place where framework adaptation takes place.

hot-spot tool: a tool supporting the development of frameworks based on metapatterns.

hypertext: a means of creating and navigating through a directed graph of documents, such as texts and drawings.

inheritance: a concept that allows sharing, extending, and/or modifying behavior offered by a class.

MacApp: an application framework for implementing Macintosh applications.

message: alternative term for method invocation. (The term message was introduced to stress the dynamic binding aspect of method calls.)

meta-information: information about objects and classes.

metapatterns: a means of capturing and communicating the design of frameworks and of actively supporting the design pattern approach.

MVC: (Model/View/Controller) a core part of the first application framework for the GUI domain.

narrow inheritance interface principle: a primary design guideline for frameworks expressing that the number of methods to be overridden for an adaptation should be minimal.

Object Model Notation: a notation for depicting class and object diagrams, proposed in OMT.

OMT: (Object Model Technique) a full-fledged OOAD methodology.

OOAD: object-oriented analysis and design.

OOP: object-oriented programming.

OOPL: object-oriented programming language.

OOPSLA: (Conference on Object-Oriented Programming Systems, Languages, and Applications) a major forum for researchers and practitioners in the field of object-oriented technology.

object: an instance of a class.

polymorphism: compatibility of object types.

recipe: an informal description of how to adapt a framework.

routine: a generic term for function and procedure.

SA/SD: (Structured Analysis/Structured Design) a widespread methodology for conventional software development; mainly based on data flow diagrams.

software architecture: several interacting software components.

subclass: a class that inherits behavior from another class.

superclass: a class from which another class inherits behavior.

template method: corresponds to a frozen spot in a framework.

Volkswagen Beetle: predecessor of Porsche 959.

X: a widespread window system available on common platforms.

Xerox PARC: (Palo Alto Research Center) birthplace of a wealth of good ideas in the 1970s and 1980s, including Smalltalk and GUIs.

Appendix C

How to obtain the hypertext system sources

The source files of the hypertext system listed in Appendix A are available at no cost via anonymous ftp from the Johannes Kepler University Linz at the following address:

Host name: ftp.swe.uni-linz.ac.at

Internet address: 140.78.42.1

Directory: Hypertext

The sources of the ET++ version that formed the basis of the hypertext system implementation is in the directory ET++3.0; the gnu C++ compiler version 2.5.4 compiled these ET++ sources and the hypertext system sources.

Have fun experimenting with this sample application and the application framework ET++!

We plan to make a prototype of a hot-spot tool for UNIX platforms available for free via ftp. If you are interested in this tool prototype, send a blank e-mail to

hotspottool@swe.uni-linz.ac.at

We will inform you how to get the tool prototype as soon as it is made available.

Bibliography

Abbott R. (1983). Program design by informal English descriptions. *Communications of the ACM*, **26**(11)

Ackermann P. and Eichelberg D. (1993). Combining 2D user interface components and interactive 3D graphics. In *TOOLS USA '93 Conference Proceedings*, Santa Barbara, California

Alexander C. (1979). *The Timeless Way of Building*. New York: Oxford University Press

Alexander C., Ishikawa S., Silverstein M., Jacobson M., Fiksdahl-King I. and Angel S. (1977). *A Pattern Language*. New York: Oxford University Press

ANSI and AJPO (1983). *Military Standard: Ada Programming Language*. American National Standards Institute and United States Government Department of Defense (DoD), Ada Joint Program Office, ANSI/MIL-STD-1815A-1983

Apple Computer (1987). *Human Interface Guidelines: The Apple Desktop Interface*. Cupertino, CA: Apple Computer, Inc.

Apple Computer (1989). *MacAppII Programmer's Guide*. Cupertino, CA: Apple Computer, Inc.

Beck K. and Cunningham W. (1989). A laboratory for object-oriented thinking. In *Proceedings of OOPSLA'89*, New Orleans, Louisiana

Blaschek G. (1994). *Object-Oriented Programming with Prototypes*. Berlin: Springer Verlag

Booch G. (1991). *Object-Oriented Design*. Redwood City, CA: Benjamin/Cummings

Chambers C., Ungar D. and Lee D. (1989). An efficient implementation of SELF, a dynamically typed object-oriented language based on prototypes. In *Proceedings of OOPSLA'89*, New Orleans, Louisiana

Coad P. (1992). Object-oriented patterns. *Communications of the ACM*, **33**(9)

Coad P. and Yourdon E. (1990). *Object-Oriented Analysis*. Englewood Cliffs, NJ: Yourdon Press

Coplien J.O. (1992). *Advanced C++ Programming Styles and Idioms*. Reading, Massachusetts: Addison-Wesley

Cox B.J. (1986). *Object-Oriented Programming—An Evolutionary Approach*. Reading, Massachusetts: Addison-Wesley

DeMarco T. (1979). *Structured Analysis and Systems Specification*. Englewood Cliffs, NJ: Prentice-Hall

Eggenschwiler T. and Gamma E. (1992). ET++ swaps manager: using object technology in the financial engineering domain. OOPSLA'92, Special Issue of *SIGPLAN Notices*, **27**(10)

Ellis M.A. and Stroustrup B. (1990). *The Annotated C++ Reference Manual*. Reading, Massachusetts: Addison-Wesley

Fenton N. (1991). *Software Metrics—A Rigorous Approach*. London: Chapman & Hall

Foote B. (1988). Designing to facilitate change with object-oriented frameworks. *Master Thesis*, University of Illinois at Urbana-Champaign

Fukanaga A., Pree W. and Kimura T. (1993). Functions as data objects in a data flow based visual language. ACM Computer Science Conference, Indianapolis

Gamma E. (1992). Objektorientierte Software-Entwicklung am Beispiel von ET++: Design-Muster, Klassenbibliothek, Werkzeuge. *Doctoral Thesis*, University of Zürich, 1991; published by Springer Verlag, 1992

Gamma E., Helm R., Johnson R. and Vlissides J. (1993). Design patterns: abstraction and reuse of object-oriented design. In *Proceedings of the ECOOP'93 Conference*, Kaiserslautern, Germany; published by Springer Verlag

Gamma E., Helm R., Johnson R. and Vlissides J. (1994). *Design Patterns— Microarchitectures for Reusable Object-Oriented Software*. Reading, Massachusetts: Addison-Wesley

Garett N.L., Smith K.E. and Meyramiles N. (1986). Intermedia—Issues, strategies and tactics in the design of a hypermedia document system. In *Proceedings of the Conference on Computer-Supported Cooperative Work*, Austin, Texas

Garlan D. and Shaw M. (1993). An introduction to software architecture. In *Advances in Software Engineering and Knowledge Engineering*, I (Ambriola V. and Tortora G., eds.). World Scientific Publishing Company

Goldberg A. (1984). *Smalltalk-80/The Interactive Programming Environment*. Reading, Massachusetts: Addison-Wesley

Goldberg A. and Robson D. (1985). *Smalltalk-80/The Language and its Implementation*. Reading, Massachusetts: Addison-Wesley

Goodman D. (1988). *HyperCard Developer's Guide*. New York: Bantam Books

Gossain S. and Anderson D.B. (1989). Designing a class hierachy for domain representation and reusability. In *Proceedings of TOOLS '89*, Paris, France

Helm R., Holland I.M. and Gangopadhyay D. (1990). Contracts: specifying behavioral compositions in object-oriented systems. In *Proceedings of OOPSLA '90*, Ottawa, Canada

Hoffman D. (1990). On criteria for module interfaces. *IEEE Transactions on Software Engineering*, **16**(5)

Jacobson I. (1987). *Object-Oriented Software Engineering*. Wokingham: Addison-Wesley

Johnson R.E. (1992). Documenting frameworks using patterns. In *Proceedings of OOPSLA '92*, Vancouver, Canada

Keene S.E. (1988). *Object-Oriented Programming in Common Lisp*. Reading, Massachusetts: Addison-Wesley

Kerninghan B.W. and Ritchie D.M. (1988). *The C Programming* Language. 2nd edn. Englewood Cliffs, NJ: Prentice-Hall

Krasner G.E. and Pope S.T. (1988). A cookbook for using the Model-View-Controller user interface paradigm in Smalltalk-80. *Journal of Object-Oriented Programming*, **1**(3)

Krueger C.W. (1992). Software reuse. *ACM Computing Survey*, **24** (2)

Lalonde W.R. (1989). Designing families of data types using exemplars. *ACM Transactions on Programming Languages and Systems*, **11**(2)

Madany P.W., Campbell R.H., Russo V.F. and Leyens D.E. (1989). A class hierarchy for building stream-oriented file systems. In *Proceedings of the ECOOP '89 Conference*, Nottingham, UK

McCabe T.J. (1976). A complexity measurement. *IEEE Transactions on Software Engineering*, SE-2

McCall J.A., Richards P.K., Walters G.F. (1977). Factors in Software Quality. In *Concepts and Definitions of Software Quality*, Vol. I-III. Rome Air Development Center

McIlroy M.D. (1976). Mass-produced software components. In *Software Engineering Concepts and Techniques* (Buxton J.M., Naur P., and Randell B., eds.). 1968 North Atlantic Treaty Organization (NATO) Conference on Software Engineering, Garmisch-Partenkirchen

Merriam Webster Inc. (1983). *Webster's New Unabridged Dictionary*. New York: Simon & Schuster

Meyer B. (1988). *Object-Oriented Software Construction*. Englewood Cliffs, NJ: Prentice-Hall

Meyer B. (1990). Lessons from the design of the Eiffel libraries. *Communications of the ACM*, **33**(9)

Microsoft Corporation (1994). *Visual C++ and Microsoft Foundation Class Libary Manuals*. Redmont, WA: Microsoft Corporation

Mössenböck P. (1993). *Object-Oriented Programming in Oberon-2*. Berlin: Springer Verlag

Parnas D.L. (1972). On the criteria to be used in decomposing systems into modules. *Communications of the ACM*, **15**(12)

Pree W. (1991). Object-oriented versus conventional construction of user interface prototyping tools. *Doctoral Thesis*, University of Linz

Ramamoorthy C.V. *et al.* (1982). Techniques in software quality assurance. In *Proceedings of the German Chapter of the ACM*, **9**, Teubner

Reiser M. (1991). *The Oberon System: User Guide and Programmer's Manual*. Wokingham: Addison-Wesley/ACM Press

Reiser M. and Wirth N. (1992). *Programming in Oberon—Steps Beyond Pascal and Modula*. Wokingham: Addison-Wesley/ACM Press

Rumbaugh J., Blaha M., Premerlani W., Eddy F. and Lorensen W. (1991). *Object-Oriented Modeling and Design*. Englewood Cliffs, NJ: Prentice-Hall

Russo V. and Campbell R.H. (1989). Virtual memory and backing storage management in multiprocessor operating systems using class hierachical design. In *Proceedings of OOPSLA '89*, New Orleans, Louisiana

Schmucker K. (1986). *Object-Oriented Programming for the Macintosh*. Hasbrouck Heights, NJ: Hayden

Shah A., Rumbaugh J., Hamel J. and Borsri R. (1989). DSM: An object-relationship modeling language. In *Proceedings of OOPSLA '89*, New Orleans, Louisiana

Shneiderman B. and Kearsley G. (1989). *Hypertext Hands-On!—An Introduction to a New Way of Organizing and Accessing Information*. Reading, Massachusetts: Addison-Wesley

Ungar D. and Smith R.B. (1987). SELF: The power of simplicity. In *OOPSLA '87 Proceedings*

Weinand A. (1992). Objektorientierter Entwurf und Implementierung portabler Fensterumgebungen am Beispiel des Application-Frameworks ET++. *Doctoral Thesis*, University of Zürich, 1991; published by Springer Verlag, 1992

Weinand A., Gamma E. and Marty R. (1988). ET++ – An object-oriented application framework in C++. In OOPSLA'88, Special Issue of *SIGPLAN Notices*, **23**(11)

Weinand A., Gamma E. and Marty R. (1989). Design and implementation of ET++, a seamless object-oriented application framework. *Structured Programming*, **10**(2), Springer Verlag

Wilson D.A., Rosenstein L.S. and Shafer D. (1990). *Programming with MacApp*. Reading, Massachusetts: Addison-Wesley

Wirfs-Brock R.J. and Johnson R.E. (1990). Surveying current research in object-oriented design. *Communications of the ACM*, **33**(9)

Wirfs-Brock R., Wilkerson B. and Wiener L. (1990). *Designing Object-Oriented Software*. Englewood Cliffs, NJ: Prentice-Hall

Wirth N. (1971). Program development by stepwise refinement. *Communications of the ACM*, **14**(4)

Wirth N. (1974). On the composition of well structured programs. *ACM Computing Surveys*, **6**(4)

Wirth N. (1982). *Programming in Modula-2*. Berlin: Springer Verlag

Wirth N. and Gutknecht J. (1992). *Project Oberon*. Wokingham: Addison-Wesley/ ACM Press

Yourdon E. (1989). *Modern Structured Analysis*. Englewood Cliffs, NJ: Yourdon Press

Yourdon E. and Constantine L. (1979). *Structured Design*. Englewood Cliffs, NJ: Yourdon Press

Index